ANGELS OF ALBION

Women of the Indian Mutiny

JANE ROBINSON

VIKING

VIKING

Published by the Penguin Group
Penguin Books Ltd, 27 Wrights Lane, London w8 5tz, England
Penguin Books USA Inc., 375 Hudson Street, New York, New York 10014 USA
Penguin Books Australia Ltd, Ringwood, Victoria, Australia
Penguin Books Canada Ltd, 10 Alcorn Avenue, Toronto, Ontario, Canada m4v 3b2
Penguin Books (NZ) Ltd, 182–190 Wairau Road, Auckland 10, New Zealand

Penguin Books Ltd, Registered Offices: Harmondsworth, Middlesex, England

First published in Great Britain by Viking 1996
1 3 5 7 9 10 8 6 4 2
First edition

Copyright © Jane Robinson, 1996

The moral right of the author has been asserted

The author and publishers are grateful to the following for permission to
reproduce illustrations: Richard Muir for no. 16 (both photographs); Basil Yalland for
no. 33; Doris Ashton for no. 7; Oriental and India Office Collections for nos. 1, 2, 13, 20, 24, 31;
the Bodleian Library, Oxford, for nos. 11, 19, 22, 23, all from *The Narrative of the Indian Revolt* and
no. 15, from *The History of the Indian Empire*; the Mary Evans Picture Library for nos. 12, 25; Hulton
Deutsch for nos. 12 and 26; Royal Collection Enterprises Ltd for no. 5; the Mansell Collection
for no. 4; Sheffield Art Galleries and the Bridgeman Art Library for no. 28; the National
Portrait Gallery for no. 18; the Maas Gallery Ltd for no. 32; the National Army
Museum for nos. 14 and 21. Nos. 8, 9, 10, 17 and 29 are from *The Illustrated
London News* of 1857; nos. 3, 6, 27, and 30 are from *From Minnie With
Love* by Jane Vansittart; no. 34 was taken by the author.

Set in 11.75/15 pt Monotype Baskerville
Typeset by Datix International Limited, Bungay, Suffolk
Printed in England by Clays Ltd, St Ives plc

A CIP catalogue record for this book is available from the British Library

isbn 0 670 84670 8

For Bruce

Contents

List of Plates

———

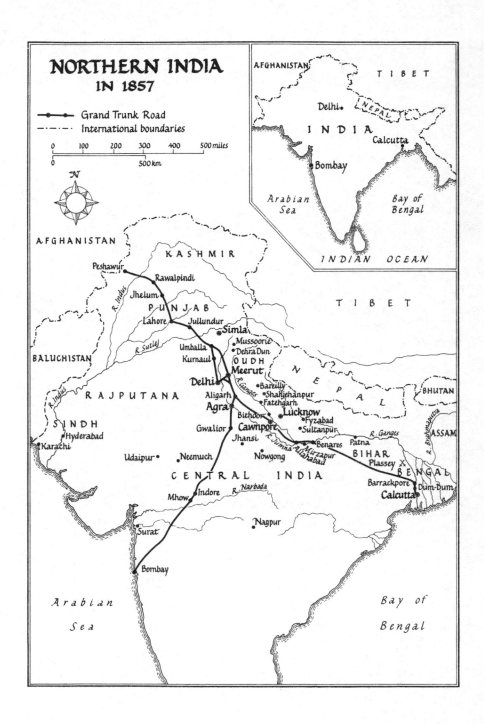

NORTHERN INDIA
IN 1857

━●━●━ Grand Trunk Road
─·─·─ International boundaries

0   100   200   300   400   500 miles
0   500 km

N

AFGHANISTAN

KASHMIR

Peshawur
Rawalpindi
R. Indus
Jhelum
PUNJAB
Lahore
Jullundur
Simla
Umballa
Mussoorie
Dehra Dun
Kurnaul
OUDH
Meerut
Delhi
Bareilly
Aligarh
Shahjehanpur
Agra
Fatehgarh
Bithoor
Lucknow
Gwalior
Cawnpore
Fyzabad
Jhansi
Sultanpur
R. Ganges
Benares
Patna
ASSAM
Nowgong
Mirzapur
Allahabad
BIHAR
R. Brahmaputra
Plassey X
BENGAL
Barrackpore
Dum-Dum
Calcutta

R. Sutlej

BALUCHISTAN

RAJPUTANA

SINDH
Hyderabad
Karachi
R. Indus

Udaipur
Neemuch

CENTRAL   INDIA

Mhow Indore   R. Narbada

Nagpur

Surat

Bombay

TIBET

NEPAL

BHUTAN

R. Ganges
R. Jumna

Arabian
Sea

Bay of
Bengal

Inset map:

AFGHANISTAN
TIBET
Delhi
NEPAL
INDIA
Calcutta
Bombay
Arabian
Sea
Bay of
Bengal
INDIAN   OCEAN

Acknowledgements

I do not really feel as though this book is mine at all, and my first and greatest acknowledgement of gratitude must be to those women to whom it really belongs: the Mutiny memsahibs themselves. While I was writing their story I was able to listen with startling immediacy to what they were saying – but they could not, of course, hear me. I do not suppose they would have taken much comfort from me if they could – but the thought was there.

I am very grateful to the staff of the following institutions for their various help: The Oriental and India Office Collections in London and the Indian Institute Library in Oxford, together with their respective parents, the British and Bodleian Libraries; the London Library; the National Army Museum; the Centre of South-Asian Studies in Cambridge; the British Association for Cemeteries in South Asia; the Indian Army Association, and the Indian Military Collectors' Society. I should especially like to thank the administrators of the Authors' Foundation (Society of Authors), who made me a grant to help fund research for this book.

For their generosity in offering family papers, anecdotes, and generally pointing me in interesting directions I am indebted to

Charles Allen, Geoffrey Allibone, Miss Doris Ashton, Pat Barr, the Lady Bellew, Kenneth Bond, Constable & Co. Ltd., for permission to reprint from Maria Germon's *Journal*, Mrs Ann Currie, Miss Mary Dodd, Diana and Stephen Evans, Byron Farwell, D. Fernley, Gordon Gay, Rumer Godden, Margaret Goostray, Christopher Hibbert, Peter Hopkirk, Captain Colin Hutchinson, Kenneth Jones, R. Johnston-Smith, Miss M. M. Kaye, Mrs Ann MacDonald, Margaret MacMillan, Judy Martin, Mrs Joyce Menzies, Peter Moody, Mrs Christina Morley, Richard Muir, Rachel Nicholson, Oxford University Press for permission to reprint from Harriet Tytler's *Memoirs*, Kevin Patience, Mrs E. Sharp Paul, Mrs F. Powers, Rosemary Raza, Mrs Pamela Seyd, Mrs Audrey Sidebotham, Mrs Sue Smithson, Judith Steward, Edmund Swinglehurst, the late Major-General D. E. B. Talbot and family, Mrs E. M. L. Thomson, Mrs Kate Twigg, Mrs Anne Uren, Andrew Ward, the late Cecil Wilkins, the late Mrs Zoë Yalland, and Mrs M. Yates.

I have been wonderfully looked after in India by many kind people, amongst whom I should mention Ram Advani, Sudhanshu Bhushan, and Partha Chaterjee in Lucknow, the late Thomas Smith in Agra, and Mrs Santosh Mahendrajit Singh in Kanpur, together with their families. Thank you to them all.

Finally, particular personal thanks must go to Mrs Helen Robinson for her inspiration and support, Peter Taylor for his unstinting and scholarly generosity (and both of them for their advice on the manuscript), to Eleo Gordon for all her efforts of my behalf, Katherine Frank for her companionship and encouragement, Rachna Bahl for her infectious love of India, Richard and Edward for their unerring sense of perspective, and Bruce – for everything.

Introduction

There is an old Moslem tradition to do with the burial of the dead which puzzled me greatly when I first came across it. I had only just arrived in India, and was being shown around the Itimad-ud-daulah or 'Baby Taj' in Agra. It seemed faintly churlish to be distracted by detail in the face of such architectural splendour, but I could not help noticing that each of the smooth, white monuments inside the Taj was decorated with a little carved figure either of a slate – the sort of hand-held tablet reminiscent of the Victorian schoolroom – or else a pen-box. I asked my guide what it meant. He was dismissive: they are only there, he said, to show whether the tomb is that of a man or a woman. I looked suitably nonplussed, and he went on to explain: women are the slates, memsahib, on which men write the history of the world.

It was a nice conceit, but the heat, even in the fretted marble shade of the mausoleum, was too new and intense for me to sort it out. Did it mean that the woman's role in history is assumed to be entirely passive, or, on the contrary, that only she can be entrusted with the safekeeping of truth? Whichever, if either, the idea of historians generally being more eager to watch the men doing the writing than read the women's words was rather appealing. It fitted in well with the purpose of my trip.

What I wanted to do in India was put into context the writings of a group of women I had discovered whilst working on a previous book about lady travellers. That was a biographical dictionary, and one of the best moments in its preparation came when I had just finished the research and decided on the final cast of characters – about four-hundred strong. I felt like royalty at one of those command performances at the theatre: all my subjects were poised in the queue and I was about to pass along from one to another, no doubt glancing at each with more or less admiration or credulity until I came (rather gratefully) to the end. I knew certain women would stand out, but because there were so many it was obvious that I was not going to be able to stay very long with anyone and I certainly did not expect to be stopped in my tracks.

I was wrong. One group of travellers I had always regarded a little derisively before as a sort of species beckoned me irresistibly beyond the queue. They were the memsahibs of British India, and in particular, those memsahibs who had had the misfortune to witness what the British call the Indian Mutiny of 1857. I was amazed to find their testimony so arresting and so *surprising*. After all, until meeting them I had wallowed with the best in tracts of recent literature on the Raj: all very interesting and colourful, but enough is enough. I could even specialize a bit, knowing something of the Mutiny, but there is only a limited amount to be said about any episode in military history, even as exciting and terrible and embarrassing an episode as this. And that is all the traditional image of the Mutiny has tended to be: a military campaign, all about soldiers and sepoys, arrogance and insurrection, strategy, politics, and heroes.

Surely there is only a limited amount to be said about the memsahib, too? I mentioned that I regarded her as a type: she was a faintly laughable creature with a ridiculously whaleboned (yet strangely stout) figure compounded of a distasteful mixture of arrogance, ignorance and intolerance, who only bothered to learn enough of the native language to issue irritable orders to the servants and spent the long, hot afternoons languishing petulantly on a horse-hair *chaise-longue*. This image – or one very like it – even obtained at the time of the Mutiny itself. In fact a few contemporary commentators, British as well as Indian, blamed the whole debacle on these harridan chatelaines of the Raj: they were the Mutiny's whoresome muses (and more of that anon). But a muse inspires in different ways, and to most loyal observers back in Britain during the upheavals of 1857 the memsahib neatly symbolized national purity. So here was another caricature: Britannia's virgin daughter, an angel of Albion whose sacrilegious violation at the hands of the mutineers became a metaphor for the violation of the Empire. British soldiers fought the Indians in blood-revenge, calling on the spirit of their murdered countrywomen to inspire them to unsurpassed heights of valour. The memsahib, meanwhile, sank into an official role as the passive, sacrificial victim of this whole passionate affair. That is what my mausoleum guide (allowing for a shift in sympathy) would consider the writing on the slate.

The words, of course, are different. Recorded in a handful of their published works and in masses of ephemeral material, the memsahibs themselves tell another story altogether. And none of them, for a start, appears to conform to the traditional image (or only a very few, and I refuse to let them stand as typical). Nor, in their eyes, is the Mutiny solely the military and political campaign I had always supposed it to be. These women hardly bother with the military news, which for all its terrible importance at the time soon became measured and a little stiff in the telling by official chroniclers, even eye-witness ones. Their journals and letters home are much more personal documents, allowed to be all the official ones were not: bewildered, compassionate, trivial, terrified, emotional – even downright disloyal. And their remarkable courage does not involve the battlefield, except in so much as their menfolk might be out fighting on it: it is more about enduring sieges, managing escapes, bearing and caring for children in the most impossible of circumstances and coping with the sudden and vicious extortion of all that made life civilized. All those handy little guides written for the mid-nineteenth-century memsahib on suitable behaviour in India did not mention what to do in the event of what was, after all, a domestic cataclysm. How to avoid one's perspiration staining one's silk bodices, or committing some blundering social solecism at a high-class dinner table, or even advising on the most economic (and least prejudicial) diet to feed one's baby's wetnurse: all this was at their fingertips. But how to survive when a random group of individuals has been thrown together by appalling violence, cut off from the support of father or husband or brother and forced to witness acts of the most fundamental inhumanity and accept them to survive: no.

Not all of them did survive, of course. One of the places that moved me most in India was the graveyard at Morar, just outside Gwalior. To get to it you pass through the dusty village where still stands an impeccably English church, built just before the Mutiny. I thought nothing could be more incongruous, as I shaded my eyes (against the heat as much as the light) to watch a bony great water-buffalo stroll around the walls of the nave and the vultures crouching in the thorn trees by the tower. But a little further on, past a few boxy huts and towards the encroaching scrub of the jungle, I noticed what looked like a tablet from St Paul's Cathedral dumped in the middle of some tamarisks. And then next to that, another, and another and another: all huge and lovingly engraved with classical scrolls and columns but set in such hard, unwelcoming soil that they were slanting and beginning to slide into disquieting little chasms at their feet. Some were already broken: a snake was basking on one of the most elaborate, I remember. It recorded the death of a baby, the son of John and Wilhelmina Murray, aged nine months and six days: it was while his funeral was being conducted by the Reverend Coopland on 14 June that the Mutiny at Morar broke out. The Reverend himself is buried there (he died the following night), and the young Stewart family, William (thirty), Jane (twenty-seven) and their infant son Robert, two years old, all 'murdered at this place by mutineers'.

They are very touching, all these long-forgotten stones, but what I found almost unbearably so was the fact that this was supposed to have been an English graveyard, a final familiar resting-place to comfort the dead and their mourners. But it cannot have been comfortable even then: it is alien and surreal, this burial-ground, and looked more out of place than anything I saw in India. Those who lie in it, exiles whilst alive, still seem somehow very far from home.

There are graves like these all over what once was British India, most, like Morar (until the kindly local chowkidar, or watchman, cleared it for us) fast being swallowed up by the scrub. But this book is not a catalogue of the dead: most of my memsahibs survived, in the most astonishing manner, and often with their spirits – even a stalwart sense of humour – remarkably intact. And however little their popular image (and that of the Mutiny) may have changed throughout the years, that the experience changed them as women is beyond doubt. But then it is hardly surprising, given the significance of those slates and pen-boxes at Agra.

I should say something about the terms and the spelling used in the text. I have referred to 'the Mutiny' throughout, although well aware that it should more properly (nowadays) be called the Sepoy Rebellion, the Freedom Struggle, or even India's First War of Independence. 'England' and 'Albion' also occasionally, and just as unfairly, appear as more general labels for Britain: I just felt that the book's integrity would best be served by sticking to the term used by those writing at the time. That goes for the orthography of place-names, too, although I have included a note of the more obscure of these with their modern equivalents within a short glossary at the end of the book.

I have tried as far as possible to tell the story of the Mutiny through the memsahibs' own words, and have not presumed to edit their often rather inconsistent spelling or syntax: it is time these women were allowed to speak for themselves.

J.H.R.

I

The Birth of British India

___

I am not very fond of Englishmen out of their own country.[1]

There was one major drawback to India, as far as Jemima Kindersley was concerned. It was an admirable place in many respects, to be sure: any visitor, like her, to Madras in 1765 could not fail to be struck by the unexpected elegance of the town, with its houses neat and pleasing (each boasting a strange and useful thing called a verandah, which shaded one by day and kept one cool and discreet at night). The streets and squares glistened with a sort of marble made of oyster shells, and all in all it was the prettiest place 'without exception' that Jemima had ever seen. Of course, being built entirely by the English, and apparently peopled by them too, it would be.

However, Jemima could not recommend it to her country-women as a place in which to settle. In a letter she sent to friends at home, after inviting their congratulations on her intrepid nature and safe arrival, she went on to explain. 'It is frequently said, though very unjustly,' she wrote, 'that this climate never kills the English ladies; and, indeed, it must be allowed, that women do not so often die of violent fevers as men, which is no wonder, as we live more temperately, and expose ourselves less in the heat of the day; and perhaps, the tenderness of our conditions sometimes prevents the violence of the disorder, and occasions a lingering, instead of a sudden, death.'[2]

But Jemima was a modern woman, an army officer's wife who had rather unusually decided to accompany her husband abroad; having made the choice, she must face its consequences. Since no eighteenth-century traveller, particularly a female one, had any right to live well and long, she supposed she may as well perish lingeringly in Madras as anywhere else so far away from home. At least it had the dignity of reminding her delightfully of Bath: there must be worse places to die than India.

Perhaps Mrs Kindersley tended a little towards the melodramatic. She expired neither in Madras nor further north in Allahabad, where she became one of British India's earliest official memsahibs by settling with her husband for a few years' residence. And although she was one of the first Englishwomen to publish a first-hand account of it,[3] and therefore might be excused soliciting the plaudits of her friends, India had been more or less closely related to England for over a century and a half before her visit.

At first it was a matter of convenience: when Elizabeth I granted 'The Governor and Company of Merchants of London' sole trading rights into the East Indies in 1600, England was still flushed with the redolence of her victory over the Armada: now it was time to extend her proven powers of enterprise and maritime endeavour towards the lucrative shores of the Indonesian Spice Islands, and so challenge the strong Dutch competition there. An Indian depot or trading post *en route* would be of considerable strategic value. Surat, north of Bombay, was the first such 'factory' port, and in 1613 trading rights were granted to the Company by the 'Shadow of God' himself, the Mogul Emperor Jahangir.

It is hardly surprising that the English adventurers should so soon be distracted from the idea of using India solely as a stepping-stone further East. The fabulous Mogul dynasty, now in its third generation, ruled richly over one of the most vast and extravagant empires in the world. The silks and cottons, jewels and paintings and all the exquisite artistry of its domain afforded the Company not only valuable trading currency but also the most luxurious of prizes to carry home: the Merchants of London looked set to prosper.

And so the relationship matured: providing it promised never to 'seek plantation by the sword' and to indulge its formidable energies only 'at sea in quiet trade',[4] England was allowed to stay. The seats of the three great 'Presidencies' or administrative areas of Madras, Bombay and Calcutta (Bengal) were all founded within twenty years of each other[5] and by the close of the century India's friendly invaders were settling in profitably.

Things were not faring so well with the Moguls, however. The dynasty had always blossomed on shallow roots, depending on glamorous imperial personalities rather than sound political consolidation, and by the time the fifth emperor, Aurangzeb, died in 1707, leaving a disaffected issue of seventeen would-be successors, none of whom had the personal or political power to survive, it withered and died.

Relishing the challenge of establishing supremacy over various European and Asian invaders clamouring over the disintegration of Aurangzeb's empire, and reeking rather of rapaciousness, the Company (now officially united to include 'the Merchants of England' as well as those exclusively of London) established the military power it had been denied before: now seeking 'plantation by the sword' became a commercial necessity. While the relicts of the Moguls warred with the invading Mahrattas, England fought off the Portuguese, the Dutch, the French, and the nawabs of several new principalities emerging from the old and disunited empire.

This period is where the history of so-called British India starts sounding familiar. Most have heard of the Black Hole of Calcutta, for instance (although what it involved is not as clear as it might be)[6] and of the heroic Colonel Robert Clive, who wrested

Calcutta from all comers (French and Indian) at the battle of Plassey in 1757. It was Clive, on the Company's behalf, who accepted the *diwani* or mastery of Bengal at the Treaty of Allahabad after having fought, taxed and levied the erstwhile Indian rulers into submission in 1765 – the year Jemima Kindersley arrived.

And so the foundations of British India were laid.

During the near-century which stretched between the Treaty of Allahabad and the outbreak of the Mutiny in 1857, despite a few local difficulties involving the Sultans of Mysore, Haider Ali and Tipu Sultan, and the tenacious Mahrattas, 'John Company', as the collective personnel of the East India Company became known, grew increasingly familiar a figure in India, whether as Lord John, presiding in splendour as Governor-General in fashionable Calcutta, or Sir John, firm-but-fair Resident in some ancient Mogul capital; as the much-respected Mr John, administering the districts of an ever-growing array of provinces beyond, or Major John, in charge of the sepoys (private infantrymen) and sowars (cavalrymen) of the three Presidencies' native armies.

Gradually Britain became not just the guardian of the territories under its control in India, but also their governor. After the India Act of 1784, which drew the Company's organization and administration towards greater governmental control, and the transformation of its personnel from traders into nabobs (entrepreneurs, or 'nobs', as they called them at home) – that is the replacement of the Company's commercial power with an integrated and highly bureaucratic civil (and military) power – the pattern was set which should ensure India grew still richer, more gorgeous, and, best of all, more *British*.

Keeping it so, of course, called for absolute dependence on the officers and men of the Company's armies, which were joined by various regiments of the king's (or, after 1837, the queen's) armies drafted from home. The latter could, of course, be relied upon unquestioningly. Until the mid-eighteen-fifties, the native armies were considered safe, too, given the ratio of British to Indian officers of one to three and a hierarchy which ensured that the most senior sepoy still ranked lower than the lowliest Briton. Even the comparative rabble of the Bengal Presidency army was unlikely to get far out of hand under measures such as these – although there had been the odd mutiny (or blip), most notably the uprising by the Madras army against new regulations at Vellore in 1806 (a matter of religion and local politics) and four involving the Bengalis between 1844 and 1857.

The reason these Bengalis were so unpredictable (in the complacent eyes of their British commanders) lay in the fact that a good proportion was of high-caste origin, Brahmins and Rajputs, unused to subordination, and over a third were men of Oudh: a fact that became highly significant after the British annexation of that proud and powerful kingdom in 1856.

Even though the India Act was supposed, amongst other things, to pledge the Company not 'to pursue schemes of conquest and extension of dominion in India', to one Governor-General, Lord Dalhousie, just such expansion was deemed not only a strategic expedient for the British but, more compellingly, a moral duty. Dalhousie was an imperious evangelist, eager to demonstrate the peculiarly British art of Progress to the poor benighted natives of India. This meant taking altruistic control, by force if necessary, of their lands and inheritance, and during the eight years of his appointment from 1848, a catalogue of states including Satara, Udaipur, Jhansi, Nagpur, the Punjab and the kingdom of Oudh were stripped of their comparative autonomy and absorbed by the feringhee (which is how Indians termed the Europeans).

To accompany the supposed reforms of annexation, and to make sure their benefit lasted, it was decided that whenever a current Rajah died without direct issue, then his property should be relinquished to the British government in perpetuity. No adopted heirs, no pretenders, and precious little compensation would be allowed. The British were proud of themselves: Dalhousie left office content that he had bequeathed to British India a stiff and loyal military force, fit for a burgeoning and tranquil empire, and the administrative means to keep it healthy and hearty for the foreseeable future.

A year later, the Mutiny broke out.

This supposedly sterling administration system was partly to blame. Indian agitators (and certain British observers) doubted its flaunted virtues. It was inherently rotten, they argued, and John Company decidedly not the decent chap he used to be. According to them his maxim throughout had been to collect as much money with as little disturbance to himself as possible. He was slyly staining the whole fabric of local life by not only allowing but also encouraging those Indians he deigned to empower to indulge themselves in peculiarly European iniquities. There are various contemporary reports of Indian agents requisitioning the unpaid labour and very meagre resources of local peasantry to carry the baggage of some governmental caravan, or join its camp followers for months at a time, while their wives left at home would be consigned to those same agents' keeping, and forced into prostitution. Following their masters' example, certain Indian court officials would boast that no desirable woman ever lost a law suit, so long as she was reasonably imaginative and, of course, compliant.[7] So much for Dalhousie's legacy.

Nor was such supposed corruption on the part of the British entirely vicarious: there is in the recesses of a library in London a rather furtive-looking notebook written carefully and closely in pencil by someone the British would have dismissed as a seditionist, which catalogues a whole list of assorted enormities revolving around the renowned sexual appetites of women such as gentle Jemima Kindersley.[8] The memsahib, it says, is totally without morals and will as eagerly seduce the servants of her husband's household as the officers and men of his regiment. Elsewhere it is documented that a respected British gentleman has turned his official Residency building into 'a scene of wholesale juvenile prostitution', and no Indian woman can be considered either too mean or too proud to be enjoyed by an Englishman. It was an Englishman who killed one of the princesses of Nagpur, after all, when her lands were annexed in 1854: she died not of injuries but insults, and sank into the grave (the legend goes) consumed by shame.[9]

It was rumours of precisely the same sort of behaviour on the part of the Indians, of course, which aroused the British to such cold-blooded vengeance after Cawnpore – but that comes later. Meanwhile, they served their own emotive purpose.

Most of the accusations of sexual outrage on the part of the British had to remain rather shadowy allegations; but their perceived rape of India's more vulnerable princely states was all too apparent, and just as potent a symbol for the putative nationalist. The insults implicit in Dalhousie's policy of annexation are obvious: in fact those angriest at its strictures, among them the dispossessed Rani Lakshmibai of Jhansi and the formidable Begum of Oudh (women both) provided the rebels with some of their fiercest fighters. The part such heroes – or villains – played as protagonists is given more or less prominence in the history of the 1857 uprising according to which commentator one reads, as does the shifting significance of this darkly swelling background of disaffection, corruption, and crass insensitivity. And while it is rather easy to become addled by the ideology of it all, the facts stand firm, and it *really* all began, the Great Indian Mutiny – or India's first and glorious War of Independence – with the curious case of the flying chupattis.

This episode, actually more reminiscent of Holmesian fiction than fact, involved the mysterious appearance in villages throughout the Bengal Presidency of quantities of chupattis, or little rounds of baked, unleavened bread. They would turn up, often in pairs but sometimes four or five together, on a desk or a doorstep, passed on from place to place multiplying as they went until, like a Chinese whisper, they completely lost their original meaning and served only to bewilder their recipients. The 'chupatty movement', as it was called by its perplexed observers, seems to have been an organized network during the weeks leading up to the Mutiny's outbreak involving local chowkidars, who would bake a number of the breads, visit their counterparts in neighbouring villages giving two each to them and instructions to bake six more; the new recruits would then visit *their* local villages and so on, with the result that the chupattis 'travelled often over 160 or 200 miles in a night'.[10] Quite why, or to what effect, is not known, but Indians and British alike strongly suspected it had something to do with insurrection.

Then there was the business of the greased cartridges. Still smarting over the implications of the General Service Enlistment Act of the previous year, which required all seventy-two regiments of the Bengal Army to abide by the same rules as those of the generally lower-caste troops of Bombay and Madras, and the new regulations that men previously retired on invalid pensions due to unfitness for active service must now accept cantonment duties instead, the sepoys were faced in early 1857 with a further and final affront.

It involved the introduction of the new Enfield rifle from England, reckoned more efficient than the smooth-bore musket it replaced. Before, the bullet and powder had had to be rammed down the bore separately; now both were combined in a single cartridge, which needed only to have the tip nipped off before being loaded and fired. No problem. Except that the cartridges were greased, for ease of passage and ignition, with animal fat. Few things could be more degrading to a Hindu than to taste beef tallow, but if pig's grease were used instead (both being cheaper than goat's or sheep's) then the burden of insult would shift to the

Moslems. Even when the British compromised by suggesting the sepoys should grease their own cartridges with whatever they pleased, and not nip but tear off the tip, doubts still persisted as to the nature of the suspiciously stiff paper used to make the cartridge itself. And so the treachery spread: the sepoys' perceived perfidy in circulating alarmist rumours about the cartridges and the British officers' in insisting they be used.

Various rumblings were to be heard well before the storm broke so savagely at Meerut on 10 May: at Dum-Dum, near Calcutta, in January and Barrackpore a month later mutiny was threatened but then temporarily quashed by the repeated assurance that no one need compromise their caste while obeying army regulations. For the next few weeks a querulous calm descended (albeit punctuated by the odd flying chupatti), but it was not a comfortable time for those with eyes, as they say, to see.

The relationship with India that Britain protested so pure and noble had in reality been curdling for years. It has been argued that the British acted as much through ignorance as arrogance: that the powers that be just did not realize the offence that would be caused to the Hindu sepoys when in 1806, in an attempt to smarten up the troops, they ordered that *leather* cockades be worn in their turbans (which led to the Vellore mutiny). Or when in 1824 sepoys were expected to sail to Burma to fight for the British, when a voyage of any length would mean intolerable conditions for keeping caste as far as eating, washing and cooking were concerned. Further disquiet was inevitable when coins were struck by the British in India in 1835 which, for the first time, were not stamped with the Mogul emperor's name.

The lack of imagination so offensively displayed by the British in such things was matched not so much by anger amongst the Indians as by fear, which was ripening into hysteria by 1857. Wild rumours began flying around of even greater outrages against their religious integrity: that the flour sold in the bazaars was

9

systematically being contaminated with ground cow-bone; that 2,000 sets of irons were secretly being cast into which reluctant sepoys would be clapped and forcibly sent abroad; that the gobbets of beef and pork uneaten at Christian dinner tables were being thrown into wells to taint the water and, more shocking still, that corruption was being bred into India both through the mass seduction of its women by British officers and men, and the forcible alliance of Crimean war widows (of which there was thought to be a superabundance) to proud native nawabs, or noblemen. A race of half-castes was being raised in the Christian tradition to deny the country its purity, dignity and identity.

These 'preposterous fables', as the British government called them, reached their apotheosis in a bizarre proclamation published on behalf of the royal house of Delhi which assured its readers that the British were thoroughly regretting what they considered to be their lenience in the past and were preparing to rectify their mistakes with a series of dramatic and fail-safe new measures. These would involve, amongst other things just as terrible, the drowning at sea of all heirs and descendants of former Indian rulers; the destruction of all Moslem and Hindu religious books and temples; the immediate cessation of military training for sepoys, and the organized intermarriage of all native daughters of rank with Britons. These things done, said the proclamation, the British would comfortably settle themselves into India for a thousand years to come. 'Oh men of Hindoostan!' it went on to urge, 'see now these Christians. How great is their enmity against you? You have been told of the future schemes of the English as related above. Now you must wash your hands, and try your best to save your religion and lives by murdering all Europeans, make your resolution firm and by the blessing of God you will succeed.'[11]

This was perhaps the greatest fear of all, this loss of identity, both personally (in the case of such nawabs and zemindars, or landowners, as could afford the luxury of an identity in the first place) and, for the rest, religiously. Proselytism had never been an official British pastime in India, and the various mission and other schools (often founded by memsahibs) which spread throughout the three Presidencies were not supposed to be subversive seminaries. But the fact that they were usually run by women, and that it was a Victorian woman's duty to her God, her husband (or failing one of those, her father) and lastly to herself to witness her Faith in all the domestic doings of her life, meant that charges of proselytism were all too easily laid.

It became convenient for critics (and still is) to generalize that the memsahib was a subtle and thorough temptress in her influence over Indian children and womenfolk, and that her attitude towards her adopted home was both disrespectful and divisive. How true this was we shall see. It is certainly embarrassing now to read the words of some of the women airing their views on the country during the twenty-odd years leading up to the Mutiny. 'God preserve me from ever having an English wife!'[12] groaned one M. Jaquemont on visiting India in 1836 – and it is rather difficult not to concur in the case of Isabella Fane, living as the daughter of the British Commander-in-Chief in Calcutta between 1835 and 1838, who insists in her letters home on sneering at the lowly humility of the ubiquitous ragged 'Blackee' and tittering remorselessly at the jumped-up gentlemen aristocrats of India whose distinguishing mark in dress, she noticed, was always to leave one bosom of enviable proportion exposed to the company. '[T]he Rajah [of Bhurtpore]'s was an object never to be forgotten.'[13]

One of the most popular of women writers on pre-Mutiny India was Emily Eden, who knew (and disliked) Miss Fane, having arrived in Calcutta at the same time. Emily's duty, as consort to her brother Lord Auckland, the Governor-General, was surely to be diplomatic or, at worst, fairly anodyne in her public observances on India and the British during what she termed her exile from home. But in private it was different:

Delhi is a very suggestive and moralising place – such stupendous remains of power and wealth passed and passing away – and somehow I feel that we horrid English have just 'gone and done it', merchandised it, revenued it, and spoiled it all. I am not very fond of Englishmen out of their own country. And Englishwomen did not look pretty at the ball in the evening, and it did not tell well for the beauty of Delhi that the painted ladies of one regiment, who are generally called 'the little corpses' (and very hard it is too upon most corpses), were much the prettiest people there, and were besieged with partners . . . How some of these young men must detest their lives! Mr — was brought up entirely at Naples and Paris, came out in the world when he was quite a boy, and cares for nothing but society and Victor Hugo's novels, and that sort of thing. He is now stationed at B., and supposed very lucky in being appointed to such a cheerful station. The whole concern consists of five bungalows, very much like the thatched lodge at Langley. There are three married residents: one lady has bad spirits (small blame to her), and she has never been seen; another has weak eyes, and wears a large shade about the size of a common verandah; the other has bad health, and has had her head shaved. A tour [a sort of toupée] is not to be had here for love or money, so she wears a brown silk cushion with a cap pinned to the top of it. The Doctor and our friend make up the rest of the society. He goes every morning to hear causes between natives about strips of land or a few rupees – that lasts till five; then he rides about an uninhabited jungle till seven; dines; reads a magazine, or a new book when he can afford one, and then goes to bed. A lively life, with the thermometer at several hundred![14]

The main argument of those who resented the presence of the memsahib not only in such stations as this but also throughout

British India, was that in the old days, when no such ladies were there (only mere women) and the depressing and judgemental terms of reference with which they constantly qualified Indian home life were lacking, it *had* been quite a lively life for a gentleman in India. A deal less complicated, anyway. Then the regiment was all the home and family he needed, and there was a manly air of affection about his relationship with the sepoys, who would traditionally call him their father, and whom he regarded as his 'babalogue', his boys. But with the appearance of 'an avatar of fair young English maidens, with the bloom of the Western summer still on their cheeks'[15] the pleasures of the parade-ground palled; the babalogue were whining interruptions all of a sudden, and the bibi, or Indian mistress, with which most officers had been comfortably furnished of old, became embarrassing and inconvenient.

The root of the problem was that women represented home. That, to put it crudely, is what the memsahibs in India were for. They were sent out as portable little packets of morality, to comfort their men, keep the blood-line clean, and remind them of their mothers. Those fitted to the part sought security in an extremely strange land in creating for themselves a hidebound home from home involving all the parochial strictures of English provincial life. Pianos and plush-draped dining tables and dismal prints of *The Monarch of the Glen* would be shipped over to furnish their parlours; there would be amateur theatricals, musical soirées, and elaborate great dinners to be endured; fashion papers, arriving months late from London and Paris, would be pounced upon, scrutinized and their patterns copied and carried off with varying degrees of much-discussed success. There was snobbery and scandal: life might almost have been bearable, in fact, were it not for the stupid heat and natives.

The heat one could provide for, given enough punkah-wallahs (men to pull the ropes of the ubiquitous household fans) and the patience to endure the fiercest hours of the day inside in the shade doing nothing. And the natives: well, the natives were a nuisance, but if properly managed need not impinge on one's social and family life too much.

And so the popular image of the memsahib takes her place in the prelude to disaster: it was she who was responsible for spoiling that cohesive relationship which had been so enjoyed by the sahib and his sepoys in the past. With her petty insularity, her home-grown prejudices and petulant dependence on her countrymen, she had succeeded, by the time the Mutiny broke out, in divorcing the officer from his man, the Collector from his clerk: Britain, in fact, from India.

2

The Memsahibs Arrive

By Pa and Ma I'm daily told
To marry now's the time,
For though I'm very far from old,
I'm rather in my prime.
They say while we have any sun
We ought to make our hay –
And India has so hot a one
I'm going to Bombay . . .[1]

The Fishing Fleet, they called it. It started sailing eastward from England during the 1670s and its cargo consisted of a selection of unmarried women – at best described as possessing but 'limited charms and beauty' and at worst as 'shrivelled and dry' and 'educated merely to cover the surface of their mental deformity'[2] – shipped out by their patron, John Company, to find a husband. Their expectations were not high at first: any gouty old nabob would do. And as board and lodging were paid for a year, and (in certain circumstances) the mortifying passage home for those unfortunate enough to be 'returned empty', it seems quite a good deal. Until one reads that an estimated ninety per cent of British males in India made native or Eurasian marriages by the mid-eighteenth century[3] (one gentleman is said to have supported fourteen wives of his own and fathered eighty children by them and various mistresses[4] – which rather throws the statistics). Sturdy Indian women were considered more hale than the pale flowers of England (think of the wilting prospects of Jemima Kindersley) and they were satisfyingly successful at bearing and rearing children, besides being gentle and biddable partners. 'I have observed', wrote one rather wistful visitor, 'that those who have lived

15

with a native woman for any length of time never marry a European . . . so amusingly playful [are they], so anxious to oblige and please, that a person after being so accustomed to their society, shrinks from the idea of encountering the whims or yielding to the fancies of an Englishwoman.'[5] So the members of the Fishing Fleet had their rivals.

Nor could they content themselves, if they failed to secure their own man, with the thought that it had all been a good adventure and no harm done. The voyage out, at least until the introduction of regular steamers, was grim. The women were forbidden to dance, sing, even talk louder than a demure murmur; they were not allowed to go ashore on any of the ship's calls and had to spend what might be a six-month (and never less than six-week) voyage locked in their cabins, gazing out of a specially barred porthole.

What little reputation these women may have had on embarking with the Fleet must surely have evaporated by the time their year was up. Then the allowance the Company made them was stopped and the rejects were faced with either supporting themselves as single women in India or coming home, on short commons, to do the same. Naturally enough, there emerged a miserable new element in the society of British India of time-expired members of the Fishing Fleet now relegated to the realms of fallen women. By late 1675 the President and Council of the Company were to be heard sputtering hypocritically to the Deputy Governor: 'Whereas some of these women are grown scandalous to our nation, religion and Government interest, we require you to give them faire warning that they do apply themselves to a more sober and Christian conversation.' Chance would be a fine thing. A few weeks later a second blast was fired, in the face, one presumes, of the first having been ignored: '. . . the sentence is that they shall be confined totally of their liberty to go abroad and fed with bread and water.'[6]

The Company's scheme to export Englishwomen was not a great success.

Come the end of the eighteenth century, the prospect of husband-hunting in India was beginning to look a little more attractive. Gentlewomen were now able to make the voyage out under their own terms. Their quarry was essentially the same (although something more promising than the ageing nabob of old, perhaps) but now they were somewhat better equipped.

Expectations were higher, for a start. The fashion was changing, and the era of the ubiquitous bibi, or native mistress, was (officially) drawing to a close. It became quite the thing for an ambitious young gentleman in India – be he in military service or civil – to acquire a wife fresh from home. Sometimes the engagement would already have been made before the lady in question sailed for India; sometimes – and this was the most romantic (or rash) – two voyagers-out would meet and fall in love between home shores and abroad, marrying soon afterwards. Otherwise, there were balls to go to, arranged in Calcutta to coincide with the Fishing Fleet's arrival each season; there were introductions to be made to eligible members of the services by one's brother or brother-in-law, or soirées and theatricals, horse-races and parades and always those interminable and lumbering dinners to go to: unofficial marriage markets all.

The passage from home was not as uncomfortable as it had been, either. Although it was not until 1917 that women were allowed to make the journey unescorted,[7] they were at least released from their dim, damp and shatteringly noisy cabins now. There would like as not be a maid in attendance, and whatever rights were due to those who had paid for their own tickets: a library, perhaps, and decorous dancing on deck. Harriet Tytler, later to witness the entire siege of Delhi from the shelter of an ammunition cart, was astonished by the profligacy of life aboard the paddle-steamer *Hindostan* on her passage to Calcutta in 1845.

'The P & O were remarkable for their princely tables in those days,' she remembered, 'but recollect they charged £150 and £153 respectively for a gentleman's and lady's first-class passage. Wine of the very best was provided ad lib. at meals. There was such waste in everything. I have seen stewards pouring good whisky into blacking bottles to clean the boots with. Champagne flowed like water on Thursdays and Sundays at dinner. On these occasions I took special care as to whom I danced with, for half the young fellows were much the worse for it.'[8]

It is as much a truism now as then that life once one has arrived out in India will be very much different to life at home. The would-be memsahibs of the mid-nineteenth century were assailed with advice – especially those who had no family connections with the place (which, as the century drew on, became increasingly unusual). Even girls who had been born out there and then sent back to Britain at the age of seven or eight to be educated might need a little help to settle in India again. Thus a modest market in guidebooks for and usually by women began to emerge (with its apotheosis in a ghastly tome called *Tropical Trials*, published in 1883).[9] These offered suggestions on almost everything from dress to deportment, etiquette to entertaining, and how to manage children, servants, and curry. (On the last point, incidentally, I have counted in a selection of 'Family Dinners for a Month' no less than nineteen different curry recipes, from the predictable chicken, prawn, vegetable and egg varieties to more unsettling concoctions of 'ball', toast, sardine and brain – and each as part of a five-course meal.)[10] Who could deny the value of such helpful hints as remembering to take particularly pretty nightdresses out to India to dazzle the doctor when the fever (inevitably) comes, or forbidding your baby's wet-nurse to eat hot chillies?[11] 'Stays require constant washing, and several pairs should be brought – not the ones with elastic, which are ruined at once by the heat, but light coutil [canvas] ones with few steels'[12] – and never put away a dress damp with perspiration: it will mildew almost in minutes. Dry it carefully instead, and so long as flannel is worn between silk and the skin, all should be well.

Women's travel accounts of the period were also furnished with useful information, often admonitory, on what to expect from others in India as well as from oneself. Julia Maitland, who published her *Letters from Madras* (1843) anonymously, warned that

. . . the officers' ladies are curiously different from the civilians. The civil ladies are generally very quiet, rather languid, speaking almost in a whisper, simply dressed, almost always lady-like and *comme-il-faut*, not pretty, but pleasant and nice-looking, rather dull, and give one very hard work in pumping for conversation. They talk of 'the Governor', 'the Presidency', the 'Overland',[13] and 'girls' schools at home', and have always daughters of about thirteen at home for education. The military ladies, on the contrary, are always quite young, pretty, noisy, affected, showily dressed, with a great many ornaments, *mauvais ton*, chatter incessantly from the moment they enter the house, twist their curls, shake their bustles, and are altogether what you may call 'Low Toss'. While they are alone with me after dinner, they talk about suckling their babies, the disadvantages of scandal, 'the Officers', and 'the Regiment'; and when the gentlemen come into the drawing-room, they invariably flirt with them most furiously.[14]

And here we are approaching the realms of Chapter One again, where the memsahib with all her petty divisiveness was cast as *agent provocateuse* . . .

I mentioned in the introduction to this book that I had initially embarked on the whole project as a sort of crusade against what I considered the myth of the memsahib: caricatured, unwarranted and unfair. It is at this stage that I begin to wonder if I have been altogether too naïve. Open almost any account by or about British women in pre-Mutiny India and you will find them full of just such unattractive characters as Julia's companions. You will find Isabella Fane, troubled by mosquitoes ('I have a place on my leg which I have over-scratched, nearly a quarter of a yard long'), an ungrateful and ungraceful guest at a hot, smelly ball ('The hostess as usual acted like a fool, but what can you expect of a pig, but a grunt!').[15] You will find pert young Dolores James, later to become notorious as the international coquette Lola Montez, deliciously scandalizing the society of Simla by playing fast (but not quite loose enough to ruin herself) with almost every male she meets.[16] And there is teenaged Bonny Byrne, a captain's daughter and ensign's wife whom the Nawab of Farrukhabad took as his mistress (after a little opportunistic pimping by her mother) just months before the Mutiny broke out, and who was subsequently judged a collaborator with her paramoor against the British[17] – so even the *dramatis personae* of this book are burdened with (frankly) the odd tart or vulgar old trout, whose shortcomings were no doubt magnified under siege conditions or in the terror of attempted escape.

It is this sort of material, plentiful as it is, that has led the historian as well as the unsympathetic contemporary to suppose that all memsahibs in 1857 were more or less the same: gorgons all, and responsible not only for the comparatively passive enormity of breaking down the old relationships of British India, but of much more active corruption, too. As that secret little notebook in the library in London put it, the English 'designate all women as flowers the scent of which whoever pleases he may enjoy . . . Indecency and fornication have reached to such a pitch under the English Government that any lecherous female who chooses to go out of her house may indulge her passions without restraint . . .'[18]

In reality, the daily round of most memsahibs in India during the decade or two leading up to 1857, the period somewhat credulously termed the 'golden calm', was very much less sensational. It was not quite as stultifying as the old image has it, however, whereby one would be woken from one's sleep (having been kept reasonably cool throughout the night by the constant fanning of a punkah) by the gentle call of a bearer, or by the parakeets whooping amongst their nests on one's verandah, and hot water would always miraculously be ready and breakfast prepared. Before the heat of the day became too much to bear, a little letter writing or needlework might be in order, and, depending on one's status in the household, instructions given to servants about the day's meals, commissions from the bazaar (a lady *never* went to the bazaar herself), and the care of the children, each of whom would have its own ayah. By now the blinds would be drawn and the punkahs busy again, and the thick, woolly hours between luncheon and dinner would be spent sleeping, reading, or composing various chitties for the evening's visits. (Somebody ought to write a thesis on the significance of the chitty in British India: no social transaction seems to have been complete without its attendant bunting of little notes to arrange a meeting, invite a guest, decline an invitation, ask a question, pass on an inch or two of gossip and so on.)

Chitty writing done, and dinner over, the day's excitements would begin. From about five-thirty onwards calls would be made and cards left (which was sometimes the only object of having made the call in the first place); then the theatricals and soirées, concerts and club gatherings, meetings and suppers and balls would all begin. It was cool now, getting dark, and the scent of the jasmine and lilies almost rank in their headiness. 'Oh, the wild happiness of those first days!'[19] exclaimed one Indian *ingénue* on being swept decorously into the social whirl of mid-nineteenth-century Calcutta.

Of course, this conventional daily round did exist, with variations, but it was not compulsory, and for those with the position – or disposition – to resist it life could be surprisingly rewarding. 'Roaming about with a good tent and a good Arab, one might be happy for ever in India.' So claimed Fanny Parks, a distinctly *un*conventional memsahib whose twenty-two years in Bengal as the wife of an ineffectual customs-officer were spent in a challenging welter of travel, exploration (of the Hindu people as well as their captivating country) and fulfilment. She used to mount her own expeditions, 'abundantly fat and lively'[20] aboard her beloved horse (the 'good Arab' mentioned above, incidentally) taking her far beyond the confines of the local cantonments into *Indian* India, where she counted 'the native ladies of rank' her friends and even went so scandalously far on occasions as to consider herself one of them. 'How I love this life in the wilderness!', she would protest, when more orthodox memsahib acquaintances congratulated her on the imminence of leaving for 'home' in 1844: 'I shall never be content to vegetate in England.'[21]

Those doubts I felt rising earlier about the unequal contest of character and caricature in the case of the memsahib are really quite easily quelled when women such as Mrs Parks are remembered (and there were plenty others of her ilk). I am almost selfish enough to have wished the formidable Fanny in India at the time of the Mutiny, not being absolutely sure whose side she would be on. There is certainly little room for the traditional old images of indolence, ignorance and intolerance which might be inferred from the 'typical' memsahib's day when one compares it with even the most mundane diary entry under siege during the Mutiny. Either nearly all the Mutiny accounts by women I have come across just happen to have been written by the most resilient, resourceful and Parks-like women in India at the time, or else the pundits are wrong in consigning the memsahib so mercilessly to Tennyson's 'soft and milky rabble of womankind'.[22] For an example, and a foretaste of what is to come, here is Mrs Maria Germon's diary entry for Wednesday 26 August:

Dearest Mother's birthday. We had had a wretched night with Mrs

Boileau's children and the firing, I actually lay [in] till seven. Dear
Charlie sent me a beautiful bouquet of roses, myrtle and tuberoses. I
went down and got my mug of tea without sugar and milk (I use
Charlie's silver mug as cups are scarce) and a chupattee, then went
and sat at the door for a little air, went and had a wash of clothes.
Today our rations are reduced – gentlemen get twelve instead of
sixteen ounces of meat and we six instead of twelve – with rather less
dal. A sentry was shot through the leg in our verandah in the night
and Dr Fayrer was hit by a spent ball. After breakfast I mended a
pair of Charlie's unmentionables with a piece of Mr Harris's habit
presented for the purpose. Charlie came for a little chat but a note
from the Brigadier called him away. A little milk punch is doled out
to us every day about one and I drank dear Mother's health in mine.
I afterwards sat at the door making a flannel waistcoat for myself – at
four we had dinner, after dinner the invalids came out and took the
air on their couches at the door – at seven I went down and made tea
for all, then sat at the door till half-past eight when we had prayers –
then to bed and I had a good night's rest, though the children were
rather squabbly.[23]

Maria was living with numerous other women and children
(who were being born and dying by her side as the days of the
siege went on) in the former dining-room of the Residency
building in Lucknow. Before the outbreak she was settled peace-
ably and comfortably in the city – one of British India's favourites,
and dubbed the 'City of Gardens' – as a Bengal Native Infantry
officer's wife. Little is known of her before the period covered by
her diary (from May to December 1857) and little afterwards –
except that both she and her husband survived and Charlie retired in 1869 having reached the rank of Lieutenant-Colonel. But
despite her obvious strength and sanguinity she obviously considered herself very ordinary. Just a memsahib.

Sadly, most of the British women involved in this book, like

Maria, only kept a record of their experiences from the date of the outbreak itself – or that particularly sensational episode is all that has survived from their life's letters and diaries – and so it is not always easy to place them before the hot weather of 1857. But of those whose pre-Mutiny history we do know, most would share the attitude of Maria Germon: they were all just memsahibs. And yet none of them would consider herself in any way standard issue.

Take Charlotte Canning, for instance. As British India's First Lady (save the Queen) since 1856, when husband Charles was appointed Governor-General, she was expected by the British élite to represent all that was most noble in British womanhood (surely a more superior cast of womanhood than any other): a sort of super-memsahib, if you like. She longed to be able to communicate with her countrywomen in India, but her rank prevented her. The charmed life she was supposed to lead in her official residence in Calcutta, a newly built edifice modelled on a Derbyshire stately home and, according to Charlotte, 'hopelessly difficult to manage', was frustrating in the extreme. Her apartments were on the top floor, above her husband's, and made her feel as though she was living as a permanent convalescent in a mouldering ivory tower. There were legions of servants, morose, mute and permanently swathed in an impenetrable fog of deference.

The Cannings had been married for twenty years when they arrived in India, and their relationship seems hardly to have been incandescent. They had no children; both were inclined towards melancholy; at least in London Charlotte had had some arguably useful and satisfying employment as Lady to the Bedchamber to Queen Victoria. But here, amongst the society of 'England in perspiration', her loneliness was acute. 'At present my solitude and idleness are unbounded, and it is anything but cheerful', she wrote from the grand and mildewed morning-room soon after her arrival. Even the countless functions she was required to attend as hostess or consort failed to divert her: once one had navigated the intractable waters of diplomatic protocol, with its dicey shallows involving who should sit next to whom, leave the table first, speak before they are spoken to and so on, there was very little to do but eat. Charlotte was too socially exalted to be drawn into conversation by other women uninvited, and all she got when she initiated it was nervous parochial small-talk. 'It really is a very proper place', she lamented: 'its greatest sin is its intense dullness.'[24]

Lady Canning's daily round was depressing, unfulfilling, and boring. Until the Mutiny, that is.

Somewhat lower down the social scale – although with an impeccable Anglo-Indian pedigree – was Augusta Becher, who was actually born aboard the *Duke of Lancaster*, an East Indiaman, off the Cape.

Augusta was a soldier's wife, brought up with the family memories of India and no doubt inculcated during her itinerant childhood with a sense of duty towards the country where it was almost inevitable she would make her home. She accordingly married the seventh son of the seventh son of one of the Company's most celebrated servants (although her husband, inevitably named Septimus, was a soldier rather than civilian) and sailed out on a troopship to Calcutta a month after the wedding, at the age of nineteen. It was 1849, and for the next few years Augusta was able to fulfil her destiny admirably, bearing (and sometimes burying) her husband's children, managing his household, taking her place amongst his colleagues' womenfolk, and generally supporting him in every way. India was part of Augusta's identity, gaudy and surreal as it sometimes seemed, and there was no yearning for the muted tones of the home counties for her. 'I was a soldier's wife to the heart's core, and there were not a few of us who felt a longing to be in the fight, women though we were . . . I think my own inner life lay dormant, being so perfectly and entirely happy. I only gave thanks, for I more than idolised him, and we were truly one in tastes and feelings.'[25] Again: until the Mutiny.

Ruth Coopland, on the other hand, might have *been* in the home counties for all the difference she saw on arriving in Gwalior (as the new chaplain's new wife) in January 1857:

My first view was a pleasing one. The cantonments consisted of a row of large thatched houses in compounds, like pretty, gay gardens, on each side of a wide road bordered with trees, and about a mile long. The road had an English look: the people were driving and riding about, and the pretty, healthy-looking children . . . also riding and driving in little pony-carriages. We passed the church, which looked exactly like an English one, and is very well built.[26]

The dinners and levées which greeted their instalment promised much in the way of comfort and familiarity. All the ladies of the station called on Ruth within days, and of course she returned every visit, and even though she was a stranger there, her Dumfriesshire blood (and, presumably, accent) worked wonders: 'for every one nearly in India is Scotch or Irish'. A celebration given in the mess-house soon after the Cooplands' arrival put the final seal of approval on this foreign land. 'The rooms were brilliantly lighted and prettily furnished, and', what is more, 'the dinner just like an English one, for what could not be procured in India had been brought from Europe; including hermetically sealed fruits, fish, and meats, and preserves, with champagne, &c.'[27]

All in all, what with the Mutton Club,[28] the Book Club, the pleasant (British) company and the congeniality of her husband's position – and if one ignored the noisy jackals and the sepoys who irritatingly fired blanks and saluted all the time – life in India was really very tolerable. There was rarely any direct need to communicate with Indians (just as well, as she 'always felt inclined to speak to the natives in German or French') and engrossed in her new husband, her new station in life (topographically as well as socially) and, no doubt, her pregnancy, Ruth was content. Once more: until the Mutiny.

And so might young Minnie Wood have been too, had her weak-willed husband had an ounce of spirit about him. Minnie (Lydia, really) would love to have been cast of the same mettle as Maria Germon and Augusta Becher, and even Ruth Coopland's short-sighted complacency would have done. She was an officer's wife married, as Augusta and Ruth were, mere weeks before the passage to Calcutta. Her letters home to mother have a brittle gloss of ecstasy about them: how wonderful a husband Archie is, how wise and brave and heroic; how tiresome her fellow female passengers are (and so how superior is she); how well she is managing her pregnancy both on board ship and once arrived in India (wearing her tightly laced stays, as advised by mama, right up until six weeks before her baby is born).

But then doubts begin to creep in. Archie is not as 'well' as he should be, she notes rather querulously. He has been in 'a great state of irritation' ever since they arrived in the comparatively remote station of Jhelum to which they have been posted. He expects her to be able to manufacture 'custards and jellies' at the drop of a hat, even though she is vastly pregnant by now, and somewhat handicapped by all the spiders, real and imaginary, who share their living quarters. 'I suppose it will all come in good time, but he is so absurd expecting me to be able to do everything as well as those who have been out here for years.'[29]

Finally Minnie's thorough disillusionment with India and all it meant to her erupted. It was meeting Archie's long-time memsahib sister (no doubt sickeningly good at custards and jellies) that did it. She had had thirteen children in fifteen years 'and now a bad miscarriage! There is a nice prospect for me . . . Oh, I *hate* this country'.[30]

Until the Mutiny, I keep saying: here are four different

women – wives before women, really: the Governor-General's, the Assistant Adjutant-General's, the griffin (new-boy) chaplain's and the disenchanted Captain's – memsahibs all, sharing not their characters, their roles and aspirations, but the fact that all are poised, for the most part facing backwards and fanned by an uneasy punkah-wallah, on the brink of catastrophe. Never mind the military derring-do, never mind the politics and the posturing and the endless analyses: their story is about enduring and coping with what amounted to a domestic calamity. Being women of their time, they were ostensibly far less fit to cope with that than the soldiers and sepoys were with the mechanics of the insurrection. The angels of Albion, they were popularly supposed to be: the passive symbol in India of all that was gentlest, purest, and most *Christian* about Britain. Catching up the blood-matted tresses of some cruelly massacred maiden as a token, with 'Remember the women of Cawnpore!' as their war-cry and spurred by an image of fair-skinned Britannia struggling like some Leda under the claws of a lascivious Indian tiger, the British soldiery was celebrated by the media of the time flying into battle as chivalrously as any crusaders. The memsahib was merely a sort of military muse, both to the Indians (in action) and the British (in defence). But passive? Symbolic?

We shall see.

3

The Spark Ignites

———

The mine had been prepared, the train had been laid, the spark which fell from female lip ignited it at once.[1]

One of the theories held about the Great Mutiny of 1857 is that it was planned, conspiratorially, to fulfil a prophecy made at the time of Robert Clive's victory at Plassey. It was said then that the feringhee would only hold sway in India for a mere hundred years. Come June 1857, on the centenary of Plassey, their subjects would rise up and topple the British from their stolen throne. And such an uprising would it be that no white man's son would ever dare to pretend power in India again. The precise date of the outbreak, allegedly arranged by secret Mutiny committee members recruited from each regiment of the Native Army, ranges according to various historians between 31 May and the actual anniversary date of 23 June. What is agreed by the conspiracy theorists, though, is that 10 May was too soon. The conflagration at Meerut caught the network of mutineers off guard – which is just as well for the British, for had the original plans been followed (they argue), there would never have been that glorious thing called the Imperial British Raj.

I doubt the theory, I must admit: the whole haphazard course of the Mutiny and lack of internal organization and of a common cause would seem to disprove it. After all, the rebels were not all the noble and idealist freedom-fighters most modern Indian scholars would have them be (although there were such admirable men and women here and there). Instead they presented a disunited and jostling mixture of disaffected sepoys, disinherited Rajahs, Ranis, and nawabs, ambitious zemindars, various malcontents bearing particular grudges against particular people, and all the opportunist badmashes (hooligans) of the local bazaars. There was precious little structure to the uprising and even less co-ordination.

If the local mutiny at Meerut did scupper the greater Mutiny, however, then the privilege of having preserved British India for the next hundred years (or so) must belong to a shadowy, beskirted figure known by the curious name of 'Mees Dolly'. Dolly – originally Dorothy (or Dolores?), I presume – was a British woman hanged by her countrymen for the murder of a couple of Eurasian women and, more significantly, for 'egging on' the mutineers. A surprising candidate for saviour of the Empire, really: she was one of those fallen women who, like the ex-members of the Fishing Fleet, had not been 'returned empty' but had instead 'gone sour'. She had never been a Fleet member herself, being country-born (a term applied to those Europeans with the poor taste to have lived in India all their lives); she was 'pure white', though, and had even managed to marry a British sergeant at one stage. But now she was widowed. It would have been most unusual had she not received further offers of marriage on her husband's death: remarriage for someone in her position was very much a matter of finance rather than romance – but something went wrong with Dolly. It is said she got into trouble for theft, which may well have disqualified her from cantonment society. In any case, she seems to have drifted into the Meerut bazaar and there set herself up as a prostitute, no doubt an exotic addition to the 'frail ones' catering (quite robustly, actually) to the appetites of the native 3rd Light Cavalry.[2]

It was the Light Cavalrymen of Meerut who set the whole Mutiny off (directly or indirectly) by refusing, at an ill-advised drill parade on 24 April, to use those supposedly contaminated new cartridges. In fact the sepoys were assured the cartridges they were issued at the parade were not the suspiciously new-fangled ones, but given the formality and ostentation of the occasion on which the commanding officer chose to present them, expecting to squash months of smouldering suspicions with one smart stamp, it was hardly surprising that the sepoys mistrusted him. Lieutenant-Colonel Carmichael-Smyth had never been popular anyway, either with his fellow officers or with the men. Why should the Cavalrymen of Meerut take it upon themselves to be the first to betray (for all they knew) the beliefs of all the sepoys of India – let alone compromise their own caste? They refused the cartridges, and when the point was uncompromisingly pressed by Carmichael-Smyth what might have rested at apologetic non-cooperation hardened into rebellion. The eighty-five troopers who had refused his orders were court-martialled. After their sentence of ten years' imprisonment with hard labour had been passed, he sent them out on to the parade-ground again, on Saturday 9 May, to be more publicly disgraced. Here their uniforms (and thus their pride) were stripped from them and fetters clamped around their ankles before a forced march, with bare heads bowed and their uselessly gleaming boots in hand, to the gaol.

There were those who doubted the wisdom of Carmichael-Smyth's relentlessness even then: not so much in punishing the men as he did, but in insisting so pompously that the cartridges be seen to be used in the first place. One young lad of the regiment, Cornet John McNabb, although he would never have been so feckless as to voice his disgust of the Colonel in public, was quite prepared to write it in a letter to his mother: 'There was no necessity to have a parade at all or to make any fuss of the sort just now . . . The men themselves humbly petitioned the Colonel to put the parade off till this disturbance in India had gone over, in fact pointing out to him what he ought to have seen himself.' The whole sorry affair would never have developed as it did had the sepoys just been 'left alone, instead of being paraded, and addressed, and all that humbug'.[3]

Another contemporary, Commissioner Cracroft Wilson, went even further, blaming Carmichael-Smyth rather paradoxically not only for the outbreak at Meerut but also – in that he thereby preempted the great Mutiny conspiracy – for the survival of British rule in India. 'From this combined and simultaneous massacre . . . we were, humanly speaking, saved by Lt.-Col. Smyth commanding the 3rd Regiment of Bengal Light Cavalry, and the frail ones of the bazaar . . . the mine had been prepared, the train had been laid, the spark which fell from female lip ignited it at once.'[4]

Which brings us back to the unfortunate Dolly. 'Female lip', says Cracroft Wilson: he is referring to the merciless fleering that is reported to have greeted the imprisoned sepoys' colleagues when, on the evening of 9 May, they made their disconsolate way to the brothels of the bazaar. The news of the shameful and degrading parade had travelled characteristically fast, and Dolly and her sisters were ready.

But the usual welcome was missing: instead taunts and sneers at their manhood. 'We have no kisses for cowards!' was the cry. Were they really men, they were asked, to allow their comrades to be fitted with anklets of iron and led off to prison? And for what? Because they would not swerve from their creed! Go and rescue them, they were told, before coming to us for kisses.[5]

And so they did. It was one of the first acts of the Great Mutiny, the liberation of the eighty-five condemned men (and assorted badmashes besides) from Meerut New Gaol. After that, the slaughter began.

The telegraph message which announced the uprising to the world (well, to Agra, actually, 130 miles down the road) did not manage to include news of the break-out at the gaol. The girl who sent it had only time, before the telegraph lines were cut by the rebels, to attend to the worrying matter of an aunt's proposed journey to Meerut:

The Lieutenant-Governor of the North-Western Provinces to the Secretary of the Government of India (Telegraphic): May 11, 1857.
Last night at 9 o'clock, a telegraph message was received here [Agra] by a lady from her niece, sister of the post-master of Meerut, to the following effect: – *The cavalry have risen, setting fire to their own houses and several officers' houses, besides having killed and wounded all European soldiers and officers they could find near the lines; if aunt intends starting tomorrow evening, please detain her from doing so as the van has been prevented from leaving the station.* No later message has been received, and the communication by telegraph has been interrupted, how, not known; any intelligence will be sent on immediately.[6]

Compared with the tight-lipped tone of this government bulletin, the telegram itself seems strangely homely. Eighteen-year-old Kate Moore had been asked by her father, editor of the *Mofussilite* newspaper in Agra, to let him know if any trouble developed in their home city so that he might be the first to publish it. Kate's brother was the Meerut post-master, which made her commission considerably easier. It was just unfortunate that her aunt should have planned 11 or 12 May to return home from a visit to Kate's father: given the mayhem that appeared to have overtaken Meerut the journey would at best be intolerably uncomfortable and at worst, downright dangerous.[7] It is difficult to tell whether Kate realized the enormity of what had just happened in Meerut. But then even the authorities found it hard to credit at first: there had obviously been some seditious scaremongering going on, and the ladies (God bless 'em) had taken fright and were imagining things. It took three days for the seat of government in Calcutta to be officially convinced Kate was in fact under rather than over-estimating the truth. And by then, the massacres of Meerut and Delhi were done.

This reluctance to believe the worst is in turn pretty difficult to understand, given all the warnings there had been. The simmering air of the cantonments had been thick with rumour (and chupattis) for months now; the minor mutinies and unwonted sepoy intransigence growing ever more evident on the parade grounds must surely have signified *something*? Just as disquieting was the apparent enthusiasm of the general ruffians of the bazaar to cash in on the sepoy cause and organize their own local riots. Looting, thieving and general lawlessness thrived under the convenient cover of insurrection.

The problem was, as J.G. Farrell's Collector Hopkins in *The Siege of Krishnapur* was only too aware, that one had to balance the dangers of publicly making preparations for possible danger ahead (building ramparts, laying down stores, making contingency plans for other goods and the women by either sending them away to the hills – a bit drastic, that – or arranging their collection into a single, safe building) thereby admitting one's present vulnerability, or airily denying that there was anything to prepare for. Krishnapur's Collector got around the problem by being notoriously absent-minded and pretending the trench he was having dug around the Residency compound was something vaguely to do with watering the roses during the hot weather, which, of course, convinced no one. There was something dishonourable about admitting weakness and for any stalwart of British society to do so must amount, *per se*, to insanity.

Farrell's character echoes somewhat that of Martin Gubbins, the Financial Commissioner of Lucknow. Poor, earnest Gubbins was considered perfectly insane by his bemused and irritated colleagues for the zeal with which he insisted on fortifying his house as soon as he heard about Meerut, and laying in stupendous stores of food and wine for the household just in case (and this was maddest of all!) of a siege. It was just as well, as it turned out, that he did.

Meerut had no such evangelist. On the contrary: its Division Commander, Major-General William Hewitt, variously described (even contemporarily) as Bloody Bill, fearful old dolt and exasperating idiot,[8] was assuring everyone right up until the first officer fell that all was steady, calm and under control – and this in the face of everything that had gone on during the fortnight before the outbreak itself.

Kate Moore's brother had reported hearing 'seditious language' amongst the orderlies sent to the post office to collect the regimental mail; Mrs Greathed, the commissioner's wife, related at a dinner party on the evening of Saturday 9 May that she had even heard of placards being posted quite baldly around the city, 'calling on all true Mussulmans to rise and slaughter the English. The threat was treated by us all with indignant disbelief.' The very morning of the Mutiny, although dawning as far as the untroubled Mrs Greathed was concerned 'in peace and happiness', was not without its omens. This commissioner's wife, perhaps locally a little more exalted than the other memsahibs of the garrison, spent the day much as usual, going to the early morning service in the cantonment church of St John, and chatting pleasantly with 'poor Mr McNab[b]', Carmichael-Smyth's critical young Cornet, afterwards. It was a particularly pleasant and serene sort of day, she remembered (although, writing in retrospect, she probably would).[9] Nothing untoward happened at all until it was time to get ready for church again at dusk.

Kate's family, stationed like the Greatheds outside the cantonment, was not so untroubled. Perhaps it lived at closer quarters with the Indian members of the household: Kate remembered her mother's cook begging her not to let the younger children out of the house that Sunday morning. Bemused at her insistence, Mrs Moore brushed her aside and sent the little ones out with their ayah as usual. Unthinkably, the family was urged, again by the cook, not to attend morning service (which, of course, they did). When time came for evening service at seven, the Moores were again implored not to go – not told why: just to stay safe behind well-shuttered windows. No doubt somewhat irritated by now, the Moores were well on their way to church before they realized what the cook had been talking about – and even then, it was not until a white face told them to get home and stay there (with the rumble of shot and the first flames beginning to lick towards them) that they did just that. 'It was then,' wrote Kate, 'that I thought it time to let my father at Agra know of what was taking place',[10] and her telegram, 'the strangest telegram that ever came, as sole warning to an Empire that its very foundation was attacked',[11] was sent.

What had actually happened at about five-thirty that Sunday afternoon was this. The evening service on Sundays was usually preceded by the regimental parade, when the officers and soldiers of the garrison marched from the lines to the church. Because it was so intolerably hot today, the parade had been postponed for half an hour and would start not at six-thirty, as usual, but at seven. The British officers on duty were just beginning to prepare for it when it became obvious something was seriously amiss. Behind the blinds, in the stifling so-called cool of the bungalows, there was a palpable air of panic amongst the servants, while outside a sulphurous streak on the horizon in the direction of the native infantry lines was growing disturbingly thicker, redder, hotter and louder by the minute. Down in the lines themselves some sort of commotion had broken out amongst the sepoys and badmashes which seemed to be concentrated on the regimental magazine. Despite bellowed orders to disperse from the officers who had managed (half dressed, in one case) to gallop down by now, the magazine was stormed and the weapons inside grabbed and flung through the increasing rabble until, with musketry firing off indiscriminately, the uproar finally exploded into riot.

The august appearance of Colonel John Finnis of the 11th Native Infantry was what triggered the Mutiny proper: fondly imagining that all that was needed to calm the over-excited baba-logue was a show of dignity and authority, he had saddled up and ridden down to the lines. At precisely the wrong moment. He arrived just as the bells-of-arms had been broken open and so supreme a figure of British imperiousness proved an irresistible focus for the Indians' whipped-up violence. First his horse was shot beneath him, and then the man himself, and what had before been a (mismanaged) matter of indiscipline was now free – on both sides – to blossom rankly into blood-revenge.

Being a proper and dutiful woman, one of the army captains' wives, Mrs Dunbar Douglas Muter, had already arrived at church while all this was going on, and found herself (metaphorically as well as physically) facing the other way when the Great Mutiny of 1857 broke out.

On Sunday, May 10th, 1857, I was at Meerut. The 1st Battalion 60th King's Royal Rifles, in which my husband was then a captain, oc-cupied the Infantry barracks. The men were parading for church at about 6.30 p.m. My husband had left me to accompany them. The sun was sinking in a blaze of fiery heat that rose hazy and glowing from the baked plain. I drove to the church and waited outside the door, expecting every moment to hear the sound of a gay march which so strangely heralds the approach of a body of soldiers to divine worship; but – I listened in vain. A dull sound, very different from that I expected, came over the stillness of Nature around; but I little heeded the holiday-making in the bazaars, holiday-making as I then thought it . . .

A gentleman accosted me. 'You need not be alarmed, but an out-break has taken place requiring the presence of the troops, so there will not be a service in the church this evening.' I replied: 'therefore I will wait a little.' But when the clock struck seven, the hour to com-mence, and no congregation was assembling, I called to my friend [and what was he doing hanging around the church at such a time as this, I wonder?] and requested him to tell my husband, should he arrive, that he had advised me to return home. Up to this, I was seated with my back to the cantonment in a little pony carriage, but the moment the horses' heads were turned I saw the Native lines in a blaze, and, in some alarm, but not the least understanding the gravity of the position, I gave the order to hasten home.[12]

Meanwhile, the wife of another captain – and one of the most popular officers in the garrison – was witnessing at far too close quarters what this 'holiday-making' was really all about. Mrs Craigie's route to St John's church led her past the mess of the 3rd Light Cavalry and as she and her companion, the sister of a Lieutenant Mackenzie, trotted by in their carriage they noticed the mess servants all leaning over the wall and craning their necks towards the native lines – the direction in which the memsahibs were heading for church. As they watched, crowds of natives, armed and bawling, began sweeping up the road towards them, preceded by a young English soldier running, as Mrs Craigie soon realized, for his life. The women managed to haul the soldier into their carriage (the Indians by now close enough to beat at the vehicle with their lattees), then they turned and pelted home, where they found Captain Craigie preparing for the parade ut-terly unaware of what was going on.

While he galloped off to muster his troops (who, for love of the man, remained loyal) his wife swapped the rescued soldier's uni-form for some clothes of the captain, but could think of nothing else constructive to do. So she and Miss Mackenzie huddled together in the hot darkness (hotter and less dark by the minute) watching the rebels' fires growing closer and closer to her own bungalow until they could not only see but also hear the arsonists' work. The neighbouring compound to the Craigies' belonged to the Chambers, an adjutant and his notably beautiful twenty-three-year-old wife. Their stables were torched first (the sound of the horses burning alive quite appalling) and then the bungalow itself. Soon the more chilling sound of a woman screaming became distinguishable over the shrieks of the horses and Mrs Craigie looked across to the verandah of the Chambers' bungalow to see Charlotte Chambers (only recently arrived in India and heavily pregnant) trapped and delirious with fear. Mrs Craigie immediately ordered her servants to climb their joint garden wall and somehow drag Charlotte out of the verandah and back with them, but it was useless. The poor woman was already dead, literally butchered (the Moslem who cut her throat with his meat-cleaver and mockingly laid her unborn baby on her chest had previously been reprimanded by his victim for bringing her bad meat – and was one of the first to be hanged by the British),[13] and now the mob was heading for the Craigies' place brandishing burning logs.

But – and although this sounds more and more like a scene out of G. A. Henty it does appear to be true – just as the first rebels leapt the wall, to be met by the Craigies' faithful servants running through the gardens waving their arms and yelling at them to remember what sort of a man was their master ('the people's friend', they called him), a four-man guard of the captain's troop galloped up to the compound, rushed to where his wife was trying to compose herself for the same sort of fate as had welcomed Charlotte Chambers, and then ignored her hands outstretched in fervent recognition and prostrated themselves on the floor, dipping their foreheads to her feet and vowing to spend their lives (if necessary) in safeguarding hers.

Even though Mrs Craigie kept desperately going out on to the verandah to see if she could see her husband coming, inviting the odd shot from the gory-looking darkness below, she managed to survive long enough for Craigie and Lieutenant Mackenzie to find their way home and arrange a temporary escape. Once the fires around had faded a little, and wrapped in dark blankets to cover the glare of their light muslin dresses, the women were shepherded out into the bungalow's grounds to hide in a tiny temple, to wait either until they were discovered there, or could move on to a safer place. If there were any.

Mrs Muter, meanwhile, was growing more and more disgusted by the minute. She had managed to get home from church – although not quite as valiantly as Mrs Craigie, having used the diversion of *two* European soldiers being chased by missile-hurling natives as cover to slip home unobserved – and was now faced by a household of panicking servants, with the khansamah, or house steward, as their spokesman.

He declared he could no longer be responsible for any property, and bringing the silver in use, he returned it to my charge. At the same time he advised me to conceal myself – a proposal he saw I regarded as an insult. To conceal yourself in your own house, in the lines of a regiment that had reckoned up a century of renown! And from what?[14]

Charlotte Chambers might have told her what. And Amelia Courtenay, the hotel-keeper's wife who was hacked out of her carriage on the way to church, and Eliza Dawson, confined to her bed with smallpox and burned there, having seen her husband shot for trying to rescue her. Or pregnant Louisa MacDonald, a captain's wife and (more significantly) an Indian's mistress, who was dressed by her children's ayah in native clothes and taken into a Hindu family for protection and yet still cut down (although her children survived) and killed. Mrs Muter was lucky.

Captain Craigie, who was spending the first night of the Mutiny cowering with his wife in a Hindu temple in his garden, had earlier that evening seen something which chilled him more than anything else. It had happened just before he witnessed Mrs Courtenay's murder (and in turn killed her killer) and just days ago would not have seemed remarkable at all. But then, just as the first, frenzied news of the catastrophe was breaking amongst the garrison's higher ranks, the sight of the eighty-five cavalrymen who the day before had been chained and jailed, now mounted, in uniform, and riding triumphantly towards Delhi, was ominous in the extreme. Especially since no orders had been given to pursue them (Major-General Hewitt considering it unlikely the mutineers would go anywhere but home, and feeling it unwise to abandon Meerut to the equally troublesome badmashes and their work). In forty miles they would reach the old Mogul capital, where they would find a king deposed by the British, a vast collection of native Indians in the bazaars and the cantonments susceptible, given a little emotive encouragement, to insurrection and, best of all, no European regiment present: both the arsenal and magazine were guarded by sepoys. The telegraph lines had been cut, and the feringhee at Delhi had no more reason to suspect Armageddon than had those at Meerut (which, incidentally, boasted the greatest European military strength of any garrison in India. And look where it got them.) It is said that the Commissioner of Delhi, Simon Fraser, was slipped a letter by a native on his way to church on the Sunday evening, which warned him of what was to happen at Meerut and might have prepared Delhi for what obviously lay ahead.[15] But Fraser received so many odd petitions on this and that: there was no reason to suppose this one was any less trivial than the rest. So he stuffed it into his pocket to look at later. It was only the next morning, when news of the mutineers' arrival reached his breakfast table, that he remembered the note, tore it open, and read the awful prophecy inside.

Fraser's first action was to order his buggy and get to the palace (within the Red Fort, where King Bahadur Shah II still reclined in straitened splendour) to warn the British officers stationed there. Captain Douglas, commander of the palace's strategic Lahore Gate, had guests that morning: the chaplain, Revd Mr Jennings, his daughter Annie,[16] and her friend Miss Mary Clifford. There are various accounts of the confusion that followed Fraser's arrival: what seems to have happened is that he and Douglas were wounded by the mutineers, and when they tried to hole up in Douglas's private apartments, were followed and killed on the stone steps that led to his rooms. Jennings had come down to see what all the fuss was about and started ranging around with a sword, but the mob soon cut him down and, climbing over the bodies, raced upstairs. It did not take them long to find Mary and Annie (newly affianced to a young lieutenant) cowering petrified in a cupboard.

The announcement of their deaths was the first of British women to reach home – news from Delhi travelled faster than from Meerut – and set the tone for all the gusty rhetoric of the months to come. The *Illustrated London News* was up there with the best: remembering the slaughter of 'the gentle mothers and wives of fair England', it vowed, would 'make the hoarse thunders of our guns' discourse sweet music in our ears, and darken even the heart's devotion, until their wrongs shall be avenged.'[17] In killing such innocents the rebels were perceived (hypocritically, as it turned out) to be grossly transgressing the rules of engagement and so surrendering the moral high ground to the enemy, whose blinkered sentimentality made it quite impregnable. But while the inspiration for some of the age's most fulsomely mawkish offerings (in painting as well as prose) was frothily fermenting back home, the mean reality – stripped of sentiment – was horrific.

Scores of Europeans are said to have been massacred in Delhi: fewer than the blanket slaughter rumoured to have wiped out the whole Christian population at the time, but enough to jolt British India out of its complacency and take the Mutiny seriously at last. Several of the comparatively favoured women who survived the first onslaught made the short, scorching journey to what was considered the safest (available) building around: the sturdy Flag-staff Tower, which still stands on the ridge that separates the old city from the cantonment. There they stayed in desperately close confinement (the building being only eighteen feet in diameter), occupied in relaying guns and ammunition to the guard at the top of the tower and taking turns to rest on the few charpoys and chairs jammed about the place until, at about six in the evening, the realization dawned that the expected relief force from Meerut was inexplicably not going to arrive (it had never been dispatched, of course) and that the only hope of survival now was to disperse in parties of varying number and fortune to the uncertain jungle beyond.

Those the fugitives left behind were subjected to atrocities quite as repellent as any the British perpetrated on the hapless Indians in revenge. There are chilling little vignettes in several accounts of the private apocalypses of ordinary women: civilian William Clark's wife, for instance, who was found in her house in the Kashmir bazaar by a neighbour.

Every minute detail is distinctly imprinted on my mind, for with that cowardly shrinking from a knowledge of the worst, which is common to us all, I lingered in the outer room and kept looking round it. At length I nerved myself and stepped into the next room which was the hall. Oh! I had indeed need to nerve myself. Just before me pinned to the wall was poor Clark's little son with his head hanging down, and a dark stream of blood trickling down the wall into a large black pool which lay near his feet. And this cruel death they must have inflicted before the mother's eyes. I closed my eyes and shuddered, but I opened them upon, even as yet, a more dreadful sight. Clark and his wife lay side by side. But I will not, I could not, describe the scene ... she was far advanced in pregnancy.[18]

It is a horrific picture, and one that was repeated throughout the Mutiny. The cold and formal memorial tablets lining St James's church in Delhi record whole families – whole dynasties, it seems – wiped out on a single day. The gloom is not unremitting, though: even in as tragic a tale as that of young Mrs Leeson, who managed to escape from one group of mutineers, simply by running away with her baby in her arms and two small children at her side, only to be met and attacked by another. A single shot killed the baby and gravely wounded her; as soon as she recovered consciousness the mutineers tore the eldest children from what they thought was her body and cut their throats, before leaving the family for dead. But Mrs Leeson, sensationally, survived, turning up weeks later on the Delhi Ridge with an astonishing story to tell and a passionate reunion with her husband to sustain her.

There is even the odd (and rather surreal) touch of humour to be gleaned amongst the general grimness. 'A widow lady narrates an extraordinary escape: before the rabble set fire to her house she was buried by her servants in the garden, her head only left above ground, and this was covered with bushes, over which straw was scattered. The latter caught fire, and not only burnt the hair of her head, but would have discovered her retreat, had not a syce rushed forward and prevented search being made, by declaring that the ground was sacred, he having buried his wife there.'[19] I can't help wondering why they didn't just leave the poor woman with her head uncovered. It would certainly pull me up short, if I were a mutineer.

A different sort of ingenuity was displayed by the Eurasian Mrs Aldwell, another city (rather than cantonment) resident:

I was residing in the part of the city known as Darya-ganj, and I got intimation of the sepoys coming from Meerut between 8 and 9 a.m. on the 11th of May.

One of my saises [grooms] came and told me that the troops had mutinied and . . . had murdered all the Europeans they met with on their way here, and recommended that our carriage should at once be got ready to take us away, as the soldiers had determined on murdering all Europeans in Delhi also. While I was speaking to the man, our next door neighbour, Mr Nowlan, confirmed the report that the sais had just brought, and asked if he could speak to Mr Aldwell. The two consulted together, and as our house was the largest and strongest, it was determined that all the Europeans in the neighbourhood should collect there, and defend themselves as long as they could, or till such time as help should arrive . . . I think we must have numbered, inclusive of men, women and children, upwards of thirty people.[20]

Nothing much happened for the rest of the morning: the Aldwells' house stood right up against the bank of the Jumna, and so the rebels clattered straight past them on their way to the city and it was not until mid-afternoon, when she heard the vast explosion following the blowing-up of the magazine, that Mrs Aldwell decided the time had come to move.

I then requested Mr Aldwell to let me and my three children leave the house, as the servants told me that the mutineers had gone for the purpose of bringing guns to bear upon it, and I was anxious to obtain concealment elsewhere. Myself and three children then dressed ourselves as natives, and left the house in two native dhoolies [covered litters], and were taken to the residence of one of the king's grandsons by name Mirza Abdulla. His wife and sister received us kindly, for Mr Aldwell and myself had known the family before. We remained there till eight that evening, when Mirza Abdulla came and said he would remove us to a house of greater security, *viz.* to one belonging to his mother-in-law. He removed us there, keeping some of our property with him, saying it would be dangerous to take it in the streets, and that I was to send my Munshi [secretary] for it next morning. I accordingly sent my Munshi for this property, *viz.* 200 rupees in money, and some silver plate; but Mirza Abdulla denied having received it, and sent word that if we did not remove from his mother-in-law's house, he would send people down to murder us . . . [21]

Thanks to the brave intervention of her munshi's mother, Mrs Aldwell was allowed by her hostess and the putative murderers (who duly arrived) to stay until the following morning. Then, hearing that the king himself was offering a guarantee for the life of every European sheltering within his palace walls, she took the children there. Once inside the Lahore Gate, the little family was imprisoned along with all the other Christians gullible enough to have accepted the guarantee (although for most of them it was Hobson's choice, I suppose).

Their names, as far as I and my children have been able to recollect them, are ... Mrs Scully and three children; Mrs Glynn; Mrs Edwards and two children; Mrs Molony and two children; Mrs Sheehan and child; Mrs Corbet and daughter; Mr Staines; Mrs Cochrane; Miss Staines; Miss M. Hunt; Miss E. Berresford; Miss L. Ryley; Master Richard Shaw; Miss Alice Shaw; Miss Ann Shaw; Mr Roberts and son; Mr Crow; Mr Smith. There was another man whose name I don't know, nor can I recollect the names of the other women and children. We were all confined in one room, very dark, with only one door, and no window or other opening. It was not fit for the residence of any human being, much less for the

number of us that were there. We were very much crowded together, and in consequence of the sepoys, and everyone who took
a fancy to do so, coming and frightening the children, we were
obliged frequently to close the one door that we had, which then
left us without light or air; the sepoys used to come with their
muskets loaded and bayonets fixed, and ask us whether we would
consent to become Mahomedans, and also slaves, if the king
granted us our lives; but the king's special armed retainers from
among whom the guard over us was always furnished, incited the
sepoys to be content with nothing short of our lives, saying we
would be cut up in small pieces and given as food to the kites and
crows . . .

Before [my imprisonment] I had a petition written addressed to
the king . . . I had stated that myself and children were from Cashmere and were Mussulmanis. On this account we had our food given
to us separately, and the king's own servants evidently believed we
were Mussulmanis, as they ate and drank with us. Since the outbreak
on Monday, I had learnt and had taught my children, the Maho-
medan confession of faith, and we were all able to repeat it. It was
from believing us Mussulmans that our lives were spared. On the
morning of the 16th of May, some of the king's special servants
attended by a small number of infantry sepoys, came and called out
to our party, that the Christians were to come out of the building,
and that the five Mahomedans were to remain; the women and
children began crying, saying they knew they were going to be murdered; but the Mahomedans swore on the Koran, and the Hindus on
the Jumna, that such was not the case, that they wanted to give them
a better residence, and that the one they were then in would be
converted into a magazine. On this they went out, were counted; but
I do not know the number; a rope was thrown round to encircle the
whole group, the same as prisoners are usually kept together when
on the move, and in this manner they were taken out of my sight,
and as I heard brought under the Pipul tree by the small reservoir in

47

the courtyard, and there murdered with swords by the king's private servants.[22]

Mrs Aldwell eventually escaped by agreeing to be held, as a Moslem, under house-arrest until being rescued by the British. She was one of the few survivors of the outbreak at Delhi to remain in the city throughout. The others were forced into becoming fugitives. As the mutineers began their inexorable (if rather haphazard) progress through Bengal, they were preceded, shadowed, dodged and deceived by increasing numbers of these fugitives. Some travelled (mostly by night, partly for the cover of darkness and also to avoid the burgeoning heat and humidity of the pre-monsoon climate) with the help of loyal servants and acquiescent villagers; others had to rely entirely on their own devices. Few of the women were accompanied by their husbands: they were either dead by now or else fighting or hiding elsewhere; many had children in their care – their own or dead friends', and several were in various stages of pregnancy, or else about to give birth. More than one baby was born in some scrubby tope in the jungle, to be covered as best as possible with scraps of petticoat to keep off the relentless May or June sun, and fed (or not) on its mother's meanly nourished milk (if her supply had not parched in the trauma of the escape) or any other food and liquid to hand. Most of the women and children had only the clothes they wore at the moment of escape, which in the case of Mary Scott meant a silk dressing-gown (she had just been having a bath); spare dresses were needed for bandages or sunshades or even for the mocking shrouds of fallen soldiers. Mind you, *anything* spare would have been a luxury, as one of them (Harriet Tytler, of whom much more anon) wistfully noted:

It was a sickening sight, knowing that all we greatly valued was lost for ever, things that money could not replace. There were relics of a beloved child that we had lost; manuscripts and paintings for a book that my husband was going to publish; all my own paintings; our plate, books, clothes, furniture, two carriages and horses; indeed all that we had, amounting to over twenty thousand rupees – a fortune for a poor military man in those days. To replace even that portion of our property which money could have bought would have cost much more than that; but our absorbing thought of escaping soon made us forget what, at other times, would have been an inconsolable grief and trial.[23]

One or two of these women even had the strength of body and character to organize their own salvation (stark courage and resourcefulness hardly being high on the traditional list of a typical memsahib's assets). By which I mean that it was the women of the party who carried – sometimes literally – any men there might be, and not always the other way around.

Take the case of the terrifyingly able Mrs Wagentreiber, for instance. The story of her escape from Delhi to Kurnaul (a popular fugitive destination about sixty miles along the Grand Trunk Road to the north of the capital) became a sort of Mutiny fable, told to prove that no matter how desperate the situation, if a Briton refuses to accept defeat, then defeat itself is done for. A daughter (more Indian than English, as it happens) of the near-mythical Colonel James Skinner, Elizabeth was able to trade on her pedigree as well as bravado and quick thinking in bartering the lives of her family (husband, fourteen-year-old daughter Julia – who wrote an account of the adventure – and baby) for the ethereal honour of serving a Skinner. Which is not to say she was not vastly heroic too: she was.

Elizabeth was married to a sub-editor of the *Delhi Gazette*. The fact that he was on the late shift that Monday morning probably saved his life: the rebels arrived before he did at the office and his wife was able to send a message via loyal servants that his carriage be turned home again. The Wagentreibers then gathered at 'a large pucca [proper] house' (their own being thatched rather than tiled) which belonged to the customs officer nearby, and from there made the chaotic and funereally slow progression that most of their fellow Delhi survivors had had to make to the supposed safety of the Flagstaff Tower. The heat and discomfort there were almost intolerable, and as soon as the first bodies were delivered from the killings at the Kashmir Gate, Elizabeth decided to chance an independent escape through the city's backstreets to the Kurnaul road.

The family's first stop three or four miles outside Delhi was at the home of a nawab who on several previous occasions had been their own guest. Although his household was most welcoming, Elizabeth was wary of the food she was offered for fear of poison, and ordered the carriage and horses to be well hidden in the garden and their wheel tracks rubbed away. She appeared, according to her awe-struck daughter Julia, to be 'guiding under Providence all our actions and words that night, [and] seemed to have extra wisdom given to her at this trying time'.

She needed it. Sepoys visited the house not once but several times during their short stay there, to check no feringhees had found their way inside, and on one occasion Elizabeth ordered that they be invited in to search. Luckily her bluff was not called, but with the suspicion that the Wagentreibers would not have been the mutineers' only victims if it had been, the family was promptly ordered out of the house and grounds.

With Elizabeth holding the reins, the Wagentreibers again hit the Grand Trunk Road, to be met after another few miles by the first of three groups of rebels, each of which was fought off by the guns and pistols Elizabeth had insisted she carry. Having survived the sepoys, the party was then attacked by a band of villagers who beat the horses' heads so viciously that – quite extraordinarily – Elizabeth turned the carriage back along the road and demanded protection (as a Skinner, I suppose) from the very sepoys they had just been shooting at. And she got it. We would rather die at the hands of soldiers, she said, than mere villagers, and faced with such nobility the sepoys could not but beat off the villagers themselves before riding off towards Delhi.

By now it was daybreak, and Elizabeth drew the battered and disintegrating carriage up at a toll-station where she demanded water to bathe the poor horses' heads. There an old fellow, recognizing a Skinner, shuffled up and took off his turban, laying it at her feet and declaring, for her father's sake, to save her life with his own. While the next band of rebels rode by she sat disguised with him (the rest of the family hidden in the carriage) gravely bowing a salaam as they galloped by. Here the baby had its first food for twenty-eight hours (a crust) and here too the Wagentreibers were joined by another party of fugitives, with whom they finally arrived at Kurnaul at three o'clock on the morning of 13 May, all utterly exhausted. Except, of course, Elizabeth who, predictably enough, instead of collapsing like the rest brewed everyone a nice, reviving cup of tea.[24]

Less breathless (but much more affecting), and to bring this story of the first stage of the Mutiny to a close, is the story of a party of more ordinary mortals than the Wagentreiber tribe. Lieutenant and Mrs Peile of the 38th Native Infantry decided to combine forces in their escape from Delhi with their friends the Woods and the Patersons. But those forces were pitifully weak:

I had no conveyance up at the Flagstaff [wrote Mrs Peile], as I went with Mrs Paterson, and my husband rode. Everybody, with the exception of one or two ladies and gentlemen, were by this time fairly off on their way to Kurnaul and Meerut. One gentleman, seeing me standing by, offered me a seat in his carriage, and, as I had my little boy, I placed him in with him, thinking to follow him with Mrs Wood. Major Paterson's coachman made off with his carriage and horses immediately we quitted it, and she was left, like myself and Mrs Wood, to depend on friends. Fortunately two empty buggies were close by, and Mrs Wood and I took one, but Mrs Paterson and her children were in another. Mrs Paterson, I am happy to say, got away with the others, and after Mrs Wood and I had proceeded a short distance we met her husband, who was being carried on a bed, he unfortunately having been shot in the face by, it is supposed, his own regiment, the 38th. The Sepoys were surrounding our buggy, but they were quite civil to us, and when they saw the doctor wounded they all stood still, and after asking them to help to assist him in his hospital dooly, which we fortunately secured on the road, one or two of the Sepoys ran to him . . .

My husband then left us to go to the quarter-guard of his regiment to see if he could prevail on his company to accompany us to Kurnaul, and we went on, the doctor being inside his close carriage, and Mrs Wood and myself following him up in a buggy. When we left the parade-ground it was about half-past six p.m., and we were the last ladies to leave the station. We had only proceeded a short distance on the Kurnaul road when some men came to us and begged of us not to proceed any further on the road as the whole of the officers and ladies who had gone before us had been murdered, and that we should meet the same fate if we persisted on our journey. We knew not what to think, and at first resolved to go on our journey let what might follow, when a very neatly dressed native, a perfect boy, made his appearance; he made us a most respectful salaam . . . and advised our taking the road he pointed out, and very kindly took us off the Grand Trunk road into some fields. We could not drive quickly as the land was perfectly rugged. We had only walked our horses a short distance when the thought struck me that the men who were surrounding us were nothing less than robbers themselves. This thought was very soon confirmed by the men coming up to us and asking for rupees. I had a few rupees in my jewel-box, but was afraid to open it lest they should see what it contained, and therefore

told them to go to our house and take anything they took a fancy to
. . . They, however, fancied we had money with us and insisted on my
showing them the seat of the buggy, and they searched every corner
of it, but still I managed to keep my jewel-box. I was driving, with
Mrs Wood by my side, and the hood of the buggy being down the
vile wretches had a capital opportunity of standing up behind, and
with the number of tulwars [swords] and sticks which they had could
have killed us in a very short space of time. Mrs Wood had a black
velvet headdress on, and as it had some bugles [glass beads] about it
it glittered a good deal in the moonlight, and when they saw this they
lost no time in tearing it from her head, and at the same time struck
her rather heavily with one of their sticks.[25]

Somehow the women managed to find their way back on to the
main road, and after being helpfully informed (when brazenly
asking the way of a passing trooper) that whichever direction they
chose would lead to death, they decided to retrace their steps
towards Delhi and hide in the East India Company's pleasure
gardens. It seemed pretty safe to assume the place would not
exactly be crawling with sepoys breathing the scented airs, and it
might indeed have proven a tolerable hiding-place had the party
not been handicapped by the wounded Dr Wood: in asking for
help for him, the women were forced to betray their whereabouts
and soon all the nearby villagers, it seemed, were converging in
their hundreds on the garden.

The gardener advised our taking shelter inside the hut, as he said
that they would be sure to kill him if they found he was protecting us.
Up to this time both charpoys were outside in the garden, for the
night was very hot. Finding that the [neighbouring] bungalows were
all in a blaze we at first feared lest the hut might be fired likewise; we
however found that, instead of its being thatched like most of them
usually are, it was tiled, and hesitated not in taking refuge. The

gardeners then locked us inside, but we had scarcely been shut up when another band of robbers, about 50 in number, made a rush at the door. We kept quite still, thinking they might leave us, but we heard them determine on breaking the lock, which was soon effected, and into the hut they rushed. I went up to one of them and implored him to save us. He asked for what we had. I told him we had lost everything we possessed, but until he had searched us he would not give credit to what we had told him. Certain it was, for even my bonnet and cloak had been taken [along with the cherished jewel-box] and the carriage horses and buggy horse ridden away, whither we knew not. They were not satisfied with taking our horses, but broke up the carriage and buggy in our presence.

Mrs Wood and I knew not what to do or where to go to. Certainly we could not remain in the gardens when daylight came; we therefore made up our minds to take the doctor as best we could and go in search of a village . . . When we reached the village it must have been about 3 o'clock a.m. on the morning of the 12th. We had to plead very hard for shelter, but when we were admitted we found the people very kind, and they gave us native bread, and the doctor some milk to drink. We tried to take rest, but sleep at a time like this was quite out of the question.[26]

Mrs Peile's narrative continues in the same rather picaresque vein: band after band of sepoys are met with and either surrendered to and bribed (she lost her wedding ring that way) or deceived by generous and apprehensive villagers. How the women managed the arbitrary choice of asking the kind country-people for help and avoiding the nasty ones is one of the Mutiny's mysteries. As is the way in which all the families involved survived intact – even the hastily dispatched Master Peile (who eventually turned up 'very well and happy' in Meerut). Messrs Peile and Paterson caught up the ladies in a village on the Kurnaul road, the former having been left with nothing by the rebels but 'a banyan [shirt] and a pair of socks'; and thanks to the unstinting efforts on the part of his wife, who dragged his bed from village to village and whose first priority on arriving was always to find fresh water to bathe his face and wash his raggy bandages, Dr Wood defied the odds, and lived.

For him, as for the families who accompanied him, the story was virtually over once the safety of dear old Simla, where they settled for the duration, was reached. Simla had succoured many a memsahib overcome by the heat of the plains in the past and its political steadfastness proved it just as welcome a refuge now.

Their Mutiny was over. But for most of British India, it had hardly yet begun.

4

Ablaze

I keep on asking God to keep my babies safe all day.[1]

Fateh-i-Islam
[*The Victory of Islam*]

It has become the bounden duty of all the people, whether women or men, slave girls or slaves, to come forward and put the English to death. The adoption of the following measures will lead to their destruction, viz.: all the Moulvees [Moslem scholars] and the Pundits [Hindu lawyers] should explain in every village and city the misfortunes which the success of the English will entail on the people and the advantages and spiritual benefit which will accrue from their extirpation. The Kings, Wuzeers [Ministers], Rajahs and Nawabs ought to slay them in the field of battle, the people should not leave their city in consequence of the entrance of the English therein, but on the contrary should shut up their doors and all the people whether men, women or children, including slave girls, slaves and old women, ought to put these accursed English to death by firing guns, carbines and pistols from the terraces, shooting arrows and pelting them with stones, bricks, earthen vessels, ladles, old shoes and all other things, which may come into their hands. They should stone to death the English in the same manner . . . The sepoys, the nobles, the

56

shopkeepers, the oil men, etc. and all the other people of the city, being of one accord, should make a simultaneous attack upon them, some of them should kill them by firing guns, pistols, and carbines and with swords, arrows, daggers, poignando, etc., some lift them up on spears, some dexterously snatch their arms and destroy the enemy, some should cling to their necks, some to their waists, some should wrestle and through stratagem break the enemy to pieces; some should strike them with cudgels, some slap them, some throw dust in their eyes, some should beat them with shoes, some attack them with their fists, some scratch them, some drag them along, some tear out their ears, some break their noses. In short no one should spare any efforts, to destroy the enemy and reduce them to the greatest extremities.[2]

It was with Jehadic proclamations such as this, issued soon after the Mutiny began, that the so-called Revolutionary Government hoped to fan the flames of insurrection in India into an all-consuming blaze. They were printed as pamphlets, for Hindu and Moslem alike, and often distributed by the mutineers themselves. Just as this one urged native women and children to join in the general blood-bath as well as men, so their victims were to include the women and children of the enemy: no one was to be spared. City, village and all the dust-brown spaces in between would be littered with the dismembered limbs of the English; the pariah dogs would grow fat and sleek on the offal and liberated India wax likewise on the triumphant spirit of its success.

That was the theory.

In fact, the spread of the Mutiny during the few weeks immediately following Meerut and Delhi was both erratic and unpredictable. Sometimes the fire swept fanatically through a station leaving only charred remains behind (as at Jhansi, where no European survived the massacre),[3] while at others it smouldered rather hesitantly, perhaps only smoking out the feringhees before either spluttering and dying altogether or else creeping off in a different direction. Hundreds of British fugitives owed their lives to the very villagers – the very sepoys, even – who were supposed to be shutting up their doors and hurling shot, shell, and shoe at them. Too many Indians were too loyal to the old order, and to their officers and memsahibs personally, for the wholesale slaughter called for to take place.

Knowing some Indian somewhere was on their side was hardly palliative to those men and women experiencing the very palpable horrors of the Mutiny first-hand, however. For the griffins like Mrs Coopland (she who had been so delighted at the Englishness of her surroundings on her arrival at Gwalior only weeks ago) one of the most difficult things to cope with was the weather. It seemed to change so quickly, like some dramatically arranged pathetic fallacy to complement the coming climax:

I was awakened one morning by the most stifling sensation in the air, and felt quite ill. The ayah and bearer said the hot winds had commenced. Really . . . it made your brain feel on fire, and all the blood in your body throb and burn like liquid fire. We drove out for a short time, and I was quite struck with the gray, lurid look of the sky: the trees looked dry and withered.[4]

To her, the news of Delhi and Meerut burst, she says, like a thunderclap. For a while, it was naïvely hoped that this was an isolated incident and that natives elsewhere would be unlikely even to have heard of it, but when it became obvious that not only had the news spread but the killing too, recriminations began. Official directives started flying across India from the Punjab to Madras, Calcutta to Bombay, with all sorts of misinformation and rumour flocking thickly just behind. In a desperately uncomfortable letter to his family at home, Ruth Coopland's Reverend husband let fly his fears:

Of course we are alarmed here. There are only about twenty English officers, with their wives and children, in the station, and about 5,000 native troops, so that we are entirely at their mercy. Already, half of our native cavalry and half of the artillery have been sent to Agra, and these were far more to be trusted than the infantry who remain. Even the Rajah's body-guard has gone to Agra. There is an English regiment at Agra, but there are many native regiments, 3,000 cut-throats in the gaol, and a hostile population; so that they would have little chance against so many enemies. And ... the Governor has called up all the native regiments, and told them that if they do not like the service, they are at liberty to leave it without molestation. Fancy such a course as this when a rising is feared throughout the country!

I do not think our lives are safe for a moment. Oh, how gladly would I send off my wife to England, or even to Agra, this moment if I could ... This is God's punishment upon all the weak tampering with idolatry and flattering vile superstitions. The sepoys have been allowed to have their own way as to this and that thing which they pretended was part of their religion, and so have been spoiled and allowed to see that we were frightened of them. And now no one can tell what will be the end of it. There is no great general to put things right by a bold stroke. We shall all be cut up piecemeal. Instead of remaining to have our throats cut, we ought to have gone to Agra long ago, or towards Bombay; and all the European regiments should have been drawn together, and every native regiment that showed the least sign of disaffection at once destroyed, or at least driven away ... I would leave for Bombay at once, but it would be death to be exposed even for an hour to the sun. What to do I know not.[5]

Actually, many of the memsahibs of Bengal *were* sent off (sooner or later) to the supposed strongholds of Agra, Lucknow, Cawnpore and, if practical, to Umballa, Lahore and the hill stations beyond – which, as we shall see, was no guarantee of safety, but the best the authorities felt they could do at the time. The first step, though, was to herd them all into the safest or least dangerous building possible, preferably fortified. For Kate Moore and those of her neighbours who had survived the initial outbreak at Meerut, this was necessarily a retrospective measure. Mrs Muter, still personally affronted by the vulgarity of the whole episode, found little to recommend the ammunition store, or Dum-Dum, in which she, Kate and Mrs Greathed found themselves billeted. 'The principal buildings were three long barracks, and the families were there grouped together during the day – the ladies at work and the children at play – eating at long tables, and living more in public than accords with English tastes. Every available spot was covered with a tent, where the nights were passed . . . and the wife of a judge, and the soldier on duty were placed in close proximity.'[6]

Planning for the future, however (as beavering Mr Gubbins of Lucknow could tell you), called for time and foresight, neither of which seems to have been in good supply during the first days and even weeks of the Mutiny's progress. In Shahjehanpur, on Sunday 31 May, all the rebels had to do was surround the church in which the parishioners were at morning service. *The Friend of India* reported what happened:

The clergyman was the first who went out to the mutineers. He was at once attacked, but managed to effect his escape with the loss of one hand. Mr Ricketts was pursued and murdered in his own verandah which he had succeeded in reaching . . . A Mr Labadoor, a writer, was killed in the church; in the confusion his wife and sister-in-law, with the bandmaster, made their escape for a time, but eventually they met with a worse fate . . . The chaplain, seeing men weeding in the fields, thought that they might be induced to help him. He accordingly left his hiding-place and offered them money if they

would assist him in reaching some place of safety. No sooner did they
see the money than they rushed upon the unfortunate man with their
sticks, and knocking him down, commenced beating him to death . . .
Dr Bowling had been allowed to visit the hospital unmolested; but on
his return, after the commencement of the outbreak, and when he
was endeavouring to escape with his wife, child, and a European
servant, he was shot by the sepoys. He was seated on the coach-box,
and fell rolling to the ground. Mrs Bowling was wounded in the
forehead by a bullet, but joined some other fugitives, who, under an
escort of fifteen sepoys and a havaldar [a native non-commissioned
officer], were endeavouring to make off. It was but for a little time
that these sepoys remained faithful; directly the plunder commenced
they deserted their charge and joined their comrades in sacking the
Treasury . . .

Those who escaped from the station [eight men, eight women,
with Mrs Bowling astonishingly the only widow, and four children]
succeeded in reaching the residence of the friendly Rajah of Poor-
byah, who lent them his elephant and sent some of his men to escort
them to the Fort of Mohumdee, which was about thirty or forty miles
distant. As the fugitives were sadly in want of money, the ladies
especially being but half-clothed, Mrs Bowling sold her carriage and
horses to the Rajah for 1,000 rupees, and upon this sum the fugitives
were to subsist for a while.[7]

Three days later the fort was taken by a company of sepoys
bringing just such an inflammatory proclamation as the *Fateh-i-
Islam* above. Captain Patrick Orr, Mohumdee's First Assistant
Commissioner, takes up the story. He had already sent his wife
Annie and their child off to the apparently sympathetic Rajah
Loni Singh at Mithowlie for safekeeping (whereupon she endured
one of the Mutiny's most astonishing adventures); now he joined
the Shahjehanpur refugees on their threadbare journey beyond
Mohumdee towards the supposed safety of Sitapur.

Well, we left Mohumdee at $5\frac{1}{2}$ p.m., after the [rebels] had secured the treasure . . . and released the prisoners. I put as many of the ladies as I could into the buggy, others on the baggage carts, and we reached Burwan at about $10\frac{1}{2}$ p.m. Next morning, Friday, the 5th, we marched towards Aurangabad. When we had come about two koss [four miles], the halt was sounded, and a trooper told us to go on ahead where we liked. We went on for some distance, when we saw a party coming along. They soon joined us and followed the buggy, which we were pushing on with all our might, when within half a mile of Aurangabad, a sepoy rushed forward and snatched [Lieutenant] Key's gun from him and shot down poor old [Lieutenant] Shiels, who was riding my horse. Then the most infernal carnage ever witnessed by man began. We all collected under a tree close by, and put the ladies down from the buggy, shots were firing in all directions amidst the most fearful yells. The poor ladies all joined in prayer, coolly and undauntedly awaiting their fate. I stopped for about three minutes amongst them, but thinking of my poor wife and child . . . I endeavoured to save my life for their sakes. I rushed out towards the insurgents and one of our men, Goordeen, 6th company, called out to me to throw down my pistol and he would save me. I did so, when he put himself between me and the men and several others followed his example. In about ten minutes more they completed their hellish work. I was about 300 yards at the utmost; poor [Captain] Lysaght was kneeling out in the open ground [with his wife], with his hands folded across his chest, and though not using his firearms, the cowardly wretches would not go up to him, till they shot him, and then rushing forward, they killed the wounded and the children, butchering them in the most cruel way. With the exception of the Drummer-boy, every one was killed . . .

On arrival at Aurangabad some of the men proposed that I should send for Annie and marching into Seetapore, put myself at the head of the Regiment.[8]

Orr did well to refuse the proposal.

Sitapur was a pleasant station on the main route between Shahjehanpur and Lucknow. Since the new year its Commissioner had been entertaining some welcome and lively guests, seventeen-year-old Madeline Jackson and her sister Georgiana, while a house was being prepared for them to live in with their brother Sir Mountstuart. Madeline was the niece of the acting Chief Commissioner of Lucknow, Coverley Jackson, and could boast a long and fairly distinguished British–Indian pedigree. Consequently, being confident, pretty, and modestly well-connected, she felt quite at home at Sitapur:

There we lived a most happy life – for about four months. At first we stayed with [Commissioner] and Mrs Christian till our house was ready – such a nice little bungalow, with a big garden and our pets Uncle C[overley] mostly had given us – our Arab, and spotted deer, and gazelles, and spotted Barbary goats, and minahs, and chicaws [a sort of partridge] and green pigeons etc. etc., and white bullocks to irrigate the garden – and my brother had a buggy and horse and his Arab.

All this time rumours of disturbances were going on . . . Then in May, Meerut, I think, began, and we all got ready, though all the officers were quite certain *their* troops were faithful! However, everybody, civilians too, went about armed, and it was settled, should there be an outbreak, that all should go to the Christians' house. Mr C. tried to get elephants to send the ladies in to Lucknow on – unsuccessfully.

One morning – the 2nd June – we had just had prayers and were at breakfast when someone, Mr Christian, I think, came in to tell us another place [Shahjehanpur] had mutinied, and the native soldiers were marching on Sitapoor; that all ladies were to go to his house, and that the men were going to defend a bridge the mutineers must cross. A number of extra men had been enrolled and drilled – they turned out worse than the rest – and all our troops mutinied that day, 2nd June 1857, and against such heaps of natives what could our few English officers do! Mrs Christian's house was full of ladies and children. One poor fellow came in to have his wounds dressed – Mrs Christian's nurse[maid], looking ghastly herself, was doing it – then all the gentlemen rushed in, saying all the troops had turned against us (they had fought their way back to the house). Then the confusion was dreadful: people could not find their husbands – Mrs Christian was looking for hers, crying, my dear sister trying to comfort her . . . The house was all barricaded to keep out the natives, but fighting was useless: the natives were hacking down the barricades in front, and we all got out at the other side of the house in hope of hiding in the jungle . . .

Well, only half of a French window door could be got open and everybody was forcing their way out, regardless of anyone else. That was how we lost Georgie [her sister]. Mountstuart's hand I had got tight hold of – and kept, though my arm was nearly broken. Directly we were out, we ran across an open plain, towards the jungles, thinking my sister was with us. Then I noticed an extraordinary whistling noise everywhere and stopped: I had never been out like that . . . in the middle of the day before and thought it had something to do with the sun! [I] said 'what's that?' My brother quietly answered, 'the bullets'. Then I got frightened and said 'Oh, we mustn't stop here!' and rushed on with him, but after a second, stopped, noticing Georgie was not with us. Looking back we saw her with Mrs Christian's English nurse, trying to quiet the baby and cover it from the sun: [it was] the last time I saw her, my poor sister . . .

Then we saw half a dozen men pursuing us, shooting now and then. Running as fast as we could, I ran into a thorny bush, and my white muslin dress was caught in tight. Poor M. threw himself on to the bush to tear it off me, and I could see all the colour leave his face as the thorns ran into him. We ran on and thought we had got away from our pursuers, when we saw them scuttling on the opposite side of a ravine. We got down into it to hide from their shots, and the last we saw of the poor Thornhills was him hiding his wife and child in a cleft, and standing in front of them. We heard afterwards that they were not killed there, but farther down the river.

We crossed through the river, calling them [the Thornhills] to follow us. I lost my shoes in it and fell on my face, and the pistol I had got wet. M. pulled me up: we had to climb a steep bank. The men saw us, yelled and fired – one shot was so close I looked to see if my arm was hurt and can almost feel the wind of it now – but we went on quite slowly – our running was over – and we thought the poor Thornhills must get killed where they were. We went through bushes and trees – one took my hat off and I did not take it again. A little further on, we sat down in a nook: no one was following us. I pulled off the muslin skirt which had been such a trouble as we sat, with our gun and pistol ready, listening.

I remember thinking how lovely the jungle was, and said to my brother I can't bear to be killed. M. said how could one bear to live, with such horror going on. We sat there a long time, then some men came – not sepoys: parsees, with bows and arrows. They used to be watchmen, I think. They saw my skirt and were evidently pitying the poor murdered people, so when they saw us we kept still and M. asked them to help us. They said they would take us to a better hiding place, which they did, and would come back at night to show us where to go . . . one man gave me a sheet to look more like a native. They told us Mr and Mrs Christian and the baby were killed: he was shot, she sat down by him crying and they went and cut off her head and the poor baby they took up on a spear and threw into the river – it was horrible – and we heard the jackals. She was very tall and graceful and sweet, and they were both so kind to us.

We walked on and I was dreadfully tired and my feet hurt, for it was not always grass, and I had lost my shoes. So M. took his boots off and made me put them on. We fastened leaves round his feet. Then the men said we were near a village and they would get us

65

something to eat – we had had nothing since breakfast. Of course we had no money – one never carries it about in India – so we gave them the pistol and we sat down and slept from sheer fatigue. It was a lovely moonlight night. They came back with some coarse 'elephant' chupatties, we thought they were, but we found out afterwards it was their usual food, with ghee [clarified butter] or dhall [split pulses] put on them. We ate and went on, the men talking amongst themselves.

At last M. [stopped] to tie more leaves on his feet – I held his gun – and one of the men came and took it from me, very politely, pretending he would carry it for me, but then he refused to give it back to M., so as we had given the pistol for food, and the sword (a Lucknow one) for showing us the way, we now had no arms, and soon after, having got possession of all we had, they said they would come no further, at which Mountstuart expostulated. After a good deal of talk one tall man drew his bow aiming it at him, saying we must go on by ourselves. I stepped in front of M. and the man lowered his arrow to my heart. I didn't like it, but laughed and turned to M. He said he supposed we must go on alone, and the men turned back to their village.

We tried to guide ourselves by the stars. Once we came to a high road and heard sepoys, and went into the jungle again. We were so tired we had to lie down: I remember we knelt first, and then actually slept. Waking, we went on and hid in some bushes as it was day and we were afraid of being seen, but we were soon found by a lot of villagers who brought their head man who made us go into the jungle and took M.'s watch and links – though they said the latter were not gold. They had been my father's.

They all had swords; they said they would come back to guide M. to Lucknow, but wanted me to stay till M. came back for me, as they said I could not go so far. M. refused and then they said they would kill us. The headman said he would let us drink some water first and took us near the river and told M. to drink. We were frightfully thirsty, so M. went. The man would not let me go too, but as it was close by I did not mind till the man put his arm round me. I put it away, saying 'don't be afraid: I shall not run away'; then he put his hands together and begged me to stop with him. I did not understand, until one word – which means wife – enlightened me: I screamed 'Mountstuart!' and he rushed back and I told him. The man looked very sorry. I touched his sword and said 'kill us' – at which he shook his head – then we heard others coming and he told us to run, which we did, down to the river and straight across it (it was not very deep). I think M. forded it, but I fell and he pulled me through. I thought how happy it would be if we might drown in it. We got out at the other side and went along the bank . . . soon dry by the sun, till we met some very poor looking men who seemed sorry for us [and] said they would guide us, and would take us to some other English people, which they did.

They were Mr Burne[s], a young officer; Sergeant Morton, a fair Englishman, who had lost his wife at Sitapoor, and little Sophy Christian, who cried to come to me directly she saw me. Mr Burne[s] told us he was the last out of the house and found Mrs Christian trying to carry Sophy and crying 'Oh, save my child! Who will save my child?' He took her, and saw Sgt. Morton just crossing the river on horseback, so gave the child to him. The horse was shot and he and the child thrown into the river: Mr Burne[s] helped them out. (They had their guns taken from them too.)

We went on much faster with guides; we had to wade through another river (M. helped me) [and] at last I sat down and cried and said I could go no further: they must leave me. Well, they helped me on and got me a pony, on which I sat with the child all that day and night, aching so. I begged them to let me lie down – of course we couldn't stop, as we were still being pursued. Once we came across more sepoys and had to almost crawl over open places for fear of being seen. Before the pony was got little Sophy cried for me to carry her – she was about three – and I couldn't, so had to hold her hand to stop her crying while one of the others carried her. One poor little arm was all burnt and festering from the sun, though they had got a cloth and covered her all over, as they thought.

Early in the morning of the 4th we got to the outskirts of Lone Singh's place: Mithowlie.[9]

The story of Madeline's immediate future, together with the Orrs', whom she met at Mithowlie, will emerge a little later. There was plenty going on meanwhile. Within two or three days of 4 June, the day Madeline came temporarily to rest, there were outbreaks (real or imagined) at Jhansi, Mirzapur, Fatehgarh and Fyzabad, Shahganj, Jullundur, Sultanpur, and Patna. These few stations alone involved hundreds of European souls, every one of them much less likely to live, given the precedents, than die.

Yet even now there were some making the perilous assumption that their troops would stay staunch and resist all the heady incitements to mutiny now swirling around Bengal. Major Kirk in Nowgong had already taken the precautions needed to ensure loyalty, he thought, by dismissing a rebellious core of native artillerymen at the end of May. The remaining soldiers certainly gave no cause for alarm. On the contrary: they were constantly avowing their faithfulness to their officers and proud, it seemed, of their steadfast reputation. But on 9 June, the news of the mutineers' rout at Jhansi, two hundred miles to the east, was triumphantly galloped into the garrison and by dusk the next day, Nowgong had gone. The only lady there (although there were a few women around) was Mrs Mawe, the regimental doctor's wife.

I was dressing when my ayah, who was standing by the window, exclaimed 'oh, what is the matter? The sergeant major is running away!' I instantly looked out and saw Lucas, with his sword raised over his head, coming towards the Bungalow; he saw me at the window, and called out – 'Mrs Mawe, fly! The men have mutinied!' I felt paralized, both husband and child out, and both at their mercy. I rushed out into the road to try if I could see either of them. I desired our punkah bearers to go and look for the child, but they would not stir, neither would our khidmutgar [butler], who was standing at the door. I heard shots fired, and feared Dr Mawe was at the hospital, and would be killed. No one would stir, as for me I was standing in the road, crying. When I saw him driving furiously from the mess house, and waving his whip, I ran to him, and saw our bearer bringing our little child . . . I snatched her from him, and got into the buggy, and drove back to the mess house, where all the officers had assembled.[10]

The mess house was not much of a refuge, however. After fifteen minutes it became clear that the sepoys were preparing to attack it and Mrs Mawe, the doctor and their daughter Lottie made off in their buggy, the first to leave Nowgong. Somewhere along the way towards Allahabad the buggy was lost and the rest of the fugitives caught up, most of whom were now reduced to walking.

Dr Mawe and I carried our child alternately. Mrs Smalley [the Band-master's wife] died near this place [Muhobah] from sunstroke. We had no food; I felt quite exhausted. One of the officers kindly lent me his horse, and Dr Mawe was lent another. We were very faint. The Major [Kirk] died on the road between Muhobah and Kubree, and was buried; also the Serjeant Major and some of the women . . .

On the morning of the 20th [ten days after they had left Nowgong] Capt. Scott took Lottie on his horse. I was riding behind my husband, as she was so crushed between us – she was two years old on the 1st of June. We were both very weak for want of food, and the thirst was dreadful, added to the burning sun; neither Lottie nor I had any head covering, and Dr Mawe only a sepoy's cap that I found on the ground at Kubree. Soon after sunrise we were followed by villagers with latties and spears; one of the latter struck Capt. Scott's horse in the leg, and he galloped away, followed by Lieuts. Franks and Remington. My poor husband never saw his child again.

We rode on for several miles, keeping away from villages, and crossed the river; our thirst was extreme, and my husband got dreadful cramps. I had to hold him on the horse; I was very uneasy about him . . . At a distance we saw water in a nullah [a ditch], and we all rode towards it; the descent was very steep; we all dismounted, and had a drink; our only drinking vessel was the cap alluded to, which I have still with me. The horses were getting water, and I was bathing my neck. As I had no stockings, my feet were dreadfully scorched and blistered, my shoes being much torn. When two latti-wallahs [characters armed with bludgeons] were seen on the hill over the nullah, they told us to go away; we were all frightened, and mounted immediately and rode off. Sergeant K[irchoff] was holding our horse, while Dr Mawe put me up, and mounted. I think he must have got suddenly faint, for I fell and he over me on the road just as we were riding off. Some time before poor Mr Barber and Dr Mawe said they could not live many hours. My poor husband felt he was dying before he reached the nullah, and told me his wishes about the children and myself, and we took leave of each other. I felt as if my brain was burnt, the relief of tears was denied me. As soon as we fell the Sergeant let go of the horse, and went away, thus cutting off our escape; we sat down on the ground awaiting our death, for we felt sure they would come and murder us; poor fellow, he was very weak, and his thirst frightful. I said I would go and bring some water in my dress and his cap. Just as I was leaving him, the two villagers came down; they took 80 rupees from him which he had round his waist, and his gold watch. I had on a handsome guard-ring which they saw. I went towards the nullah, and drew off my wedding ring, and twisting it in my hair, replaced my guard; they came to me and pulled it off my finger. I tore part of the skirt of my dress to bring the water in, but it was of no use, for when I returned my beloved's eyes were fixed, and though I called and tried to restore him and poured water into his mouth, it only rattled in his throat; he never spoke to me again. I felt frantic, but could not cry; I knew the being I had idolized nearly fifteen years was gone, and I was alone; so I bound his head and face in my dress, for there was no earth to bury him. This thought wrings my heart day and night.

The pain in my hands and feet was dreadful, so I went down to the nullah, and sat down in the water on a stone, hoping to get off at night and look for Lottie. When I came back from the water, I saw they had not taken her little watch, chain and seal; so I took it and tied it to the string of my petticoat under my jacket. It was a parting gift from Lieut. H. Campbell of the 52nd N.I., when he left the regiment in November 1854, to take our four little girls to Ireland.

I had been about an hour in the nullah when some thirty villagers came in search of me; they dragged me out of the water and took off my jacket to search for money. Though I told them they had taken all from Dr Mawe, they found the little chain, and took it; then they dragged me to the town of Munnapore, one and [a] half miles distant, mocking me all the way, and wondering to whom I was to belong. They had sent on some of their party, and when we arrived the whole village was out to look at me, men and women. I asked for a charpoy, and laid down outside a door. I asked them for some milk, as dozens of cows passed, but they refused; at last when night came, and the village was quiet, an old woman brought me a leaf full of dhall and rice, but my throat was so parched I could not eat; she brought me a small earthen vessel with some drink, which she told me was made from bhang [hemp – or cannabis].

Next morning some of the men came and told me I was to go to Banda. I refused, and said I would go to Allahabad; but about an hour after the Nawab sent a palkee for me, and the sowar gave me the grateful news that a little child was there and three sahibs. How I hoped it was Lottie!

On arrival I found my poor little one: she was greatly blistered from the sun . . . We were there fourteen days after I arrived, and we were well watched and guarded, not allowed to speak to anyone, but kindly treated . . . The Begum sent for me some days after I arrived, and talked a long time with me, for she said she could understand me. The night we left she sent for me again, and gave me some English clothes, stockings, &c., for Lottie, and a pair of earrings on a little silver plate for myself."

The Begum's kindness was obviously welcome, but little reparation for what Mrs Mawe had gone through. Because of the state of her feet on arrival at Banda, she remained 'partly a cripple' for the rest of her life, and like all those who survived escapes like this, she was reduced to the charity of her countrymen and women, not only to tide her over until her eventual voyage home, but to restore to her children some souvenir of their father. What she most missed were his medal and clasps, which should have gone to her twelve-year-old son. With luck, once the school fees back in Ireland were somehow paid, she might one day be able to get copies: people were very kind, after all.

By the time Mrs Mawe reached Banda at the beginning of July, the first stage of the Mutiny was over. There could be no more surprise attacks: most stations liable to insurrection had already risen, and the action (on both sides) was beginning to set into a pattern that would continue for the rest of the year. There were still prolonged and gruelling journeys of escape going on, under cover of night and with the help of elderly villagers and loyal sepoys; little pockets of Europeans might be hiding out in the cowsheds of some friendly Mofussilite Rajah, perhaps realizing that what they thought was sanctuary was in fact a prison, while some had already reached the comparative safety of areas outside the main arena and could afford to sit it out – although rarely without the stress of worrying about family elsewhere. British troops were beginning to arrive, many weary and jaded from the Crimea, and an organized military campaign was underway.

Trapped in the middle of all this were those memsahibs who had either been sent or else had escaped into the three elected centres of British refuge in northern India: Cawnpore, Lucknow and Agra. What happened in the intrenchment at Cawnpore and the Residency compound of Lucknow was hardly ever less than harrowing. In Agra, however, the only one of the three to avoid all-out siege, the story was a little more relaxed.

Altogether there were 924 European women and children inhabiting the Mogul emperors' vast and beautiful Red Fort by the end of July 1857. With a whole city of palaces and pleasure gardens within seven-feet-thick and mile-long perimeter walls, and a long, lazy view of the sacred river Jumna and the Taj Mahal beyond, it was, as it turned out, just about the safest place any local Christian could be at the time. But such comfort is all comparative, and to Ruth Coopland, who arrived there in a state of shock and spent her first ten days' incarceration 'with a wet towel wrapped round my head, utterly stunned',[12] it was barely better than death.

Ruth's disillusionment with India had been budding for some time: Gwalior was growing disappointingly less and less like rural England every day. It blossomed during the outbreak there on 14 June, when her husband was amongst the many to lose his life. It was hardly a relief to be told by the sepoys that they were only interested in killing sahibs. It would be a waste of time to do away with the mems as well: as one stricken widow recorded, 'I begged of them to shoot me . . . No, a wretch replied, we have killed you already, pointing to my darling on the ground.'[13] Ruth, now almost eight months pregnant, was left to make the sixty-mile trek into Agra as best she could. There was at least one elephant on which as many as two ladies and four children might be perched, with just an umbrella, constantly being blown inside out, against the sun; the rest were reduced to riding horses without side-saddles ('. . . it was well we were not obliged to become familiar with [that]')[14] or being trundled along in carts – or merely walking.

It was a terrible journey: five days spent under a sky burning during the day like 'a canopy of fire'[15] and at night sultry and thick, and there was little rest. Even when young Mrs Gilbert's baby was born in a convenient bungalow along the way, the party paused only a few hours before moving on. It was all too much for one poor woman, the ironically named Mrs Quick: 'at last [she] fell down in an apoplectic fit, and became black in the face; some of the ladies kindly stayed with her, but in a quarter of an hour she died. The natives crowded round, laughing at her immense size, and mocked her. We asked them to bury her; but I don't know whether they did, as we left her body lying on the road.'[16] The Gwalior refugees did at least have an escort, though, otherwise none of them is likely to have survived, and once they were ensconced inside the vast walls of the fort they were safe.

One of those who watched the pitiful arrival of Ruth and her party in their 'night attire',[17] with shredded slippers and their feet all thorny and torn, was a very small ten-year-old girl. Edith Sharpley's mother had recently made the journey to Agra from Bhurtpore, where her husband had been engaged by the local Maharajah to form a private regiment (and was later killed). Mrs Sharpley had travelled with Edith's three elder sisters, one of whom was married with a baby son, and her own baby daughter as well as Edith; like Kate Moore's aunt, however, once arrived in Agra she was not allowed to return home. It was too dangerous. The family was split further, and billeted with various friends and relations:

We three younger sisters were living with my elder brother, for whom the eldest girl was keeping house. Living in the house was a male cousin of ours also. We were staying there so that we could attend a day school, kept by an American couple, which was known as 'The High School'.

I was very short in stature for my age. One day at school I was placed on a bench, as was usually done in my case, to enable me to point out certain places on a big map during the geography lesson. Then suddenly, there were rapid footsteps and several gentlemen, all armed, walked into the room. I was lifted up in my cousin's arms. He called my two elder sisters and rushed us all out of the room. He hurriedly told the teacher that the mutiny had broken out, advising her to make her escape as quickly as possible.

While on our way home, for we ran all the way, we saw a native who appeared to be a Hindu priest, running towards us. His long flowing hair was covered with ashes and flying loose all over the upper part of his body. He was shouting curses on the Europeans and brandishing a naked sword. As soon as my cousin saw him, he put me down on the ground and told us three sisters to get close behind him. He then drew his own sword and we all walked forward. The priest passed by us but pretended not to see us. We also passed by without interfering with him . . . After this day of many exciting incidents, three houses were selected as 'Houses of Refuge'. As many people as possible collected at these houses, where they had their meals together and lived permanently. Each of these houses were guarded by armed volunteers.

We were all drilled in various ways. Every woman had to learn how to load muskets. In those days, the powder and ball had to be rammed in separately from the muzzle. The children were taught to get the caps, powder and bullets to take to the women when they required them.[18]

While all this was going on, John Colvin, Governor of the North-Western Provinces and based in Agra, was busy vacillating. It was the old problem: whether to admit weakness and take the memsahibs and their children into the fort, thereby risking a siege, or flaunt British confidence (however far pretended) by leaving them, suitably guarded, in the city. According to Mary Vansittart, an Agra resident, Colvin was not a popular man:

Wise Sir Henry Lawrence is causing a feeling of security at Lucknow by meeting and preparing for every contingency. Would that he or someone like him were here in the place of this panic-stricken Mr Colvin . . . I think [his] conduct so base – he orders ladies into the Fort then he sends their Husbands away to a distance, but as soon as they have left Agra . . . he orders their unprotected wives and children out of the Fort to take care of themselves as they can!¹⁹

At last it became obvious, given the news flying to Agra from all directions, that the resident Europeans would be far safer one side of the massive walls than the other, and so the considerable acreage inside was organized for the influx.

Our quarters [wrote Mrs Coopland] . . . were on a piazza, supported on pillars, and we not only had to divide it, but to screw [screen?] the front with 'jamps' [hurdles of woven bamboo], so as to form small rooms. The floor was of [beaten earth] and the doorways were closed by chicks, or screens made of thin split reeds, which admitted light and air; but as the 'jamps' did not reach the roof, which was formed of massive blocks of sandstone, the partitions had the appearance of a long range of stalls. Our quarters were characterised 'stables above, and pigsties below'; the half-castes being beneath us.

Our furniture consisted of two narrow soldier's cribs, with very hard mattresses and but scanty bedclothes, a small camp table, two or three chairs, and boxes to contain our stores and meagre wardrobe; and in one corner were the cooking vessels, and earthen pots for water. Our toilette apparatus consisted of a small chillumchie [brass

1. *Madras Landing*, 1837, by J. B. East. Despite the inelegant disembarkation arrangements, Julia Maitland found the city reassuringly 'English'.

2. The 'typical' memsahib of the immediate pre-Mutiny period sits cocooned in her Indian home-from-home, fanned by a punkah, and bored.

3. The cantonments of British India had an air of Georgian charm about them. But for the heat and natives, said Ruth Coopland, one might almost fancy oneself in Surrey…

4. 'How the Mutiny Came to English Homes', a cartoon from *Punch*, 1857.

5. Charlotte, Viscountess Canning, drawn by Edward Matthew Ward. Charlotte lived in the relative calm of Calcutta throughout the Mutiny, the 'Burra Mem', or first lady, of British India.

6. Minnie Wood, long-suffering wife of the dissolute Archie, almost welcomed the Mutiny as a respite from her dismal domestic life.

7. Edith Sharpley, veteran of the siege of Agra, in old age.
She was only ten in 1857, and delighted her granddaughter (who lent me this snapshot) with her vivid memories of life in the fort.

WHO WILL SERVE THE COUNTRY?

Recruiting Sergeant. "NOW, BRAVE BOYS, WITH THOSE WHISKERS AND SHOULDERS YOU SHOULD
BE WITH US, AND—I'M SURE THE LADIES WOULD EXCUSE YOU!"

8. 'WHO WILL SERVE THE COUNTRY?
RECRUITING SERGEANT: "Now, brave boys,
with those whiskers and shoulders you
should be with us, and – I'm sure the
ladies would excuse you!"' Not only
would the ladies excuse them to fight the
mutineers in India but, it was suggested
in *Punch*, they might even take over
the vacant jobs themselves.

"O GOD OF BATTLES! STEEL MY SOLDIERS' HEARTS!"

Henry V., Act IV.

9. Queen Victoria felt a particular sympathy for what she called her
'fellow countrywomen' killed during the Mutiny: the memsahib was, after all,
her domestic representative in India.

10. It smacked rather of shutting the stable door
when the survivors of the Meerut outbreak were herded into
the hastily fortified Artillery Laboratory for safety.
The mutineers never returned.

DESTRUCTION OF A BUNGALOW AT MEERUT.

11. Amongst the first British casualties of the Mutiny were
Charlotte Chambers and Eliza Dawson, both killed by the rebels
in their burning bungalows in Meerut.

12. A particularly melodramatic Mutiny scene: the 'daring seizure' by Captain Hodson of the King of Delhi.

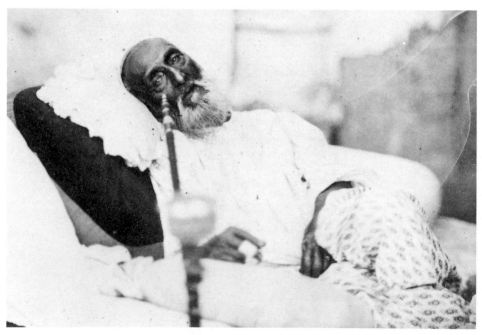

13. In fact the 'puppet king', Mohammed Bahadur Shah Zafar – 78 in 1857 – was merely the titular monarch of Delhi. It was to his court that the rebels raced from Meerut and in his name they fought their war, but the man himself was impotent.

14. The Flagstaff Tower, a sturdy building some eighteen feet in diameter,
where scores of survivors (mostly women and children) spent the
first stage of the Mutiny in Delhi.

15. A particular treat during the quieter moments of the siege of Agra was
a visit to the Taj Mahal, pictured here just across the River Jumna.

16. Helena Angelo (*left*), the last British woman to leave Cawnpore before the siege, is pictured here nearly fifty years after the Mutiny at the christening of her great-grandson. Helena's daughter (*standing*) was with her on the escape to Calcutta in 1857.

Helena's husband, Frederick (*inset, above*), a lieutenant in the 16th Bengal Native Infantry, who insisted – much against her will – that she leave Cawnpore with their three children. He was killed soon afterwards.

pot], and a cracked looking-glass. A lamp, a few cups and saucers, plates, knives and forks, completed the *ménage*. This 'den' and its furniture I shared with Mrs Innes; and it is a sample of all the others . . .

A lady's life in India . . . though very luxurious, is not so useless and frivolous as some imagine. We had to cook, wash our clothes, and clean out our 'dens', and those who had children [which, from a month after her traumatic journey from Gwalior to Agra, included Ruth herself] had the double task of attending to them and keeping them inside the 'dens', as it was dangerous to let them be outside on the stone walk alone, the parapet was so low: little Archie Murray did fall over into the court below, a distance of twelve or fourteen feet, but happily escaped uninjured.[20]

Although one of the memsahibs' main worries was the welfare of their children (together with the meagre supplies of dhall and rice which formed the staple ration for everyone), to young master Bagley – amongst others – the whole episode was quite thrilling. He was five at the time.

My world was inhabited, firstly and chiefly, by my mother, a tall, graceful, and quiet woman engrossed in household duties, including the care of three children, of whom I was the eldest. I know there was a brother three years younger than myself, but of him as one of us at the time I have no recollection whatever. There was another brother, a baby born in the preceding February, remembered clearly as he formed the subject of interesting speculations as to whether he would be spitted on a bayonet, or covered with oil and burnt alive when the 'baghis' (rebels) came . . .

No servants were allowed to come into the fort with us, or for some time after, and during that time I can realise now that life must have been a hard struggle, and in many cases a prolonged agony to the women, especially of families in my position . . . To me, however, hunger and heat and discomforts mattered nothing, and it was all, in my eyes, a most glorious picnic . . .

The mothers talked gloomily of what they would do if the mutineers got at the children . . . The more hopeful put their trust in the '40-pounder' at the gates, and in the militia guards; but all expressed distrust of the 'Sikhs,' who were 'foolishly being treated as loyal.' My mother said she would not live herself, or let her children live to fall into the hands of the cruel rebel murderers, and would throw the boys and herself out of the window if they got in. On hearing this, I got up and stalked promptly to the window, and looked out to measure the prospect, causing amongst the grown-ups a general sickly smile, the only one probably seen that day. I calculated that we should certainly be killed by such a fall, and did not at all approve of my mother's programme, but it was greeted with quiet consent by the other mothers as the only possible course, so I said nothing, and resigned myself to my fate . . .

There was at one time an issue of wheat instead of flour, which we were supposed to grind and make into chuppatties. This was difficult without a 'chukkee' (hand-mill), and it was easy for me to annex a handful of the grain. It seemed to me that while there was much talk of impending starvation, little was being done to prevent it, and I was filled with the idea of appearing one day as the saviour of the family. I found a small unused room, dark and smelling of bats, and carefully digging up the earth floor with an improvised spade made out of an old plank, sowed my handful of wheat with great expectations of reaping a noble harvest and much self-praise for my forethought. It came up all right, and grew to a length of three or four inches, but the want of light and air resulted in a change in the colour of my wheatfield from deep green to a pale and anaemic colour which shortly became almost white, and it finally withered up and died, to my bitter disappointment.[21]

Little Edith Sharpley was finding life no less absorbing:

The soldiers were very good and kind to us children. They would come round in the evening and ask our parents to be allowed to take us out for a walk along the ramparts. It was the only walk we could indulge in and the only way we could get some fresh air . . .

On the 5th of July, we had our first battle in the vicinity of Agra. It took place in a village called Shahgunge, about five miles away from the Fort. This was really a drawn battle as neither side decisively defeated the other. Our men were few in number and ran short of ammunition. The mutineers were also short of ammunition. It was very lucky for us because, had we been defeated, the Fort would have been taken and we should all have been massacred [or hurled out of the window by grim-faced mothers].

I have never forgotten that day and also the night! We watched the soldiers and volunteers leave. Then we heard the battle commence with sounds of gun and musket fire. This was followed by silence. Some time later we saw our men marching back. The gates were opened and in they came. Oh! the poor bodies, covered with blood, carried in doolies or covered stretchers. We all crowded round them with glasses of water which they all eagerly drank, both the wounded and the unwounded. I was also there and an officer caught me up in his arms, saying, 'you are far too small a little girl to do this work . . .' Then he carried me to where the water was kept and made me stand there. Almost every woman in the Fort was helping the wounded throughout the night in the hospital. Later some people came round collecting delicacies, to which everyone gave some daintily-cooked food, so as to give the soldiers a good supper . . .

Nine days after the servants were shut out of the Fort, we heard a shouting and cheering crowd coming towards our block. It came nearer and nearer. Then we saw a crowd of people around a man who was holding aloft a leg of mutton! They were cheering him as it was the first piece of mutton brought into the Fort since the gates were shut to the natives. All in our block joined in the cheering and much to our astonishment the man came and presented the leg of mutton to my mother. She was almost overwhelmed with the gift and the honour!'[22]

Come the third or fourth months of the so-called 'siege' of Agra, with events like the coming of the mutton growing less novel, the atmosphere inside the lawns, galleries, and courtyards of the fort began to lighten a little. There were even balls and dances (although a proclamation was issued to ban excessive 'singing and playing of flutes'); there were picnics, parties, and towards the close of their six-month residence occasional jaunts for favoured memsahibs outside the walls of the fort to take the air and look at the Taj Mahal. In fact life seemed almost normal. Except that sooner or later this world within a world would have to be abandoned, and the real and turbulent world outside faced again.

5

News Spreads

A Rachael's Holy Innocent was every hewed-up child!
And every outraged woman died a Virgin undefil'd![1]

The fort of Agra was like an asylum for the six months from July to December. Not only were those memsahibs within given sanctuary from the 'row' going on outside, but they also found themselves virtually out of communication with anyone beyond the walls. Mrs Innes did manage 'to entrust a very tiny roll of thin paper now and then [which was usually rolled up inside a quill and stowed up the anus of a trusty spy] . . . in the faint hope of its being eventually carried on to Lucknow',[2] where her husband, Lieutenant-General Mcleod Innes, was besieged – and one such missive actually arrived at its destination, 'the only private letter received during the siege of Lucknow'.[3] But most had neither the influence nor the opportunity for correspondence.

'Row', by the way, is one of their euphemisms, not mine:[4] for those memsahibs not directly involved in the violence, it was still one of daily life's available pleasures to play the part of imperial chatelaine to a household of scallywags. Even when such violence was threatened, the Marchioness of Sligo, for example, was sure enough of her position in British India as to be almost dismissive of the mutineers. Patna, where she lived, was on the eastern fringe of the Mutiny arena in Bihar, and largely avoided the sort of insurrection so widespread in neighbouring Oudh thanks to its Commissioner, William Tayler. As soon as the news of Meerut and Delhi reached him he had all potential ringleaders arrested before they had a chance to co-ordinate any local rebellion. But appropriate measures still had to be taken to protect the memsahibs of the station, just in case.

The Marchioness had spent the first six years of her girlhood in Patna before being sent back home to be educated in 1842; when suitably 'finished' in England she returned to India at the age of seventeen and married Lord Ulick Browne, son of the Marquis of Sligo, two years later. She was back in Patna by 1857, with a baby son (conventionally consigned for most of the time to his ayah), enjoying the fruits of her upbringing: a succession (she says) of 'golden hours' filled with amusements, leisure, and the strict and satisfying observance of social niceties.

The news of Meerut did not reach Patna until the end of May, and the first indication that anything was seriously amiss came when Tayler and his sworn enemy, the opium agent Mr Garrett, were spotted one day in earnest conversation. As soon as it became clear what had happened (however far away) it was decided that the ladies of Patna should collect their children from the servants and station themselves in Tayler's house, which was hastily fortified with a few sandbags. They were all to sleep together on the roof. No chance, retorted the Marchioness: her baby might catch fever from the morning dew, and the Lord knew what else from such unhealthy proximity to other children. So she stayed below with her ayah, whom she had promptly retrieved after embarrassingly having to be told (by a *gentleman*) that the reason her son was always crying was nothing more nor less than hunger. She did not think much either of the order during the next few weeks that everyone should repair to the opium godowns (warehouses) in the event of an emergency. It was bad enough trying to keep up standards while sharing a room with a punkah-wallah who only had a plank of wood with which to do his work. She had had to swallow her pride on that occasion and rig up portions of her underlinen to create a better draught, but enough was enough. As for the vulgar suggestion (common during the Mutiny) that she should keep a loaded revolver under her pillow – not just to shoot sepoys but, *in extremis*, herself – it was preposterous. The whole episode was preposterous, come to that, and the Marchioness did her best to ignore it, which under the circumstances was quite a virtuosic feat. Who else would have managed to fall asleep during an early-morning false alarm between the putting on of one stocking and the next?[5]

In acting with such stern foresight in Patna William Tayler was following the same sort of pattern as the blessed Sir John Lawrence of Punjab. Lawrence was the first Briton to be elevated to the hagiographic ranks of Mutiny Hero (alongside his elder brother Sir Henry, and Sirs Colin Campbell and Henry Havelock). Immediately the telegraph announcing the start of the Delhi massacre arrived in Lahore and Peshawur, action was taken by Lawrence and his staff to disarm as many of the fifty thousand native troops garrisoned in the Punjab as might be considered 'unsafe', and to replace them with local Punjabi soldiers and tribesmen from the North-West Frontier. With this new and dedicated force he was able to maintain a 'Moveable Column', an army permanently on the march to quell any sign of rebellion before it ripened into war. So the sepoys of the Punjab were disarmed and stayed quiet – no doubt persuaded as much by the salutary sight of unsound comrades being bound to the barrels of cannon and fired through by thigh-slapping British officers ('very satisfying . . . The pieces were blown about in all directions')[6] as anything else.

That telegraphic message, dispatched just before the lines were cut from Delhi to Umballa, was soon relayed throughout the stations of northernmost India. Simla was one of the most popular of these stations, and still retained its reputation as a fashionable and picturesque resort right until the end of the British Raj. It was to Simla that the ladies repaired (and their gentlemen, when at leisure) when the weather in the plains became too hot. During the Mutiny it became a refuge not just from the sun but from the flagrant mayhem burning down in Bengal; but now, in the harsh light of May 1857, it felt as vulnerable as anywhere else in British India. After all, one lady there had reported being approached by a native who actually *twirled his moustache* at her, and when another complained to the milkwoman that supplies were being watered down, she was told that it hardly mattered since all memsahibs would shortly be having their throats cut anyway.[7]

Augusta Becher (whom we met on her voyage out to India in 1849) had settled into Simla well. She took her turn, in the absence of commanding officer General Anson's wife and daughter in England, as Burra Memsahib – first lady – with the other European women there. On the evening of Tuesday 12 May, it was Mrs Chester's turn. During dinner, a telegram was brought in to the general. Like the true sahib he was, he tucked it under his plate until Mrs Chester had led the ladies out after the meal; only when he had discussed it over port and cigars with the gentlemen were Augusta and her companions told what was in it.

While Anson was busy deferring to Lawrence on the business of dealing with the 'row', the memsahibs were kept in readiness to fly the station if necessary. All across the region there were women doing the same, including the fragrant wife of an officer in Neemuch who did not dare take off her clothes for thirteen days and nights in a row for fear of being caught unprepared.[8] In Augusta's case, the word to decamp came on her wedding anniversary the following Friday, when after some trouble in the bazaar there was a short and unlovely episode of sheer and craven panic amongst the authorities and she and her companions were sent to a staging-bungalow further up in the hills.

When we got down to the river the poor ayahs sat down and cried; they had forgotten their shoes and could go no further. We sent them back and I mounted Sep's [her husband's] horse (astride, for the road was too rough to keep on otherwise) to cross the water and rest a little, for the May sun is no joke, and walking is not an exercise one keeps up in India. We put Miss Olpherts on by turns with me, and Sep now and then took a turn on the barebacked horse. Of course the dilemma had found me dressed in the most unsuitable manner, for the weather was hot and I was caught in the midst of hot work, and I was clad in a thin muslin dress with flounces! We had to cross and re-cross that river perpetually. I was wet up to the waist and my thin boots getting pretty bad. We went on till it was too dark to see in that narrow valley, about ten at night I should say, and the men were tired out, and proposed to wait some two hours till the moon rose. We had no food with us, but mercifully the children slept, and my little Phil, as I was nursing him, did well . . . Presently appeared two of our kitmutgars, bringing a decanter with a little wine in it and some biscuits, tied up in a duster, and some bread, not much. They said they had much more, but some 'Sahibs' had stopped them and eaten up the children's food. We found this to be true, and knew who those men were . . .

Next morning we moved into a little bungalow [in Dagshai] belonging to one of the younger officers who had marched with the regiment, and we got the children washed, poor things, and Mrs Sloggett got me a nice woman from the Barracks to come and help me. But it is strange to lack everything – no brush, no sponges, no shoes, no clean clothes – nothing! I found a pair of scissors and cut off Bessie's mass of curly hair, having no brush to keep it clean. And I tore the skirt of my petticoat to make something to wash and dry the children with. That evening . . . as soon as lights were dim, swarms, clouds, of bugs assailed us! The poor children could not rest, and Mrs Lennan and I spent all night in going from one to the other to keep them partially free from their tormentors . . .

After a little time cholera showed itself . . . In one day three children died, and the next day in our room the young wife of a civilian in Bengal fell ill, and died in a very few hours of painless cholera. We had been twelve days at Dagshai when very early in the morning I was crossing the barrack yard with Bessie (my boots by this time had no vestige of sole remaining and my dress hung in rags), when Sep met us, returning from his duty. He cried, 'What is wrong? You are perfectly grey!' Someone had already said so, but I felt nothing in particular. He, however, went straight away into the Bazaar, managed to collect sufficient coolies, and insisted on starting for Simla, no matter what was going on.[9]

Nothing much *was* going on, it seemed (nor had ever been), and soon all the surviving memsahibs were sent home again to the comforting familiarity of Simla.

Like the Marchioness in Patna, Augusta and her country-women in the Himalayan foothills could afford at least a little confidence (once this little flurry was over), which was a luxury denied those fighting to survive elsewhere. Printed in one of the newspapers of the day is a letter from a nineteen-year-old girl from the hill station of Murree, in present-day Pakistan, which gives (according to the editor) 'a wonderful example of the spirit which has been excited by the treacherous and basely cruel conduct of the Indian army'. She reacts splendidly to the news she's heard of Delhi ladies being 'cut into pieces before each other's eyes': 'It makes me so ferocious to think of it, I long to go and fight the wretches myself.'[10] I wonder. She, like us, was lucky enough just to spectate. Yet there were memsahibs around whose mettle when tried proved just as sterling as any sahib's. Sarah Fagan of the Punjab was one.

Sarah must have been made of the same stuff as the missionary Annie Taylor who, on finding herself faced by murderous Tibetans in 1892, calmly informed them, 'I am English and do not fear for my life.' Both women put their faith not in themselves and their class (like the Marchioness of Sligo) but, unquestioningly, in God. Sarah had the additional protection of God's representative on earth, her husband, who had told her not to leave their bungalow in Jullundur whatever happened. This injunction made things rather difficult when fires broke out on the evening of Sunday 7 June: all the other Europeans had gone down to the barracks for safety and Sarah, with her five younger children (the very youngest of all being four weeks old), was the only memsahib left at home.

It occurred to her that the best thing to do would be to summon the officer in command of the local guard. Addressing him with his full title ('an act of courtesy too often neglected by the English'),[11] she informed him that he was responsible for the family's lives and that they entrusted themselves and their property entirely to his care, and asked him politely what his plans were. The first thing to do, apparently, was put the lights out and dismiss the punkah-wallahs. Only Europeans used such menials, and once they were gone it would be assumed that their employers had left too. The risk that the children might wake with the heat and mosquitoes and cry had to be taken, and this is when God stepped in with the first of several miracles: 'I believe He bade their guardian angels fan them with their holy wings', and they all slept all night. Meanwhile, soon after midnight, the noise of shouting and shots Sarah had been hearing since the first alarm grew suddenly nearer, and visions of her 'five most precious darlings' being used as shuttlecocks on the mutineers' bayonets momentarily tempted her to despair. But the guard stayed loyal – even when sepoys were seen huddled in the Fagans' summerhouse sharing out the treasure they had managed to loot from neighbouring bungalows, and a party of cavalry rode up to the gate demanding Sarah and her children be handed over. The miracles were falling thick and fast now: at three o'clock in the morning an astonished Sarah heard the voice of a friend in the garden asking the guard if there were any Europeans left alive inside – all the other bungalows had been burned, and some poor memsahib found bayoneted 'like a pincushion' nearby. Sarah called out joyfully that there were 'lots of us' left, that they were all ready to fly (having already packed a silver teapot, some linen and wraps for the children) and quite calm and collected: he need not fear hysteria. There follows a passage in Sarah's memoirs of pure Victoriana: ' "Too plucky by half, Mrs Fagan. Too plucky by half!" said Captain Sankey. "Why were you not in barracks?" "Because my husband bid me stay at home with my children. No woman is too plucky who only obeys her husband." "You're right. Quite right." '

On arrival at the barracks after an exhilarating dash through the moonlight in a carriage guarded by 'noble Afghan horsemen' and six bluecoats on either side, Sarah allowed herself one or two tears of relief – 'only a few' – before helping the other women there to nurse the wounded (she sang hymns to lull them to sleep) and after three days she was allowed home again, the sepoys having now passed on. All danger was not over yet, however, for a week or two after returning, Sarah noticed a plant in her garden strangely stripped of its leaves. Her ayah told her the leaves were used to burnish daggers, whereupon Sarah ordered a search of the household and the culprit, who had commissioned a number of weapons from the local blacksmith, was found and taken off. After this episode, Sarah ordered all the household staff to give up their arms (even the most loyal) and was told by one old retainer, as he knelt at her feet with prized sword in hand, 'what I would give up to no man I do to a woman who is alone, and yet is doing her duty without fear.' Only now was Sarah able to afford a little self-congratulation, thanking God for allowing her brave husband to 'feel proud of his old woman, because she had not disgraced his name'. Sarah was a real sahib's memsahib: the perfect example of submissive stoutheartedness. And I admire her.

Generally speaking, the further away one got from the Mutiny action, the more extreme were the reactions to it. Within British India, of course, it depended on how far away the nearest massacre was, and how reliable the means of communication. Once the telegraph line was cut, truth and rumour became perilously tangled, giving plenty of opportunity for the gossip of station society so beloved of days gone by to take a decidedly grim and mawkish turn. A ghastly Mutiny pantomime would be enacted again and again in the minds of the ill-informed with tableaux of maidens in distress swooning beneath the shadow of some snarling native brandishing a tulwar; their soulful eyes would be raised to heaven and their hands clasped at a milken chin, while the sepoy prepared to savage them in as many different ways as possible. God knows the truth was desperate enough, but rumour had it worse. The euphemistically termed fate worse than death was popularly supposed to have been one of the mutineers' favourite weapons against the memsahib (and, by implication, her husband); in fact the official inquiry instituted after the Mutiny[12] could find no substantiated case of rape at all.[13] For Hindus it would break caste anyway, and for Moslems it would be intolerably unclean. There are different ways to violate a woman, as the dead of Delhi knew.

The fear of rape was widespread throughout British India during the Mutiny – and was, incidentally, one of its chief legacies to the women of the Raj during the ninety years that followed it. It became a sort of metaphor for a more generalized fear of the unknown. On 24 May it was Queen Victoria's birthday. The customary junketings were cancelled around Delhi, of course, but way over in Calcutta, where the Viceroy's wife, Charlotte Canning, admitted in a letter to a friend 'it would be absurd to be frightened', the celebratory grand ball was held as usual. Yet even here one young lady is reported to have refused to go in case it should be gate-crashed by lustful and blood-thirsty sepoys, while another somewhat rashly hired a series of sailors to sit up through the night in her house to guard her – until they got drunk and started frightening her more than any imaginary enemies could have done.[14] Staunchness was never as infectious as panic.

Charlotte Canning's correspondent was none other than Her Majesty herself. Victoria was wise to rely on such a sensible witness to what was going on in India: the time-lag involved in getting hard news of the Mutiny home inevitably led to much discussion, speculation, and misinformation. Lady Canning never relayed news she could not verify, and was not interested in jingoistic propaganda. Perhaps because she was writing as woman to woman she was able to temper her account of the Mutiny as few other 'official' reporters could. Nowhere else, for example, can I find any mention of the unfashionable tale of Mrs Maude:

She has a thriving boy, born not six weeks after all her perils and sorrows . . . When the mob surrounded her [quite where, I cannot tell], and the Rajah's people came to fetch her and protect her, they asked her if her husband was killed, and she told them he had *died*. They asked her to point out who had robbed her. She would not and said, 'They were young, none but the young would do so,' and immediately the little chain and seals she cared so much for were thrown to her by an unseen hand from the crowd.[15]

This strange little vignette turns on its head the received wisdom of memsahib as victim: it was typical of Charlotte to have noted it, and brave, too. It was hardly politically correct, after all. An Englishwoman publicly sympathetic to her masters' and sisters' murderers? I wonder how many more there were like her, embarrassing the cause.

The first reaction in the British press to the strange and terrible news delivered by mail steamer on 26 June was, of course, one of blustering outrage. The *Illustrated London News* spoke for many:

The state of affairs in India may well excite the alarm of the nation; but it will do more: it will excite its courage and its wisdom. At one time, and before fuller details had corrected, explained, and supplemented the curt and fragmentary announcements of the electric telegraph, the intelligence created a feeling of dismay. But that speedily wore off, and the prevalent feeling is no longer of dismay, but of anxiety. The full extent of the danger is seen and appreciated, and the means which are in existence to meet and subdue it are obvious and palpable, and ready to our hands. Our house in India is on fire. We are not insured. To lose that house would be to lose power, prestige, and character – to descend in the rank of nations, and take a position more in accordance with our size on the map of Europe than with the greatness of our past glory and present ambition. The fire must be extinguished at any cost. All ordinary considerations give way before the greatness and suddenness of such a danger. Fortunately the Indian Government has vigour enough for the emergency, and if it have not means will be supported by all the wealth, power, energy, and resources of Great Britain. In this case there will be no grudging. The nation knows its work, and woe betide the statesman who shall stand between it and the consummation! . . .

By the next mail we shall in all probability hear that the Mutiny has been confined to the one Presidency in which it originated; that it has been quenched in the blood of the mutineers; that every native regiment that took part in it has been annihilated; that the murders of Englishmen, women, and children in Delhi and Meerut have been signally avenged; and that such an example has been made as will strike Terror into the minds of the native population, and keep it there for a century to come. Whether it were desirable that we should win India by the sword is no longer a question. Having won it we must keep it. The sword procured it, and the sword must guard it.[16]

The whole damned episode was probably the work of the

Russians (how could mere Indians be capable of such successful insurrection alone?) and if so, ran the editorials, it could turn out to be an extremely useful public relations exercise after the mess in the Crimea. For Britain was sure to win – had probably already done so, in fact.

When the next mail came, though, and the next and the next, each charged with news and speculation more shocking than the last, the press began to grow sickly-sweet with propagandist senti-ment. Sentiment is always a useful tool against a struggling parlia-ment (and Viscount Palmerston and his men certainly seemed to be struggling) – what better subject for it than the plight of that allegorical angel of Albion, the memsahib? Thus reams of mater-ial started appearing, from the beginning of August onwards, ranging from syrupy commentaries on the virtue of British womanhood to salacious accounts of how that virtue might be tested to its limits. We are back at the pantomime again. Here is a letter written to *The Times* from a clergyman in Bangalore early in July:

The cruelties committed by the wretches exceed all belief. They took 48 females, most of them girls from 10 to 14, many delicately-nurtured ladies, violated them, and kept them for the base pur-poses of the heads of the insurrection for a whole week. At the end of that time they made them strip themselves, and gave them up to the lowest of the people, to abuse in broad daylight in the streets of Delhi. They then commenced the work of torturing them to death, cutting off their breasts, fingers, and noses, and leaving them to die. One lady was three days dying. They flayed the face of another lady and made her walk naked through the street . . . I do not believe that the world ever witnessed such hellish torments than have been inflicted on our poor fellow country-women.[17]

And while they suffered, they really did lie back and think of England:

In times of sickness and sorrow we know of old no true woman's heart ever fails, nor do her spirits flag till the evil day be overpast; but in scenes of horror and bloodshed human eyes have rarely looked upon, we are hardly prepared to find our sisters acting with a calm devotion, and meeting their cruel deaths with a proud submission which while it must have nerved the arms of their countrymen . . . with superhuman strength (alas, that in so many cases it should have been so unavailing!), may well cause us who stand by in security – powerless to aid, while listening to the tale of their bitter wrongs – to wonder, while our eyes are dimmed and our throbbing hearts beat high, if the land that has been thus hallowed by such a baptism of our country's blood shall ever be allowed to pass from the hands of their descendants. Does not the deep heart of England respond, 'God helping us, never!'[18]

Perhaps the apotheosis of all this super-sentimentality is to be found in some of the poetry of the day. The tag at the beginning of this chapter is taken from an offering by Martin Tupper, entitled 'Who Shall Comfort England?' I shall not subject you to it all: two or three stanzas are enough to get the gist.

> Ah, who shall comfort England for her daughters and her sons,
> Her gentle and her generous, her own heroic ones
> Polluted, tortured, murdered – intolerable fate
> To be the sport of demons in their lust and in their hate! . . .
>
> There is deep comfort; heed ye well, that those are *Martyrs all*;
> For God and for their country they were killed at Duty's call;
> A Rachael's Holy Innocent was every hewed-up child!
> And every outraged woman died a Virgin undefil'd! . . .

All glory to those Martyrs! the blessed children slain,
The holy women, soon redeemed from all that shame and pain;
The brave good men, baptised by their own soldiers in their blood;
Oh, glory to the Martyrs, for they are all with God![19]

Angels of Albion indeed. Charles Arthur Kelly added his two pennyworth in *Delhi*, a work of almost epic proportions which included long verses on the Mutiny redolent of high Victorian pathos!

O for a Byron's fire, a Milton's might,
To wail our woes in words of living light;
To chant the death-dirge for their souls, who fell
By Delhi's marble palaces of hell;
Where England's mothers (hear it, England!) kneel,
But find no mercy save the accursed steel;
Where children's wailings load the tainted air,
And angels shudder at the old man's prayer.

Weep for the golden tresses steeped in blood,
Weep for the woes of England's womanhood,
Weep for our murdered infants' stifled cry,
Weep for the strong man's silent agony,
Weep for the loved ones early doomed to part,
Weep for the anguish of the pure in heart!
For fairer suppliants never bowed the head,
Since Rachel's tears would not be comforted;
And slaves more bloody never drew the brand,
Since Herod's vengeance cursed his red right hand![20]

It is almost impossible to read such material without visualizing one or other of those vastly popular narrative paintings also spawned by the Mutiny. For the fashionable artists of the day the subject must have been irresistible, combining almost endless opportunity to capture a single, telling 'moment', and an inspiring richness of brave, pale, inviolable women to choose for heroines, all against the clarity of light and colour of the orient. Chief amongst them all must be Sir Joseph Paton's *In Memoriam*, in which our brim-eyed angel is seen huddled with her six children and an ayah in a rough, dusty tykhana, or cellar. Each child is reacting according to its age: the two youngest are innocently asleep, the next sits on her sister's lap more bewildered than afraid, while the two eldest daughters cling to their mother, half supporting, half supplicating, as though they are past terror now and resigned to death. In the original painting the artist suggested just how imminent was that death by showing the cellar door flung open behind them and a rabble of frenzied mutineers bursting through. This was considered by critics and public alike to be verging on indecency, however, and for exhibition purposes Paton replaced the sepoys with sturdy Highland soldiers striding in to answer the mother's prayer. He dedicated *In Memoriam* to 'the Christian Heroism of the British Ladies in India during the Mutiny of 1857, and their ultimate Deliverance by British Prowess' and the religious magnificence of its subject moved one critic to suggest its own chapel be built more suitably to house it.[21]

A welcome antidote to this gaudy surfeit in print and picture is to be found in the slightly more astringent columns and cartoons of the satirical periodical *Punch* during the late summer and autumn of 1857. 'England's Womanhood', which the memsahib had come so sacredly to represent, was enjoying a relatively high profile at the time, what with the modern Divorce Bill and its (meagre) measure of rights for wronged wives. There was also much discussion going on about the thorny subject of women and work. Two full-page cartoons posit a timely solution to the controversy: the first shows a recruiting sergeant in a draper's shop, eager to enlist the gentlemen behind the counter for service in India. 'Now, brave boys,' he urges, 'with those whiskers and shoulders you should be with us, and – I'm sure the ladies would excuse you!'. The second cartoon has the same shop full of banner-waving females ('Women for Women's Work'), one of whom looks suspiciously to be sporting a pair of trousers under her knee-length skirt, proclaiming 'We'll serve the shop.'[22]

Just in case its readers should think it too radical, *Punch* tempers all this with a running commentary throughout the year on the size, strength, and significance of that most fashionable of feminine accoutrements, the crinoline. Nor is it free of the angel of Albion syndrome, with sketches of a statuesque Lady Justice bestriding the bowed heads of terrified Indians (including women and children) with sword raised ready to cut them down,[23] and the British Lion savaging a Bengali tiger who in turn is astride a slender, big-eyed memsahib.[24] And so it goes on. Charging an already volatile image with the added piquancy of satire (in this case against the perceived pussy-footing of so-called 'Clemency' Canning), it celebrated the ghastliest of all Mutiny massacres, supposedly perpetrated by one Nana Sahib, with this bitter little ditty:

> Who pules about mercy? The agonized wail
> Of babies hewn piecemeal yet sickens the air,
> And echoes still shudder that caught on the gale
> The mother's, the maiden's, wild scream of despair.
>
> Who pules about mercy? That word may be said
> When steel, red and sated, perforce must retire,
> And for every soft hair of each dearly-loved head
> A cord has dispatched a foul fiend to hell-fire . . .

And woe to the hell-hounds! Right well may they fear
A vengeance – ay, darker than we ever knew,
When Englishmen, charging, exchange the old cheer
For 'Remember the women and babes whom they slew' . . .

Our swords come for slaughter; they come in the name
Of Justice; and sternly their work shall be done;
And a world, now indignant, behold with acclaim
That hecatomb slain in the face of the sun.[25]

The poet is talking, of course, of Cawnpore.

6

The Cawnpore Massacres

Nothing has ever happened in the world like this.[1]

Most Mutiny episodes have been chronicled more or less thoroughly by witnesses. A good percentage of its British survivors wrote about their Indian adventures, either in letters and journals at the time or else later, in memoirs and narratives published (or not) in the calm comfort of home. With Cawnpore, however, it is different. The word alone is enough to conjure up the most brutal images of suffering, violence and treachery; what happened there in 1857 stands out in imperial memory with as much clarity (for what that's worth) as the old Black Hole and the Charge of the Light Brigade.

Cawnpore was not merely a matter of military affront: it struck deeper than that. It was all that was most vicious about the Mutiny stripped bare: the first time the women of England had ever been slaughtered in the history of battle. The British response was a tribal one – even atavistic – and still fuels bitter debate both here and in India itself. So what little authentic testimony there is of what really happened there during the long weeks following the first alarm on 14 May is invested with even more poignancy and fascination than the remarkable stories of other goings-on nearby. Only a handful of accounts by survivors exists; the rest, almost immediately posthumous, carry an emotive freight that frequently threatens to overwhelm:

[Wheeler's entrenchment, Cawnpore, 9 June]

I write this dearest Henrietta in the belief that our time of departure is come – the whole of the troops rose here and we took refuge in a barrack. We are so hemmed in by overpowering numbers that there seems no hope of escape, only about forty European soldiers are left of one hundred and twenty men, a sad, sad number to hold out against such an awful enemy . . . they have six guns against us, the walls are going, this is an awful hour my darling Henrietta. Jessie, Emily and Georgie [the writer's children] cling to us, dearest George [her husband] has been well up to today but he is, I grieve to say, obliged to abandon his post. This is to me a grief. Many brave men have fallen today . . . let this be a warning to your government never again to place British officers and men in such a pitiable position, only 120 European soldiers at Cawnpore! [I]t is sad and painful to reflect on that our lives are to be sacrificed in such a condition. Give my love to my sweet girls [her elder daughters at home] – tell them that there is but one thing needful . . . faith sure and steadfast, an anchor of the Soul. Conny darling, your Mama has longed to see and know you – seek your God and heaven in *spirit* . . . Alice my sweet child, remember your Creator in the days of your youth. Seek him till you can say I have found him – Ellen my little lamb, I must not see you again in the flesh, but remember I will look for you where sorrow or disappointment can never enter. Henry dear boy, my heart grieves over you, oh dear boy if you saw the position your little brother and sisters are in at this moment . . .[2]

This is a folded, faded letter, so worn as to be almost illegible, and it continues in farewells to family and friends, stiff with religious formulae but with a desperately moving undercurrent of terror and resignation. On the back there is a note:

Written by Emma Ewart, wife of Col. George Larkins, Bengal Artillery. Given to her faithful Ayah, who escaped through the Sepoy Troops. After many vicissitudes this letter reached England a year and nine months after the massacre. On reaching Calcutta Col. Will. Larkins, sitting on a Court Martial, refused to see her, giving no credence to her tale. Bursting into tears she called on Heaven to witness her Faithfulness, gave the packet to a servant and weeping, turned away never to be heard of again.

Emma's name is on the mass memorial tablet in the church of All Souls at Cawnpore, together with those of her husband and children – and more than a thousand Christian souls besides. What they had gone through was perfectly clear to one appalled British visitor to the city soon after their deaths. It was quite simply the most terrible thing that had ever happened.

The approach to the Satichowra Ghat, about a mile away from Emma's 'barrack', or entrenchment, was described towards the end of 1857 as looking obscenely like a little corner of Surrey, with a white picket fence by the gate and a winding lane through the trees to the river. It still does, give or take the odd water buffalo and palm tree, and there is a sense of pastoral quietude about the long path which follows the nullah in its shallow ravine down from the main road to the bank of the Ganges. But once at the waterside, any sense of familiarity is lost: contrary to those penny-dreadful woodcuts of what happened there on 27 June with their usual welter of crude horrors set amidst an evergreened Rhine-like landscape of rocks and defiles, the sacred river here stretches complacently almost to the horizon; there are bathers by the littered shore, their clothes in heaps on the terrace of the

Fishermen's Temple nearby, and water-melon beds disappear into a hot grey haze on the other side. Here, over two long weeks after Emma wrote her letter, hundreds of British were killed – shot, hewn, burned or drowned – and ever since, the Satichowra Ghat has been a place of morbid pilgrimage.

The other shrine to the dead of Cawnpore should be one of the most affecting sites in British India. It is the well, down which the remains of the 200-odd women and children who survived the Ghat massacre were supposed to have been tossed once the butchers of the Bibigarh (or Lady's House) had done their job on 15 July. Soon after the Mutiny ended a sanctifying white marble surround was commissioned of the fashionable sculptor Baron Marochetti, featuring an angel (after a design by none other than Charlotte Canning) to stand guard over the well itself; the whole edifice was to have stood in the newly founded Memorial Park as a simple, graceful and very moving commemoration of the victims lying below.

Now, if you look carefully in a smoggy corner of what has become the Nana Rao Park in the middle of Cawnpore, you will see a cracked expanse of concrete next to a wire-netting fence at the back of a neighbouring factory. It is where the local lads play cricket to the incessant accompaniment of car and rickshaw hooters round about. They dribble the ball along shallow steps surrounding a stained white plinth on which teeters a ludicrously tiny bust of Tantia Topi, Cawnpore's rebel hero. Occasional chipped stone frogs sit at intervals round the steps (or in pieces at the bottom of them) and there is an air of municipal shabbiness hard to reconcile with the knowledge that this, today, is the Well of the Innocents. It is not moving at all.

The screen and Marochetti's beautiful angel (whom Tantia Topi supplanted just weeks after independence in 1947) still exist: they are well cared for in a garden at the back of All Souls Church, itself built to commemorate the fallen garrison. Perhaps it is appropriate that it should be here after all: the church stands on the edge of the entrenchment where Emma and her compatriots endured a three-week siege before being led down to the Ganges to make their way, they thought, to Allahabad and freedom. Even now, a flat and scrubby expanse with its two wells (one for water, one for a grave) and the sound of practice gunfire floating over the scorched and grubby air from a barracks beyond, the entrenchment is an inexpressibly melancholy place.

In the old days, of course, the days before the Mutiny, Cawnpore was one of the gayest and jolliest stations in India. From the middle of the eighteenth century it had been steadily growing not only as a garrison city but as the 'Manchester of the East': a flourishing centre for merchants and traders of textiles and leather. The European population was large and a motley of military and civilian, and even though the frothy waters of social hierarchy must therefore have been rather difficult to navigate at times, life seems to have been remarkably full and entertaining. Amateur theatricals were a great thing in Cawnpore, and there was a capital club, a reading room, racquets court and racecourse; balls, dances and parties in the fine assembly rooms were given all the year round.

One of Cawnpore's greatest local attractions was its local Mahratta Maharajah Dhondu Pant, familiarly known as Nana Sahib. He was the adopted son of the dispossessed Mahratta King Baji Rao II, whose inheritance had been forcibly mortgaged to the British in return for a pension and certain rather meagre privileges. A pale, plump and rather sybaritic-looking Brahmin of thirty-five or six, he was patronized by officers, nabobs and memsahibs alike as an eager if eccentric host and benefactor. His palace twelve miles upstream at Bithoor, with its comfortable Residency building alongside, was a well-known pleasure spot where favoured guests might enjoy a sumptuous dinner (served with and on a bizarre collection of rather jaded European equipment) followed by a game of billiards, perhaps, or where ailing English children were invited with their mothers to convalesce in comfort. He was generally considered a harmless enough fellow: given to arguing with the British government over his ancestral rights, it is true, but that was probably just a matter of form and family pride. He would settle down soon enough.

The Nana's invitations to Bithoor were possibly more attractive to the gentlemen of Cawnpore (especially his fellow Freemasons)[3] than their ladies: they had their own amusements meanwhile. When Louisa Chalwin arrived with her husband from Meerut, one of her greatest preoccupations was the delay of her beloved piano in following them. Somewhere along the Grand Trunk Road it had been mislaid. When the Nana heard of Louisa's distress, he immediately offered her one of his own to play until hers turned up. As it happened, there was hardly time to play at all, what with the household to organize, the dinner parties, the sewing evenings, discussion of station gup (or gossip) and, of course, the writing of letters home. Hers were happy and carefree:

I have wonderfully improved in housekeeping since I came to Cawnpore – things are so much more easily procurable here . . . The hot weather is keeping off wonderfully and we are most thankful that we are so fortunate in this season as Cawnpore is a notoriously hot place . . . What do you think? My hair is falling off. I have commenced rubbing my head every day with an *onion* . . . We are going to a ball next Wednesday, given by a bachelor in the Engineers, who is smitten with the eldest Miss Lindsay . . . I think I shall wear my blue tarlatan.[4]

This Miss Lindsay was one of three daughters of a judge's widow; they had, like Louisa, only recently arrived in Cawnpore and had come to join relations there. The only thing that spoiled their return to India after a sojourn at home in Kent was the depressing attitude of the eldest of them, Caroline, who had wept bitterly at being instructed by her mother to come and remained rather jittery ever since: something unnamed but awful was going to happen to them, she said.

It took four days for the news of Meerut to reach Cawnpore. These were shocking tidings, to be sure – especially when one remembered that at Cawnpore there were at least ten sepoys for every European soldier – but hardly relevant enough to merit the sort of action Sir Henry Lawrence and the diligent Gubbins were taking over the river (and forty miles away) in Lucknow. Major-General Sir Hugh Wheeler, the officer in command, was a popular man with the sepoys: his wife was half Indian, after all, and she was related to our friend the Nana Sahib: even if all else failed, Nana could be trusted. A dispatch to the Governor-General on 18 May showed just how confident Wheeler was: 'All well at Cawnpore', it ran. 'Quiet, but excitement continues among the people . . . Calm and expert policy will soon reassure the public mind. The plague is, in truth, stayed.'[5]

Not everyone shared Wheeler's optimism (or *naïveté*): this 'excitement' amongst the 60,000 native population of Cawnpore was leaching into the cantonments and civil lines and little poisonous eruptions of panic were beginning to explode. More rumours of what the mutineers were doing to friends and family elsewhere came in every day, and the bazaar was reported restless and volatile. Gradually, and somewhat shamefacedly, families living out of cantonments moved into safer houses with friends, and the tone of their letters home began to shift. Emma Larkins had admitted in an earlier one that she 'may run home for a few months', but felt it prudent to add 'say nothing of this'. As an officer's wife she would no doubt be expected to follow Lady Wheeler's example by refusing to be frightened by what was going on. The Burra Memsahib had declared that nothing would make her agree to the cowardly plan mooted in certain circles to send the ladies and children of the station downriver to Calcutta for safety.

Emma was hardly alone, however, in worrying and privately wishing herself far away – or even as far as Bithoor, where it had been arranged that the Collector's pregnant young wife, Lydia Hillersdon, and her children should be sent if there should be any 'trouble' at Cawnpore. Never can living in India have seemed so much like an exile. 'Oh, what a humiliating state of things.' wrote Lydia, in the perplexing absence of a summons to his palace from the Nana.

Fancy us, the governors of the country, obliged to shelter ourselves behind guns . . . Oh! how I wish we were with you, and out of this horrid country. May God spare us, and may we live to see each other again. And, however severe our trials may be, may we have strength given to bear them. I send you some of the dear children's hair . . . Tell dearest [G] to keep the two little books Bishop Wilson gave me for my sake, and never to forget that in the midst of life we are in death . . . Oh! it is a hard trial to bear, and almost too much, but the sight of the children gives us strength and courage.[6]

Mrs Ewart, a kinswoman of Emma Larkins and the Hillersdons' temporary hostess, was finding it even harder to be stoical:

You will scarcely be able to realize the fearful state we are in: we can scarcely do so ourselves. No one can say how or where the trouble is to end. Mrs H[illersdon] is a sweet companion in affliction; we shall stick close to each other as long as it pleases God to spare us. Last night [31 May], after much fatigue of mental torture, and several nights of imperfect rest, I fell into a state of stupefaction. Body and mind alike refused to be longer active . . . And there was my child, so restless! and Mrs H. took her and walked about with her, and soothed the little thing, that I might not be disturbed . . . Such nights of anxiety I would never have believed possible, and the days are full of excitement. Every note and every message come pregnant with events and alarms. Another fortnight we expect will decide our fate ... May we be preserved from the evils that the incapacity of our leaders naturally entails! If these are my last words to you [and they were], you will remember them lovingly, and always bear in mind that your affection and the love we have ever had for each other is an ingredient of comfort in these bitter times.[7]

The British were losing control.

Mrs Ewart was the wife of one of the highest-ranking officers present at Cawnpore; poor Mrs Wiggens, another officer's wife (and one impugned for his own wavering fortitude at the time) had 'quite lost her reason from terror and excitement'.[8]

It must have been extremely hard not to be envious of those few women who did abandon ship during the last couple of weeks in May. Mrs MacDowell, one of Cawnpore's three European milliners, upped and went as soon as she could, despite being owed about £500; a Mrs Martin rather unfortunately chose Mynpoorie for a refuge, arriving there just in time for its own mutiny. The most successful fugitive from Cawnpore was Helena Angelo, the pregnant wife of a lieutenant posted to Cawnpore on 14 May. She and her two daughters were still living on the boat that had brought them there when, on 26 May, they were called into the entrenched camp Wheeler had hastily prepared for emergencies. And just to parenthesize for a moment: no one has ever been quite sure why Wheeler chose the entrenchment site in preference to a perfectly good, strong magazine further towards the European centre of Cawnpore. Why should he find a wide, four-acre expanse of unsheltered plain perilously close to the native lines so much more attractive than a massively walled enclosure near the seven-mile stretch of cantonments? Perhaps because it was close to the Calcutta road, whence reinforcements were sure to be coming soon – or maybe it was all some giant gesture of mis-placed faith? The risk was not worth taking.

Helena Angelo had found the entrenchment quite jolly when she arrived: 'a singular scene – parties of officers and ladies singing and laughing in one place – gentlemen assembled in the open air – all noise and bustle and one would imagine it some gay assembly.'[9] Her husband was not deceived, however, and very bravely (for he must have been scorned for it at the time) he told her to leave. Her diary entry for 28 May suggests how mortified she was by the decision: 'Fred absolutely determined that I and the children should go to Calcutta ... so we are to start this evening much against my wish but he seems to wish it. I can only pray God that this step is blessed by Him and turns out to be beneficial to us both, yet in my opinion husband and wife should separate as little as possible. Started at 6 p.m. Oh! my God keep and protect my beloved husband.' The gharry (carriage) which carried Helena and her three girls away from the city (guarded by two faithful sepoys of her husband's regiment) was the last, it is said, to leave Cawnpore before the siege.[10]

By the morning of 31 May, it became clear that the crisis had come. The troops at Lucknow had mutinied; here the sepoys were obviously ripe for action and a siege, it seemed, was imminent. Wheeler ordered everyone into the entrenchment, managed to find enough provisions (he thought) to last a month, and settled in to wait for help, either from the Nana or the British. This order acted as a catalyst: all the barely suppressed panic of the last two weeks was suddenly let fly. It gave the signal too – just as Wheeler had feared – for mutiny.

For the first few days of the siege the rebels occupied them-selves with sacking and firing the cantonments, and taking pris-oner any Christian stragglers they could find, including this poor family whose arrival in Cawnpore could hardly have been more ill timed:

A lady,[11] a girl and three young children who were coming from the western direction in a Dak-Gharry [mail carriage] were seized by the troopers of the 2nd Cavalry, on their entering Cawnpore, and carried before the Nana (the husband of the lady had been previously murdered on the road but the murderer spared the lady and children and allowed them to proceed on their journey). The Nana ordered that they should be killed. The lady asked him to spare their lives but the coward refused to do so. They were then taken to the middle of the *maidan* [an open square], the sun was hot, and the lady asked them to let her and her children into the shade. The wretch paid no attention to her request. The children clung to their mother, and asked her to take them to a bungalow; they said that they were suffering from the heat of the sun. Eventually their hands were tied, they were taken to the middle of the *maidan* and fired on, all were killed at the first volley, except an infant. It was rolling about on the dead bodies taking the hands of the corpses, was lifting them up and was saying 'why have you fallen down in the sun?' At last a trooper killed it with his sword.[12]

Caroline Lindsay's bleakest premonition had come true: there is about the whole of the Cawnpore story (from the Indian as well as the British standpoint) a cold and corrupt air of utter, forlorn cruelty.

On 6 June, the mutineers' attention turned to the entrenchment itself. Perhaps in deference to his relationship with Lady Wheeler, Nana Sahib very sportingly sent Sir Hugh a message to inform him the firing was about to begin. There was precious little the British could do about it, though: for every man available to fight there were ten women and children, and not nearly enough weaponry to go round. Nowhere around the enclosure were the mud walls more than four feet high, and nowhere inside were the trenches deeper than eighteen inches. There were a few frail buildings, but far too many people to shelter within them. All that was left to protect the others from a sun so relentlessly hot that it burst the muzzles of guns, was the odd tattered tent and ladies' parasol. And no morale at all.

I did say in opening this chapter that first-hand accounts of the Cawnpore massacres were hard to come by. One of the few that does still exist was written by Amelia (or Amy) Horne, the eighteen-year-old step-daughter of an agent of the North-Western Dak [Mail] Company there. Amy was the eldest child in a family which included another three daughters and two sons, ranging in age from ten months to ten years; even at the best of times her days were fully occupied by domestic duties. Now, with the growing suspicion that her mother was joining Mrs Wiggens (and many others) in the dark realms of dementia, her responsibilities were almost intolerable.

[O]nce within the entrenchment walls we thought ourselves perfectly safe, though, I confess, this was not the general belief. It appears that more than one officer had dissuaded General Wheeler from taking up the position he did. Their opinion from the beginning was that the spot and buildings would never stand a siege. Even those who had little pretensions to military tactics perceived the utter insecurity of the place, and pointed out that the magazine was better adapted for defence. It stood on the river bank, and was surrounded by walls of substantial masonry. But General Wheeler seemed to take a far different view of things. He thought the danger exaggerated, and as proof of this, brought into the entrenchment but six guns of small calibre, only one-third of the ammunition, and not a single shell, leaving a well-stored magazine for the mutineers, and so providing them with the means for our destruction . . .

It was not, however, till Sunday, the 7th of June, that our troubles really commenced, as on the previous day the rebels were hard at work mounting the siege guns, and by noon on Sunday they got ready a cordon of seven batteries, which opened such a hot and incessant firing on us that Captain Moore . . . remarked that he had never known such heavy and continued cannonading. Our brave solders were quite resigned to face such terrific odds, and were game to fight to the bitter end. It was one of the most terrible sights which our eyes now beheld; the whole surrounding country seemed covered with men at arms, on horse and foot, and they presented a most formidable appearance. They seemed such fearful odds to keep at bay from our Lilliputian defences.

The site of our entrenchment was surrounded by large and substantial buildings, from three to eight hundred yards distant, occupied by the rebels, and from roof and window, all day, a shower of bullets poured down upon us in our exposed position. Shells likewise kept falling all over . . . One shell killed seven women as it fell hissing into the trenches and burst. Windows and doors were soon shot off their sockets, and the shot and ball began to play freely through the denuded buildings . . .

The agonies we endured during the siege are indescribable. The men were out in the trenches, under the burning rays of a June sun . . . where the temperature in the *shade* is as high as 110 to 115 degrees Fahrenheit [one day during the siege it was actually thought to be as high as 138 degrees]. It was not the heat alone that caused us intense suffering, but also the lack of food, water, and rest.

In regard to the first, although the commissariat and regimental messes did the best they could in respect to the provisioning of the place, yet the aggregate amount of food was out of all proportion to the thousand mouths that were to be filled. As to the second, the only source of supply was a single well, which soon became the target of the rebel artillery, and it was only at the risk of life that any water could be drawn. Notwithstanding the danger, cheerfully would the men go and draw it rather than see us perish from thirst . . .

The firing became so hot that very soon no water could be drawn out of the well during the day, and we had to wait till late at night, when the firing abated somewhat, and water could be drawn. We had to practise great economy in respect to our water rations, and had to drink in sips, not knowing when the next supply would be forthcoming.

Our stress for water can be imagined, when on one occasion we were obliged to drink some mixed with human blood, which had fallen into our vessel from the wounds of a native nurse or 'ayah' who, while standing near by, had both her legs carried away by the bursting of a shell. Water to wash there was none, of course . . .

Our troubles hourly increased; and we began to feel the pangs of hunger, our provision-room having shared the same fate as the other parts of the building. My poor little brothers and sisters, wee little things as they were, felt the want of food dreadfully, and would have eaten the most loathsome thing had it been served up as an article of diet. Infants were starved to death on the maternal breasts, which famine had dried of their nourishment.

Our last meal was a horse, which was lying wounded. His flesh was converted into soup, and many cheerfully partook of it. All we had to live on now was a handful of parched gram [a pulse usually reserved for feeding animals] which had been brought for the horses. This was served round once a day with a little rum . . .

Half our number had lost their reason; my dear mother (who was then seven months *enceinte*) being one of the afflicted. I used to sit and listen to her ravings, muttered in broken sentences. Her one theme was her mother whom she wanted to see. At one moment she would be calling for a conveyance to take her to her mother, and the next her mind would wander away to something else. Her dreadful affliction rendered me heartbroken, and her cries haunt me still. There was a clergyman among us who died raving mad through the combined effects of heat, exposure, and fear, and used to walk about stark naked. His condition was pitiful to see.[13]

As if there were not enough for the dwindling population of the entrenchment to cope with, a shell started a blaze on the thatched roof of a crowded old hospital building one day. Amy was there:

There was a high breeze at the time, and the material with which the roof was built being so inflammable afforded not the least chance to save anything. The scene that ensued was awful. The women and children were panic-stricken; confronted on one side by the burning building, and on the other by the shot and shell from the enemy's guns, which fell like hail on every side, they knew not where to run for protection. The soldiers had to keep their place in the trenches, it being a critical moment for the garrison, as the enemy were preparing to storm the position. The cries of the sick and wounded to be saved from the flames and the falling building were heart-rending. The rebels, guided in their firing by the blazing pile, poured a continuous volley of shot and shell into the burning building, the occupants whereof were dragged out without any regard to the excruciating pain occasioned by their wounds. Several were burned alive. My sister, a little girl of five, had her leg fractured by a falling block of masonry. A woman had half of one foot torn off, and as all the hospital stores were destroyed both these poor sufferers had to stay as they were. Mother and I were both wounded in the head . . . Every drop of medicine in the building was destroyed, and the consequences felt almost immediately, and bitterly too, for, putting recovery out of the question, no relief whatever could now be afforded to soothe their dying moments, not even a drop of water . . . It was now that our skirts were in demand. We tore every vestige, even to our sleeves, to supply bandages for the wounded. Great God, was it possible that human beings could endure so much! Gladly would we have laid down rank and wealth for our freedom, but we saw no hope, and our strength was growing less and less daily.[14]

The hellish entrenchment was fast assuming Dantesque characteristics by now, being a stinking, rancid and rat-infested chaos of human degradation. Lydia Hillersdon – days away from giving birth – was still doing her best to minister to those even less fortunate than herself, still 'sweet, calm, and gentle'[15] and 'a favourite of all'.[16] Another sterling soul named Bridget Widdowson spent one glorious episode (fairly early on during the siege) guarding a group of eleven captured mutineers when no one else could be spared to do the job: the terrified men are said to have 'sat quietly on the ground like good school-children, while the matron walked up and down in front of the row, drawn sword in hand'.[17] As soon as she was relieved by a soldier, of course, they all ran away. Such gleams of the old familiar spirit were diminishing fast, however. Lydia herself was killed two days after witnessing her husband's death when a vestige of the ceiling collapsed on her whilst in labour in one of the last remaining sheltered corners in the camp. One of the women whose fate speaks most eloquently of the rank futility of the whole episode was a private's wife, Mrs White. She was walking one day at her husband's side with a baby twin in each arm when a single shot screamed towards them, breaking both her elbows, injuring one of the twins and killing their father. She was seen a few days later lying on her back with a child at each breast: there was no other way to support their suckling but on the filthy floor. She died, with the twins, soon afterwards.

In a list that survives of how the victims of Cawnpore perished, there is one plaintive entry that stands out from all the rest. A baby died at two days old merely, it says, 'of itself'.[18] The Lindsay girls, Emma Larkins,[19] Mrs Ewart and Amy, meanwhile, were still, somehow, alive. Amy takes up the story:

[W]e held out for about three weeks, and were at the last gasp when, on the 25th of June, a message was brought to us from the Nana by Mrs Henry Jacobi,[20] who was well known to most of us. She was the wife [widow] of a watchmaker. It was a source of unbounded delight to us to see a white face from over the border, and we invited her to stay; but [this kind offer of hospitality from a reeking, half-starved, half-dressed and hollow-eyed Amy and her mad mother being probably the most unlikely she had ever received] she said she could not, as the Nana had kept her children and would kill them if she did not go back.

The message she had brought, as I learned later, was written on a slip of paper in the handwriting of Azimoola Khan, the Nana's secretary, and was addressed 'To the subjects of Her Most Gracious Majesty Queen Victoria'. It was to the effect that all those who were in no way connected with the acts of Lord Dalhousie and were willing to lay down their arms would receive a safe passage to Allahabad. Or, in other words, we were to give up the treasure and guns, and to walk out as we stood, and would be provided with forty boats, provisions, and an escort to see us safely landed at Allahabad . . .

Mrs Jacobi spent the whole day in the entrenchment, while the deliberations on the message she had brought were being conducted. Every soldier in the garrison revolted at the idea of surrendering, knowing well the treacherous character of the Nana. Moreover, the thought of white men surrendering to the blacks [was] most abhorrent to British prestige. Most of the officers, too, were for fighting to the bitter end, as was likewise General Wheeler, who still entertained hopes of help from Sir Henry Lawrence.

The situation was critical in the extreme. On the one side, our numbers were fearfully reduced by death and disease, gunshot, privation, and hunger; our guns had been considerably damaged by the enemy; and even had they not been, they could make no adequate reply to the heavy fire of the enemy's guns. Our ammunition was fast coming to an end, and our food supply had run out. With starvation staring us in the face, and black despair at our hearts, who could blame the wisdom of the decision that was at last reluctantly arrived at, in favour of capitulation?

The day following – *viz*, the 26th of June – was a great day for us.
The flag of truce was hoisted, and the roaring of cannon having
ceased, a weight seemed to have been taken off our hearts. The joy
was general, and everybody seemed to have at once forgotten their
past sufferings. It was such happiness to quit a place so fraught with
misery for all of us, and haunted with the groans of the wounded
and the dying. Poor deluded fools that we were . . .

The soldiers were singing and dancing, and they tried to get up a
little fun for the children. It was the first time since we entered the
entrenchment that the little ones were allowed their liberty, and they
soon made up for lost time. A cask was converted into a drum and
belaboured with a stick; one man whistled a jig, while the others
started to dance. The children, though very much broken down and
emaciated, yet gathered round the dancers and tried to show their
appreciation of the entertainment got up for them. We walked about
that evening enjoying our freedom; no creeping about on all fours,
and having to lie flat on our faces every now and then in fear of the
shells.

We sadly needed clothing, for, as I have already said, our dresses
had been torn up for bandages. I went into the entrenchment with a
dress made up of frills from the waist downwards, as was the fashion
in those days, but when I left I had only the body, the entire skirt
having been torn up . . . Our boxes were used to strengthen the barricade, and when restored to us were in as disreputable a condition as
ourselves. We selected from them a few necessary articles of clothing,
and left the rest for the Nana's benefit. Those who had jewellery
concealed it about their persons.

At dawn on the morning of the 27th of June we fell into order,
though no bugle was sounded. Behold us as we then appeared, like
so many ghosts, tattered, emaciated, and begrimed! Many a woman
and child whom I had seen enter with beautiful and smiling countenances now looked old, haggard, desperate and imbecile. There they
stood, shoeless and stockingless, and destitute of all the finery so dear

to the heart of a woman – objects fit to make the angels weep! The old – battered and bruised, like ships that come into port after being buffeted by storms – babbled like children; others had a vacant stare in their eyes, as if they beheld visions of the future. Many a little child was raving mad, and it was pitiful to see their singular behaviour.

Although we had all been driven to most horrible straits, still every woman retained her modesty and refinement to the last. In this con- nexion I would say, situated as we were in the entrenchment, it was not possible to observe etiquette and decorum, for we had to witness sights that often shocked us. Many a night I have been astounded on waking up to find a soldier sharing my *charpoy*, where the poor fellow had thrown himself down in utter weariness! . . .

It was about seven o'clock when we left for the Ghat, mounted on elephants, like sheep being driven to the shambles, the rebel army escorting us. The elephants provided for our conveyance were not allowed by their *mahouts* [the men who managed the elephants] to sit down so that we might mount in comfort. We were therefore obliged to climb up by their tails, and you can imagine the brutality of such a proceeding (instigated by the Nana), when the wounded and sick had to adopt this mode of ascent and fell to the ground. This nearly cost my poor mother her life, for, hampered as she was by her *enceinte* condition, and weakened by hunger and privation, the task was a most Herculean one for her to perform, and she fell heavily. How much better that she had died then and so have ended her sufferings . . . My only consolation is that she and my little brothers and sisters were not among the victims of the Nana's bloodthirstiness as dis- played in the Slaughter House.[21]

Reaching the Ghat we found that the boats were not very close to the shore, and the task of getting on board was a most difficult one. We had to wade knee-deep through the water, and it was pitiful to witness the difficulty of the aged, the sick, and the wounded in clam- bering up the boats' sides . . .

Under the awning of our boat were seated my step-father, two brothers and two sisters, and an Indian nurse; while on the deck or forepart were two soldiers, my little sister, and myself. In the hopeless scramble and confusion that ensued, and also on account of the want of room in our boat, my poor mother was conveyed to another boat a short distance away . . .

After all had embarked – which took about two hours to accomplish – the word was given to proceed. Instead of the crew obeying these orders, a signal was given from the shore and they all leaped into the water and waded to the bank, after having first secreted burning charoal in the thatch of most of the boats. Immediately a volley of bullets assailed us, followed by a hail of shot and grape which struck the boats. The two soldiers seated alongside of me were wounded, and crept into the shelter of the awning to escape being made further targets of. In a few minutes pandemonium reigned. Several of the boats were seen to be wrapped in flames, and the sick and wounded were burnt to death. Some jumped overboard and tried to swim to the opposite shore, but were picked off by the bullets of the sepoys. Others were drowned, while a few jumped into the water and hid behind their boats to escape the pitiless fire. But the guns continued their vile work, and grape and musketry were poured into the last-mentioned people from the opposite bank which soon became alive with rebels who had been placed there to intercept refugees to that shore. A few succeeded in pushing their boats to the further side of the river, and were mercilessly slaughtered.

The cavalry waded into the river with drawn swords and cut down those who were still alive, while the infantry boarded the boats . . .

The air resounded with the shrieks of the women and children and agonised prayers to God for mercy. The water was red with blood, and the smoke from the heavy firing of the cannon and muskets and the fire from the burning boats lay like dense clouds over and around us. Several men were mutilated in the presence of their wives, while babies and children were torn from their mothers' arms and hacked to pieces, the mothers being compelled to look on at the carnage! Many children were deliberately set fire to and burned, while the sepoys laughed and cheered, inciting each other to greater acts of brutality!

My poor little sister, the one who had had her leg fractured in the entrenchment, moaned piteously, crying out the while 'Oh, Amy, don't leave me!' A few yards away I saw the boat containing my poor mother slowly burning, and I cowered on the deck overwhelmed with grief, not knowing what horrible fate the next moment had in store for me. My heart beat like a sledge hammer, and my temples throbbed with pain; but there I sat, gripping my little sister's hand, while the bullets fell like hail around me, praying fervently to God for mercy, and every second expecting to be in the presence of my Maker!

The sepoys quickly boarded our boat, and a few trinkets I had with me were forcibly taken possession of by one of them. These not being sufficient to satisfy his avarice, he had the barbarity to fetch me a blow on the head with his musket. Shortly after I was beckoned to by a sowar who was on his horse riding alongside of our boat, the water reaching up to his saddle. I turned sick with fear, but paid no heed, pretending I had not seen him. He then levelled his carbine at me, but finding that it had not the effect of frightening me into submission to his wishes, and unable to approach near enough to the boat, he shouted out to another sepoy who was on the boat to throw me into the water. I was thereupon brutally seized round the waist, and though I struggled and fought wildly, was quickly overcome and tossed into the river.

The cries of my poor little sister, imploring me wildly not to leave her, still ring in my ears; and her last look of anguish . . . has haunted me ever since. That was the last I ever saw or heard of my family . . .'[22]

The first massacre of Cawnpore was over.

One boat happened to escape unnoticed by the rebels in the general frenzy: as it began to float through the hot, sour fog hanging over the Ganges it was joined by one Lieutenant Mowbray Thomson. He had leapt off his own burning craft, grounded on mudbanks like the rest, and sacrificing his most treasured possessions (a medal of his father and his mother's portrait) had managed to clamber aboard.

Now the crowded state of our poor ark left little room for working her. Her rudder was shot away, we had no oars, for these had all been thrown overboard by the traitorous boatmen, and the only implements that could be brought into use were a spar or two and such pieces of wood as we could in safety tear from the sides. Grape and round shot flew about us from either bank of the river, and shells burst constantly on the sandbanks . . . Mrs Swinton . . . was standing up in the stern, and, having been struck by a round shot, fell overboard and sank immediately. Her poor little boy, six years old, came up to me and said, 'Mamma has fallen overboard.' I endeavoured to comfort him, and told him Mamma would not suffer any more pain . . . He cried out, 'Oh, why are they firing on us? Did they not promise to leave off?' I never saw the child after that.[23]

Another boat was captured a day after the massacre and its eighty-nine passengers – sixty men, twenty-five women and four children – sent back to Cawnpore. There the sahibs were shot (and one of the memsahibs, Dr Boyes's wife Kate, who refused to be torn away from him at the end). The remaining women were taken down to a sad reunion with the relics of the entrenchment.

Emma Ewart was dead by now: she and her wounded husband had been killed by taunting sepoys as they trailed at the end of the awful procession to the Ghat. So was Louisa Chalwin, the one who had been so worried before about the loss of her hair and her piano: she died on the boats, like the Burra Mem Lady Wheeler.

The Lindsays, however, had managed to survive. They were seen being led from the Satichowra Ghat, dazed and dull-witted, to the old orphanage known as the Savada Koti that served as the memsahibs' prison for the next three days. Their progress from the river, with a vast and spurious sepoy guard, was a well-attended spectacle. Some of the women were wounded and bleeding; others had had their earrings torn from their ears in the water and bound their heads with handkerchiefs; all were dressed in soiled and stinking remnants, with the exception of a few naked children. There was no male present over the age of about fourteen.

On 1 July the prisoners were moved again, this time to the Bibigarh, a poky little bungalow built for the mistress of some long-gone British officer, thirty yards from the hotel Nana Sahib had requisitioned as his headquarters. I suppose the site of it must be just about where that dingy factory backing on to the Nana Rao Park is today.

Here, in two rooms measuring about sixteen feet square, 206 women and children were incarcerated for fifteen days. The numbers had been swelled by the addition of those Christian women like Mrs Jacobi who had escaped the entrenchment episode by being imprisoned by the Nana elsewhere, and by a consignment of refugees from Fatehgarh, about eighty miles up the Ganges, who had taken to the water as soon as mutiny threatened in the middle of May. About 126 of them had miraculously managed to find their way in boats down to Bithoor, hoping to find both safety and support. Instead all but three of the men were shot straight away; those whose lives had inexplicably been spared were then packed off with the women and their children to await the rebels' pleasure.

After the Mutiny, a series of official depositions was commissioned to try to sort out (necessarily from the native or Eurasian point of view) what really happened at Cawnpore.[24] Several of them had it that the memsahibs of the Bibighar were seen forcibly washing their own clothes and grinding grain – both significantly menial tasks far too degrading for the memsahib of old. The ladies were supposed to have been supervised by Hosainee Khanum, a woman of the Nana's household known simply as the Begum. She looked odd: tall, fair-skinned and grey-haired (although only in her late twenties); it was her job to bring food every day (chupattis and dhall) and provide decent clothes for those in her charge. But although meat was promised every Sunday, no one ever saw it. One day milk had been provided for the infants – but never again. The starving memsahibs and their children slept wherever they could find the space in the dirt, and it took twenty-five deaths from cholera and dysentery during the first week alone for them to be allowed out on the verandah for an occasional (and very public) breath of air. In fact it was not until the last day of their confinement that the Begum showed any particular enthusiasm for her work. That afternoon, Wednesday 15 July, she was bright-eyed, brisk and businesslike: she had an announcement to make to the squalid assembly inside.

The British were coming.

This was the news that finally put an end to the misery of the memsahibs of Cawnpore. No doubt those with any spirit left had been praying for Sir Henry Havelock and his men to arrive: nothing else was likely to save their lives. It was all nearly over at last, thank God.

And so it was. They had been valuable hostages until now, these wives and children of the oppressor, but now it was decided they were more useful dead than alive. If they were killed, they would obviously be unable to testify against particular rebels (as rumour had it some were already attempting to do in letters smuggled out to Allahabad); the British would be absolved, too, of the need to fight their way into Cawnpore to liberate them, and thus save the Nana's increasingly uncertain military resources for another day.

It is not unreasonable to assume, either, that the rebel camp had caught some of the rumours flying around ahead of the British advance, which would make the second massacre as much a matter of direct retribution as anything else. The first might have been a glorious and sacred sacrifice (according to certain Indian historians):[25] the public consummation of India's first concerted struggle for religious and political independence. But it had not worked: news was coming in of persecution far keener than it had ever been before at the hands of one Brigadier-General James Neill. Scarlet with wrath and huge with patriotic prejudice he was reported to be making his progress from Allahabad towards Cawnpore like some vengeful great juggernaut. In his wake there stretched a billowing cloud of cruelty and waste just as deadly as any that engulfed the British. It was his policy (supported by the government back home) to raze to the ground any village that might have had some connection – however tenuous – with rebellion; he burned not only their houses but also whomsoever was inside them at the time: women, children, the old, the sick, anyone. 'In two days', reported W. H. Russell of *The Times*, 'forty-two men were hanged on the roadside, and a batch of twelve men were executed because their faces were "turned the wrong way" when they were met on the march.'[26] Even the eminently orthodox historian Sir John Kaye had to admit that 'Englishmen did not hesitate to boast, or to record their boastings in writing, that they had "spared no one" and that "peppering away at niggers" was very pleasant pastime'.[27] Why should a few worn-out memsahibs be spared in the face of such wholesale slaughter as this?

Those Cawnpore depositions collected so diligently by the British authorities suddenly turn tight-lipped come 15 July. Thanks to the testimony of John Fitchett, a Eurasian drummer in a sepoy regiment who had been imprisoned in the grounds of the Bibigarh, we know that it was the Begum's job to inform the ladies of their fate, and that when one of the memsahibs queried Hosainee's orders with the jemadar (Indian officer) in charge of the guard, he told her not to worry: they were safe. But by then the three sahib survivors from Fatehgarh had been taken out, with one of the oldest children in the Bibigarh (a lad of fourteen), and shot. It was also the Begum's job to give the order to the sepoy guard to fire on the rest – but they refused to do so, aiming instead at the ceiling. They were summarily dismissed while Hosainee Khanum went off to tempt more willing recruits, whom she found in two Moslem butchers, a couple of Hindu peasants, and her own lover, who was a member of the Nana's bodyguard. First a few sepoys pushed their way around the Bibigarh to find what booty they could, then, says Fitchett, the killers entered with their swords. The sun was just going down.

The lady who spoke to the jemadar was at the door, she was the first cut down. I saw her fall, but could not see further than the door; I heard fearful shrieks. This lasted half an hour or more. I did not see any of the women or children try to escape.

The sowars were posted at the trees near the house. A Velaitee [stranger from a long way away: Hosainee's lover], a stout, short man, and fair, soon came out with his sword broken. I saw him go into the Nana's house [the hotel] and bring back another sword. This he also broke in a few minutes, and got a third from the Nana . . .

The groans lasted all night . . . At about 8 o'clock the next morning, the sweepers living in the compound, I think there were three or four, were ordered to throw the bodies into a dry well, near the house. The bodies were dragged out, most of them by the hair of the head, those whose clothes were worth taking, were stripped. Some of the women were alive, I cannot say how many, but three could speak; they prayed for the sake of God that an end might be put to their sufferings. I remarked one very stout woman, a half-caste, who was severely wounded in both arms, who entreated to be killed. She and two or three others were placed against the bank of the cut by which bullocks go down in drawing water from the well. The dead bodies were first thrown down. Application was made to the Nana about those who were alive. Three children were also alive. I do not know what order came, but I saw one of the children thrown in alive. I believe the other children and women, who were alive, were then thrown in . . .

[T]here was a great crowd looking on; they were standing along the walls of the compound. They were principally city people and villagers. Yes, there were also sepoys . . . [T]hey were fair children, the eldest I think must have been six or seven, and the youngest five years; it was the youngest who was thrown in by one of the sweepers. The children were running round the well, where else could they go to? and there was none to save them. No, none said a word . . .[28]

7

The Cawnpore Survivors

---

*I do not like sending you these horrid stories, but still
you will read and hear worse . . .*[1]

Henry Havelock's men had already been marching for five hours
when the last of those terror-stricken children was loaded into the
Bibigarh well to suffocate amongst their mothers. Although tantal-
izingly close for the British, the timing was impeccable from the
rebels' point of view: the plan had been for all the hostages to be
gone by the time the troops arrived – the massacre being the fruit
of Havelock's own success, after all – and that very morning, 16
July, he was scarcely twenty-five miles away from Cawnpore. He
and his 1,200 men had mustered soon after 3 a.m.; they then
breakfasted on a few boardy biscuits and a gulp of porter after a
march of some twenty miles, and went on to meet the Nana's
10,000-strong force hungry, tired, and clad in thick, dusty uniforms foul with sweat. The heavy, pre-monsoon heat was vicious
enough to sear their fingers whenever they touched metal. Yet so
inspirational was their general that they all seemed to acknowledge a single, grand purpose. Havelock had hammered it in in the
dark before the dawn, when news had come through from a spy
that the hostages were still alive: 'By God's help, men, we shall
save them, or every man die in the attempt.'

That afternoon, while the Bibigarh stood reeking, quiet and

empty, the battle of Cawnpore was fought and won by the British. Nana's men broke up (he fled to Bithoor himself) and those of Havelock's who had survived the fighting lay down and slept where they were, ill-fed and uncovered, ready to march the two miles needed next morning to liberate the ladies of Cawnpore.

An advance party was sent out into the city at sunrise on 17 July. What they witnessed made them physically sick, appalled, and incensed.

I was directed to the house where all the poor miserable ladies had been murdered. It was alongside the Cawnpore hotel, where the Nena [sic] lived. I never was more horrified! The place was one mass of blood. I am not exaggerating when I tell you that the soles of my boots were more than covered with the blood of these poor wretched creatures . . .[2]

[I found] quantities of dresses, clogged thickly with blood, children's frocks, frills, and ladies' under clothing of all kinds, also boys' trousers, leaves of Bibles, and of one book in particular, which seems to be strewed over the whole place, called *Preparation for Death*, also broken daguerrotype cases only, and hair, some nearly a yard long; bonnets all bloody, and one or two shoes. I picked up a bit of paper with on it, 'Ned's hair, with love,' and opened [it] and found a little bit tied up with riband . . .[3]

All the way to the well was marked by a regular track along which the bodies had been dragged, and the thorny bushes had entangled in them scraps of clothing and long hairs. One of the large trees . . . had evidently had children's brains dashed out against its trunk . . . and an eye glazed and withered could be plainly made out . . .[4]

I have looked upon death in every form, but I could not look down that well again.[5]

The well was some fifty feet deep, and narrow; all that could be seen of the victims within was a white and tangled mess of naked limbs choked up to within about six feet of the top. It was ordered that it be filled in almost immediately.

Several of those who made it to Cawnpore with Havelock knew former members of the garrison personally. One of these was a Captain Moorsom, desperate to find clues to the fate of some particular friends of his. He came across a few dismembered books on his grisly search through the Bibigarh with the odd relevant inscription inside, but the most affecting relic was a scrap of paper found clotted to the floor of what was hereafter known as the Slaughter House with a terse and chilling little list on it in pencil:

> Entered the barracks May 21st
> Cavalry left June 5th
> First shot fired June 6th
> Aunt Lilly died June 17th
> Uncle Willy died June 18th
> Left barracks June 27th
> George died June 27th
> Alice died July 9th
> Mama died July 12th

It was written by Caroline Lindsay, she who had been so reluctant to come to Cawnpore with her excited mother and sisters, for fear of something terrible happening to them all.

She died, with her sister Frances, in the final massacre.

There were supposed to have been other messages from the dead, too, amongst the general detritus of Cawnpore, and it is with these that the great raft of apocryphal evidence of what really happened there began to welter out of control. Patently, the intended rescue of the angels of Albion was no longer possible; now what mattered was vengeance, and any incitement, wherever it came from, was welcome. 'Discoveries' were being made, amid much morbid sensationalism, of graffiti gouged in shell-pocked plaster or traced in blood on the walls. 'Countrymen and women, remember the 15th of July, 1857! Your wives and families are here, misary [sic]! and at the disposal of savages, who have ravished both young and old. Oh! my child! my child!'[6] ran one – or, more pathetically, 'Dear Jesus, send us help today, and deliver us not into the hands of our enemies.'[7] In fact, there were no such messages there at all when the first men went in on 17 July.

A popular rumour at the time, which rapidly joined the ranks of Cawnpore folklore, involved the finding by Highland soldiers of a young woman's head behind a bush on the way to the well with all its lovely hair intact. They divided the tresses up amongst them with the solemn vow that for each strand they held, a mutineer should die. Something just as mawkish but probably true, this time, happened a few weeks later when a thrilled soldier reported having found 'a quantity of females' hair' outside the Bibigarh, declaring that he would have kept some (and sent it home to his family as a particularly high-class *memento mori*) had it not been a little 'too rotten'.[8] Wherever one turned in Cawnpore, it seemed some dreadful vision was at hand. Someone searching some room somewhere reported coming across 'fifty pairs of men's feet in their shoes, and thirty pairs of women's'[9] neatly arranged along the wall. A friend of a friend had found a number of infants speared to the walls in the Bibigarh, or hanging on hooks from the ceiling, and some charred boxes into which babies had been packed, alive, and burned; 'others were spitted on bayonets and twisted round in the air, and to make the tortures more exquisite all this was done in the presence of the mothers who were compelled to look on . . . in a state of nudity'.[10] It was arousing stuff, enough to move the mildest man to blood-revenge.

General Neill was hardly that: when he landed in Cawnpore on 21 July, having been practising all the way from Allahabad, he was raring to go:

Since I arrived here I have been hard at work to get order re-established. I have now put a stop to the plundering I found going on by reorganizing a police. I am also collecting all the property of the deceased, and trying to trace if any have survived, but as yet have not succeeded in finding one. Man, woman, and child seem all to have been murdered. As soon as that monster Nena Sahib heard of the success of our troops and of their having forced the bridge about 20 miles from Cawnpore, he ordered the wholesale butchery of the poor women and children. I find the officers' servants behaved shamefully, and were in the plot, all but the lowest caste ones. They deserted their masters and plundered them. Whenever a rebel is caught he is immediately tried, and unless he can prove a defence he is sentenced to be hanged at once; but the chief rebels or ring leaders I make first clean up a portion of the pool of blood, still two inches deep, in the shed where the fearful murder and mutilation of women and children took place. To touch blood is most abhorrent to the high caste natives, they think by doing so they doom their souls to perdition. Let them think so. My object is to inflict a fearful punishment for a revolting, cowardly, barbarous deed, and to strike terror into these rebels. The first I caught was a subhadar, or native officer, a high-caste Brahmin, who tried to resist my order to clean up the very blood he had helped to shed; but I made the Provost-Marshal do his duty, and a few lashes soon made the miscreant accomplish his task. When done, he was taken out and immediately hanged, and after death buried in a ditch at the road side. No one who has witnessed the scenes of murder, mutilation, and massacre can ever listen to the word 'mercy', as applied to these fiends.[11]

What Neill refrained from mentioning in this letter to a newspaper in (of all places) his native town of Ayr, was the method used to 'clean up' the blood. It involved the often arbitrarily condemned 'fiend' having to kneel down on the floor of the Slaughter House, and *lick* the congealed blood, which was dampened square foot by square foot for the purpose. Every effort was made to break his caste, including the force-feeding of pork and beef, while an audience looked on to jeer him as one of the 'cursed women-slayers'. There was the odd emollient voice heard whispering persistently in the background, like that of the level-headed Mr J. W. Sherer, one of the first Europeans into the Bibigarh after the massacre and later Magistrate of Cawnpore. He found what had happened just as harrowing as anyone else, but realized – and warned against – the danger of exaggeration. The implication was that the British must avoid accusations of the same sort of behaviour indulged in by those savage Indians: as *Punch* put it in a moment of unwonted gentleness:

> Who babes and women slew with lingering pain,
> Upon the wretched slave thy vengeance feast.
> There stop; nor let his guilt thy manhood stain,
> But spare the Indian mother and her child.[12]

There were few there, though, being men of their time, who could weep without personal resentment (and plenty wept): anyone who could diminish their virility like that, as well as com-mitting the enormities of rape and femicide – anyone who could break *their* caste, in fact, as proud and honourable Englishmen, deserved to die. The Empire had been cuckolded by a bunch of uncivilized and ungrateful cowards.

Or had it? The question of rape (by Indians) comes up again. It figured gaudily in the apocryphal tales of Cawnpore, of course, and Havelock's men would no doubt have found it easy to believe it happened. The native depositions taken by Colonel Williams, though, give no evidence of what was euphemistically termed 'dishonour' at all. Nor could Commissioner Sherer and Magis-trate Thornhill come up with any credible example during their official investigations. Even Sir John Kaye, perched on the high moral ground of authorized imperial historian some twenty years later was unable to see anything more distinct than rumour. Certainly, the massacre of Britain's women and children, he said, was unforgivable.

But beyond this wholesale killing and burying, which sickened the whole Christian world, and roused English manhood in India to a pitch of national hatred that took years to allay, the atrocity was not pushed. The refinements of cruelty – the unutterable shame – with which, in some of the chronicles of the day, this hideous massacre was attended, were but fictions of an excited imagination, too readily believed without inquiry and circulated without thought. None were mutilated – none were dishonoured. There was nothing needed to aggravate the naked horror of the fact that some two hundred Christian women and children were hacked to death in the course of a few hours.[13]

There was one exception, however, acknowledged by all these reports. And she, sensationally, was the Commanding Officer of the garrison's youngest daughter, Miss Ulrica Wheeler.

There is an immediate qualification whenever Ulrica is mentioned: she was, as Kaye so delicately put it, 'by no means of pure English blood' and so, statistically, hardly counted. But because of her father's position and the mystery that surrounded her story she fascinated both the Indians and Europeans even then, and has continued to do so, no one yet being absolutely certain what became of her and when.

Sir Hugh Massy Wheeler had ten children altogether, by his Eurasian wife – and kinswoman of the Nana – Frances Matilda (née Marsden).[14] He was sixty-eight in 1857, yet still to be seen in the weeks before the Mutiny on family expeditions out jackal-hunting by horseback, cantering along beside his children and a pack of Scotch deer-hounds. Three of those children were in

Cawnpore with their parents when the entrenchment was occupied in May: Godfrey, a lieutenant and his 'favourite darling
son', Eliza Matilda, and the youngest of his daughters, Ulrica.
Godfrey was killed during the siege in the most horrific circumstances: he had been wounded on duty in the trenches and was
lying on a sofa being tended by his mother and two sisters, and
fretted over by Sir Hugh, when a round shot suddenly whistled
through the doorway and blew the lad's head from his body. Physically, the others were unhurt. But it was said that Sir Hugh's spirit
was broken after this, and what it must have done to Frances and
her daughters, even in the horribly heightened atmosphere of the
siege, is hard to imagine.

Several witnesses saw Sir Hugh and the ladies on the slow
procession from the entrenchment to the Satichowra Ghat on 27
June: Ulrica was wearing a green dress,[15] they remembered, and
somehow managed to become separated from her parents and
Eliza during the boarding of the boats. What happened to her
next was to become the stuff of legend. Several legends, in fact.

Most accounts had it that Ulrica was dragged off her boat, like
Amy Horne, by a sowar of the 2nd Cavalry. Amy actually saw her,
crouching and shivering on the riverbank during the massacre,
before both girls were hurried off by their respective captors.
Then the stories of this Mutiny heroine begin to differ. One of the
most popular was first published by one of Wheeler's native spies,
who knew the family well enough to regard eighteen-year-old
Ulrica as little 'Missee Baba'.

This was her circumstance. As they were taking the mem-Sahibs out
of the boat a Sowar took her away with him to his house. She went
quietly; but at night [and he implies elsewhere that she had, meanwhile, been raped] she rose and got hold of the sowar's sword. He
was asleep; his wife, his son, and his mother-in-law were sleeping in
the house with him. She killed them all with the sword, and then she

went and threw herself down the well behind the house. In the morning, when people came and found the dead in the house, their cry was, 'Who has done this?' Then a neighbour said that in the night he had seen someone go and throw himself into the well. They went and looked, and there was Missee Baba, dead and swollen.[16]

Elsewhere, however, Ulrica was supposed to have been seen levelling a pistol at her captor, presumably just before carefully decapitating herself (since the angelic head those Highlanders were said to have found in the bushes was recognized, of course, as hers). All this is somewhat difficult to reconcile with the florid testimony of a Lucknow balladeer, who swore the fair Ulrica had survived the first massacre and then valiantly committed suicide during the second:

> From midst the house of slaughter
> I see a lady fair
> Rush forth with screams of terror,
> And wild dishevelled hair.
> With compressed lips and bloodless cheeks
> She dashes through the door,
> And flies as straight as arrow shot
> To the old well of Cawnpore.
> The rebels see their prey is lost,
> And raise a fiendish yell
> As Ada [sic!] Wheeler nears the edge
> Of that deep yawning well.
> 'Tis reached at last she looks aloft
> To Heaven's eternal sky,
> That virtuous Angels breathe a prayer,
> To God's bright throne on high
> And then a leap an awful plunge
> And death has claimed its own.

> The life God sent for a time on earth
> To the giver back has flown . . .[17]

A common thread in all these accounts is the girl's decent response to the sham, with which the sowar burdened her, whether that shame was related (as most thought it was) to rape, or not: she chose to die.

In reality, Ulrica preferred rather to keep quiet. The British government did try to find out what had happened to her, even sending spies up to Nepal, where the Nana was said to have made his eventual refuge. The faithful Fitchett, now riding with the rebel troops as a pretended Moslem, claimed to have seen 'a European lady with the sowar's women'.

She was in native dress, silk pyjamahs and a chuddur [veil] over her head, but was riding on a side saddle. I heard it was General Wheeler's youngest daughter, the sepoys were talking about her. I saw her every day during the march . . . I cannot be sure it was General Wheeler's daughter, as I had never seen her before, and was not allowed to speak to her; but heard from everyone that . . . [it] was . . . I heard one day that Ahmed Yar Khan [a rebel leader] had demanded the European lady; the sowars refused to give her up, they said she had been saved at the risk of her protector's life, and had become a Mohomedan. We then heard that the 41st Native Infantry, and the new levy raised at Futteghur under Ahmed Yar Khan's orders, would fight the sowars, who were quite determined to defend the lady with their lives; they said they would be cut to pieces before they gave her up.

The next day I saw two sowars pass our camp on the road to Cawnpore. The European lady was with them, and from that time I missed her. I do not know where she was taken to.[18]

One researcher, the son of one of the Bibigarh's victims, said in

1878 that Ulrica had indeed been taken to Cawnpore and was living there still.[19] Certainly there is evidence that a Mr and Mrs Clarke, who settled there in 1880, used to receive visits from an Englishwoman living as a native in the bazaar. They got to know her through their ayah, and were intrigued to find that on her arrival at their house she would whisk off her Indian clothes to reveal Western ones beneath. She could never admit her identity, or reveal exactly where it was she was living, for the shame it would bring her family, she said. And besides, she owed too much to her husband to betray him.

And then there is a postscript, in some information given by Florence Leach, a missionary doctor in Cawnpore. She recalled being summoned one night to the bazaar in about 1907 to attend an old, dying woman. This woman told Florence, in perfectly modulated English, that she was indeed Sir Hugh Massy Wheeler's child, that she had married the sowar who rescued (rather than abducted) her from the Satichowra Ghat, and that now she was dying and needed a priest. A Roman Catholic father was called from the bazaar for her comfort: perhaps, long widowed by now, she wore her native Christianity like her native dress, hidden and ready beneath her Moslem self.[20] She must have been very lonely at the end.

The soft-focus romance of Miss Wheeler has tended to eclipse harder news of the escape of other women (mostly of mixed race) from the Ghat. The massacres have always been regarded as atrocities of the most complete kind: well-authenticated news of survivors rather spoils the effect from a British point of view. Nevertheless, there are official statements in the government annals of, for example, a Christian girl named Elizabeth Spiers. Her evidence is succinct:

I am the daughter of Joseph Spiers, drummer; we went into the entrenchment with General Wheeler, and when the treaty was made with the Nana, we went with the others to the ghat. When the firing began we jumped into the water. My father, my brother, named David, 27 years old, band sergeant, and a little sister, about nine years old, were all killed there.

One sister, named Charlotte, about fourteen years old, was taken away by the sowars, and I have never heard anything more of her. I saw several ladies taken away, amongst them Mrs J— of the 67th, Mrs B— of the 2nd Cavalry [both later supposed to have been given up to the police] and Miss G—, the sister of Mrs B— of the 53rd. I knew these ladies, as they had been living in the same barracks in the entrenchment. I don't know what became of them afterwards . . .[21]

Elizabeth and her mother, together with a little brother and sister, were eventually hidden by a native doctor in Cawnpore. Two more musicians' widows, Eliza Bradshaw and Elizabeth Letts, were pulled out of the Ganges by the rebels and stripped before escaping, with their two daughters-in-law, first to a native burial ground, then (when discovered) to some elephant sheds for the night, to which they were admitted on swearing themselves to be Moslems. They found refuge the next morning with an oil-seller's wife from the bazaar and then a sweeper from the Cawnpore Free School, who cared for them until the Mutiny was over.[22] A Mrs Murray and Mrs Stewart whose husbands were in the same regiment as Bradshaw and Letts, and who were in the same boat as Eliza and Elizabeth, are also said to have survived, along with a young girl whose story took Mr Magistrate Sherer's particular fancy:

Did I mention [he wrote in September 1857] the poor child Victoria Anderson? She was the niece, I think, of Mr Banter, of Humeerpore, Clerk in the Collector's office. All her family were slain, and she herself wounded with a sword-cut. The native doctor, Ahmud Yar

Khan, protected the poor creature (she is about 10 years old), and concealed her in his house. He had written to me once or twice about having her brought in, but the pergunnahs [communities of villages] were then too disturbed. At last, through the good offices of Beharee Sing of Burreepal, she was brought safely to this place [Cawnpore]. She is quite recovered and placed under charge of Mrs Jones, wife of Fife-Major Jones, and I propose sending her to Calcutta to be put to school by the Relief Fund.[23]

Elizabeth Spiers mentioned in her deposition three women who had been 'taken away' by sowars in addition to Ulrica Wheeler: their names have remained as mere initials ever since. 'Mrs J— of the 67th' and 'Mrs B— of the 2nd Cavalry' were subsequently surrendered, she says, to the British; of poor 'Miss G—, the sister of Mrs B—' we hear nothing more at all.

Unless, that is, she is the unnamed young lady (for the sake of a shattered reputation) whose story was published in *The Times* in February 1859. 'I was sixteen years of age', she says, 'when I accompanied my sister and her husband to Cawnpore, about six months before the mutiny broke out, and suffered with the Christians under General Sir Hugh Wheeler.' She barely survived the siege, but thought she had been granted just reward for her fortitude when the order came to go to the Ghat and board the Nana's boats for Allahabad.

Like the rest, she was soon disabused. A party of sepoys clambered on to her grounded boat almost as soon as the firing started, and after being robbed by them and intimately searched for any further booty, Miss G. (for want of a better name) fainted and was thrown into the river, presumably for dead. When she came round she managed to scramble to the shore, where, like Amy Horne, she found a patient and petrified Ulrica Wheeler waiting for the end.

Our agitation and fear, however, were so great that we had not much
of consolation to offer each other. We had not been together more
than an hour, I should suppose, when a party of the enemy surprised us. We were dragged in different directions, and of Miss
Wheeler's fate I knew nothing till very lately. I was pushed and
dragged along and subjected to every indignity. Occasionally I felt
the thrust of a bayonet, and on my protesting against such treatment
with uplifted hands, and appealing to their feelings as men, I was
struck on my head, and was made to understand, in language too
plain that I had not long to live; but before being put to death, that I
would be made to feel some portion of the degradation their
brethren felt at Meerut when ironed and disgraced before the
troops. After a walk of about four hours I was brought to a place
about four miles from Cawnpore, very near Bithoor, where some of
the mutineers were encamped. I was almost in a state of nudity, for
my clothes had been torn to pieces when I had been dragged along
by the men, and I had the mortification of being made a spectacle
before these heartless and cruel wretches' clapping of hands and
cries of 'khoob kee!' (well done!) burst upon my stupefied senses. A
circle formed round me. I sunk on the ground and buried my face in
my hands. Oh, the agony of those moments! At length I heard a
voice speaking to my persecutors in rather a conciliatory tone. Spare
the poor creature, and have compassion on her. Let her alone; she
seems dead already. I looked up, and saw an African. There was
something mild and compassionate about his look. He relieved me
in a great measure from the shame I was suffering, by throwing a
covering or chuddur on me. He asked me to accompany him. I
immediately followed and was ushered into a tent, where I was
desired by my benefactor to take rest. He made me understand that
he would do all in his power to have my life spared. I thanked him
for his kindness. After a while he procured me a suit of native
clothes, which he said I should put on. 'You are very unwell,' he
said, 'your eyes are bloodshot, and face very much flushed.' I knew

138

that I had a strong fever on me, and felt exceedingly weak. I replied that a little sleep would perhaps do me good. I laid my aching head on the mattress and fell fast asleep.[24]

This African, whom Miss G. christened almost affectionately her 'sable benefactor', was in fact a eunuch, a courier from that great patroness of the mutineers Begum Hazrat Mahal of Oudh in Lucknow, and soon disappeared on official business. She was left amongst the Nana's camp-followers outside Cawnpore, 'treated brutally', until orders came on 15 July for the rebels' women and children to be evacuated and herded off towards Lucknow. That, of course, was the day of the second massacre.

Once in Lucknow, after a circuitous march (literally) via Bareilly, Rohilcund, Fatehgarh and Shahjehanpur, Miss G. was reunited with the eunuch, who suggested she should appeal to the charismatic rebel leader, Moulvee Ahmadullah Shah, lately arrived from Fyzabad (where, as Amy Horne was to note, he had summarily dispatched all the Europeans he could find). The Moulvee was a fanatic: provided he could be persuaded of Miss G.'s total devotion to Islam and renunciation of Christianity, he would be bound – sacredly bound – to keep her safe.

The girl applied herself well, smuggling messages out to him written in charcoal begging him in the name of Mahommed to relieve her from the cruelty of the native soldiers amongst whom she was slowly dying. She was duly sent a suit of clothes 'similar to those worn by Mahommedan ladies of distinction' and installed in the Begum of Oudh's palace.

I shall briefly pass over the particulars of my conversion to the Mahommedan faith and installation as a lady of the household, as I feel pained to think of this period of my eventful existence; suffice it to say that I had to contend with sufferings enough to subdue and bend any woman. The effect of the ill-treatment I endured tended to make me a downright hypocrite. I could have been made to do anything, and I played my part as a convert to the Mahommedan creed in a style at which I feel astonished now. I was obliged to learn by heart portions of the Koran ... and had mornings and evenings to get through my devotions.[25]

Yet, she goes on to say, her health rapidly improved under the strict regime, 'and the desire to live was now strong in me. I was well aware that the British would relieve the garrison of Lucknow, and that troops were on their way from England to punish the mutineers.' Miss G. stayed in the palace – thanks, she says, to her own superior hypocrisy – until the imminent arrival of those forces at the beginning of November turned the Begum danger-ously sceptical and 'irritable to the last degree'.

On the approach of the Commander-in-Chief, her equanimity en-tirely forsook her. She treated me with great severity, and abused me frequently, calling me kaffir or unbeliever, a hypocrite, a slut, and a serpent who would yet sting her benefactors. Her treatment of me at last became cruel, I tried to bear up with her ill humour as well as I could, for to have said a word to her would have been useless. Death, I knew full well, stared me in the face should my conduct be in the least offensive.[26]

At last it was decided to take no chances with this feringhee changeling, and Miss G. was told that tomorrow, she would be shot. Her narrative closes with a brisk account of her subsequent night-time escape in the hands of a sympathetic servant to whom she had been civil (which was more, said the servant, than anyone else had ever been); a surreal glimpse of the Moulvee's forces mustering the next morning to the rebel bands' sterling rendition of 'The Blue Bells of Scotland' and, of all things, 'God Save the Queen'; and her eventual journey to safety at Allahabad under the guise of a native ambassador. There she was reunited with an astonished uncle, who did not at first recognize this excitable female with its 'Mahommedan costume, sun-burnt face, and emaciated form'. But as soon as he realized who she was, the welcome was warm.

Still the shame, once the euphoria of having survived wore off, must have been crippling – not just for Miss G., but for the remains of her family too. It was very much the pukka Victorian point of view that '[t]he right kind of woman would accept death rather than give up her position as an Englishwoman':[27] Miss G. (mourned the commentaries surrounding the publication of her story) had mortgaged her reputation merely to stay alive. The poor girl was disgraced.

So, by implication, was fourteen-year-old Miss Sutherland, another Cawnpore escapee. According to an account published in *The Indian Planter's Gazette* in 1890,[28] she and her family (father, a general merchant, mother and twelve-year-old sister) had been with the party of fugitives from Fatehgarh who managed to reach Bithoor before being apprehended by the Nana and either killed on the spot or imprisoned. It was Miss Sutherland's fortune to survive the fire set by the rebels in the long, parched grass by the banks of the Ganges at Bithoor to smoke out (or burn up) those from the boat who had hidden there when the shooting began: she fell into a 'deep hole', she says, while trying to run from the flames, and dislocated her ankle. Twenty-four hours later she was discovered by a subhadar and brought water to drink while he bound her swollen foot with a strip of turban. He then took her to a native nurse, keeping her survival a secret for fear of reprisals, and once she had recovered enough, kept her in a covered dhoolie as his personal pet – until Havelock arrived. For once the poor general can be credited with saving the life of a Christian woman in Cawnpore: Miss Sutherland's saviour-cum-captor deserted (or, at least, the dhoolie-bearers did) and she was found by the advancing British and restored, like young Victoria Anderson, to safety.

There is, of course, one final memsahib of Cawnpore whose story is better documented than all the rest – at least by herself. Amy Horne (or Haines, as she was sometimes called, and later, Mrs Bennett) wrote at least two accounts of what befell her after first entering Wheeler's entrenchment in May 1857. The first part of her narrative, up to the point at which she was abducted from the Ghat, she has told already. Now comes the part almost every Mutiny novel ever since has poached (more or less sensitively) to add a little gaudiness to the otherwise blankly grim story of Cawnpore: her forcible conversion to Islam by the sowar's spiritual superiors, and subsequent ten months' captivity as concubine in the hands of the mutineers.

It was commented when Amy first attempted to tell her story that she was able to give 'a very connected account . . . up to the massacre, but whenever she reaches that point she becomes mad.'[29] Judging by her rather mannered published account, it seems she had to sacrifice any sense of immediacy about the events that followed in order to cope with the truth. And even then, the truth is difficult at times to distinguish: she had become an embittered woman full of prejudice and resentment by the time she wrote it all down. If one can resist such distractions, though, and look at what happened to Amy through the eyes of the girl she was then, it is a very affecting tale. It could hardly fail to be: the heroine is an intelligent eighteen-year-old English girl (even though she may never have actually *been* to England), the sole survivor of what had seemed a couple of months ago a happy and burgeoning family, well placed then for a modestly successful and confident career as Queen Victoria's ambassadress in India (which is what every memsahib, in her more patriotic moments, considered herself to be). What emerged ten months later, according to a report in the *Bengal Hurkaru*, was 'a lady, whose name we do not give . . . in great distress of mind, often in tears, [who] has forgotten much of the English language, and looks prematurely aged'.

Poor Amy.

We left her being tossed into the Ganges during the carnage at the Satichowra Ghat on 27 June, with the cries of her little sister Florence ringing in her ears; Amy was dragged to the shore by the sowar she had seen beckoning her from the boat. He was from the 3rd Cavalry, about twenty-eight, and named (she later learned) Mahomed Ismail Khan. 'His face was badly pitted with pock, and was adorned with a black beard divided in the centre. His eyes were the most striking feature in his face, being black and piercing, and capable of driving fear into one.' After dumping her on the bank (where she encountered Ulrica), Ismail Khan took Amy by the hand and pulled her along beside his horse

. . . drenched to the skin, bare-footed and bare-headed. I was conducted to a subadar's [sepoy officer's] hut a distance of about three miles from the Ghat. Here I was given a change of clothing of varied hue, consisting of the garments worn by the upper classes of native females . . . Disguised in this costume, and my face tanned from exposure to the hot sun while in the trenches, it was easy enough for my captor to move me about from place to place – as he later did – without exciting comment; otherwise the sight of an English girl in the train of a Mohammedan would have attracted such attention as would have terminated both our lives.[30]

Next, Amy was taken before two Moulvees, or Moslem holy men, by now feversome, dazed, and exhausted.

And now occurred the most dramatic episode in my life. I found myself in a large tent, which had originally been Government property and used as an officers' mess. It was scantily furnished, a *durrie*, or Indian carpet, being spread on the floor, and a few chairs scattered round; the Moulvies sat with solemn faces on a wooden dais, each having a drawn sword by his side. They looked for all the world like marble effigies stained in black, seated quite motionless, with their eyes cast down, and as if not daring to breathe. I was not granted the courtesy of a chair, but was made to squat on the ground; and I can only presume that the sanctity of the Moulvies' presence would not permit of such gross familiarity as the idea of a seat on a chair would have involved . . .

Here was I, a young, cultured English girl, forcibly clothed in native costume, seated crouching on the floor, at the foot of the dais on which the Moulvies sat. Behind me stood a horde of wild-looking, fanatical Moslems who had assembled to witness the *tamasha* [entertainment]; while towering over me, with a drawn sword in his hand, was another fanatic who seemed to be the Master of Ceremonies. The bright, mid-day sun lighted up the scene and the countenances of the actors and audience, some expressive of sullen indifference, others of religious frenzy and cruelty, and a few of vulgar curiosity at the sight of an English 'Missee' being placed so entirely in their power.

A deadly silence reigned, and the followers of the Prophet began the ceremony of my forced 'conversion' to their faith. A 'blessed' pomegranate was broken in halves, one section of which the Moulvie-in-chief partook of, while the other was handed to me to eat. A glass of sherbet was then partially drunk by him, I having to dispose of the remainder. Prayers were then recited in a loud voice, after which a female attendant, taking me by the hand, led me out of the tent to an improvised bathing place, where she undressed and bathed me. This was done in the way of 'purification', as previous to it I was, from the religious point of view, held to be 'unclean'. A new suit of clothes of the same type as the previous one was given to me to wear, and after dressing myself I was brought back to the tent, where I was made to stand and recite with bowed head a prayer termed the *Kulma*. This ended the ceremony, and my captor took me back to the hut where I had been lodged.[31]

There she stayed for several days, fed on a daily diet of dhall, chupattis, and the quickly muttered and terrifying reports of what enormities the memsahibs of the Bibigarh were even now experiencing: the native bandmaster's wife who had been appointed to attend Amy was also, apparently, ministering to the other surviving memsahibs.

When the rebel army moved for Allahabad, I was carried a prisoner along with them. I was asked to be their guide, on their arrival in Allahabad, as I knew the place well, for the purpose of showing them the easiest approach to the Fort, which it was their intention to seize. I thought to myself that that was easier said than done, and had determined in my mind to mislead them as much as I possibly could. However, on arriving at Futtehpore, the rebels very unexpectedly came upon a column of our troops, under the command of General Havelock, as I afterwards learned. What anguish it was to be so near our soldiers, and not to be able to effect my escape! I was too closely guarded, however, to dream of making the attempt. General Havelock's column, proceeding up to retake Cawnpore, soon routed them, and they retreated hastily. I then heard that some of the mutineers had cut up their women and children, for fear that they should fall into the hands of the British, who, they expected, would ill-use them, in the same way as they had done ours.

I also learned that an exceedingly fair girl, with light hair and blue eyes, was sitting on the roadside, and on inquiry was told that she had been abandoned by a sepoy to whom she had been married from the Assembly Rooms [she means the Bibigarh], on account of an order from the Nana that anyone found to have an English girl with him would be severely dealt with. What became of the poor girl I do not know.

While crossing the Panday Nuddee (or canal) I saw, to my horror, a
pair of child's boots, enclosing a portion of the legs . . . The poor little
thing must have been fleeing with its parents, when the sepoys over-
took them and cut off its legs.

The greater portion of the mutineers made for Delhi, taking me
along, but, ere they could reach that place, were informed of its
having been retaken by the British, which, however, I learned later
was not the case at that time.[32]

It was then decided by the rebels to change course for Farrukhabad, where they arrived soon after the massacre of Europeans by the Nawab there and Amy was informed that she too
was to be killed:

But they had arranged a better programme this time, and one in
which the whole town could participate. I was to be blown from the
cannon's mouth! One hundred cavalry and the same number of
infantry were to be paraded to see the unique spectacle of an English
girl being consigned to perdition in the quickest possible manner.
Fortunately for me, the same Moulvies who had 'converted' me were
at that time heading the mutineers at Farrukhabad. They had here-
tofore protected me only in consequence of my conversion to their
faith, but were now forced to give a proof of their allegiance to the
Nawab by assisting to murder me. Almighty God, however . . . did not
forsake me . . . and the Moulvies, while pretending to acquiesce in the
Nawab's wishes, moved to compassion for me sent for my captor and
concerted with him for my escape. I was conveyed to Lucknow that
very night, and there concealed for two months in a dyer's hut situated close to the Residency.

On one of the stopping stages we came across a picket of native
soldiers, and the sowar, being challenged as to the occupants of the
dooly in which I was being conveyed, replied that they were ladies of
his zenana, and, in corroboration of his statement, a black female

hand was immediately thrust out of the dooly. He had very 'cutely provided against a contingency of this nature by sending a black woman to accompany me in my flight . . .

My place of concealment was a most wretched hovel. I, who had been reared in the greatest comfort and luxury, who had been the petted and spoilt child of loving parents, had now to live like some trapped animal in a cage. There was hardly room to move about in, the hut being large enough only to accommodate a charpoy. There was no ventilation whatsoever, and the heat was intolerable. I felt every minute as if I would have died of suffocation, and doubtless I should . . . were it not for the fact that I was sometimes permitted to emerge from my den to take the air for a few minutes at night.

From this hut my captor was obliged to remove me, as some women had discovered my existence, and, not being convinced that I was really a convert to the Moslem faith, threatened to betray the sowar to the authorities. My captor thereupon took me to a bungalow in some other part of the town, which had originally been the residence of a Mr Simpson, and the native name of which was 'Tha-ra-walla Kotee' (Observatory). Here I was secreted in the kitchen, which seemed a palace contrasted with the hovel I had recently occupied. In the building itself now dwelt Sha-ah Hum o Dilla [Miss G.'s Ahmadullah Shah], the Moulvie of Fyzabad, who had brutally murdered every European in that town . . .[33]

He was not to remain for long, however: the advance of the British meant that it was unsafe for the Observatory to be used as his headquarters any longer, and he and his men fled, leaving Amy quite alone.

I would have made an attempt to escape, but for the fact that the whole city of Lucknow was in possession of the mutineers, and had I been discovered on my way to the Residency I should have experienced a horrible death.

For three days I had neither water nor food – only a few dry betel leaves to chew; but the hope that the English, who were not far off, might come that way, after dispersing the rebels, sustained me through my troubles. But a bitter disappointment was in store for me, as, instead of British troops coming my way, the rebels returned. Although they had been engaged in a slight skirmish, their losses had been heavy, which infuriated them to an alarming extent, and momentarily I expected them to wreak their vengeance upon me. The babel of noises that ensued on their return, and their appearance, which was something fiendish from the large quantity of *bhang* (an intoxicant made from hemp leaves) which they were consuming, frightened me to death, and, to escape observation, I concealed myself behind a pillar in the kitchen.[34]

There follows an episode in Amy's history disquietingly like another in Miss G.'s:[35] she was found by her captor still hiding behind the pillar twenty-four hours later, and taken by him to 'one of the mothers-in-law of the King of Oude', who, although promising to protect Amy at first, then changed her mind. Amy's only hope of survival now was to appeal personally to the Moulvee of Fyzabad – he whose strict religious code had forbidden him already to dispose of the hapless Miss G.

Obtaining an interview with him, I imposed on his credulity so successfully that he admitted I had claims on his protection, and, before I left his presence, made me take an oath to comply with all their religious observances; and, to test my sincerity, administered the 'sacrament' to me at once, by making me partake of a sweetmeat of which he ate one-half and handed me the other. He then declared me his 'Moreed' or disciple. I thus had become bound to follow him wherever he went, to observe all their festivals, and rigidly keep every fast.

It was with considerable loathing and repugnance that I went through the above ceremony, being, as I have been all through my life, a devout Christian; but life is sweet to the young, and the end justified the means.

As a result of the above-mentioned farce, I had to pray five times a day, and the hours appointed for the aforesaid prayers were most unseasonable at times; for instance, at midnight and before dawn, thus disturbing my rest. I had also to recite endless petitions as lustily as my lungs would permit. All this was done in the Hindustani language, in which I had now become thoroughly proficient.

The Moulvie was residing in All Nucky [Naqi] Khan's palace, situated on the banks of the river Goomtee, close to Gow Ghat and Jummun Neah Bagh, where I stayed a month. The palace was a square building, surrounded by out-offices, which formed the boundaries. In the centre of the courtyard stood a small one-storeyed building, containing a very spacious room, where the Begum of Oude used to hold her Kutcheri or court. In the middle of this room there was an underground cellar, where the treasure of the King of Oude, consisting of personal and State jewellery, money and other valuables, amounting to three crores of rupees (or, roughly, four hundred and fifty million pounds sterling) was hidden. When the inmates fled, on the arrival of the British into the town, and deserted the palace, they left the treasure behind, merely covering it over with a layer of rubbish and a large green-painted wooden blind, such as you see in the verandahs of houses in India . . . [It] was discovered by the British the year following . . .

The Moulvie allowed me two meals a day, a light at night, and a room to myself, all of which were esteemed by me as great privileges indeed, after all that I had gone through before. I must not forget to mention that he used to converse with me in English. He had been to England, and seemed a highly educated and intelligent man. Among other things he told me was that Bombay belonged to his forefathers, and that by right he ought to be Sultan of it. He also boasted that once when on a visit there, he was so highly respected and esteemed by our countrymen, that one of the officials had offered him his daughter in marriage![36]

Amy stayed under the Moulvee's protection until he advised her himself to leave, 'for he had strong suspicions that some of his men would either poison my food or murder me' (which may well have been an excuse just to relieve himself of her). He suggested she return to the king's mother-in-law again, there being quite simply nowhere else to go.

I followed his advice, and bent my steps back to the house of this heartless woman. I must confess that I went with a dismal foreboding of evil; but I was by now somewhat indifferent as to what became of me . . . The only thing that terrified me, in connexion with death, and which weakened my nerve whenever I had to face it, was the awful manner in which one met it in those horrible days, where one – and more especially a woman – was submitted first to such fearful out-rages, indignities, and tortures that made the heart quail and the blood curdle.

The rebels in Lucknow now mustered about ten thousand strong, but the advance of the English just then, making the place too uncom-fortable for them, caused a general move. I had hoped that, in the confusion and flight, I would have been left behind, and our column was so close that there was every chance of my being rescued. The sowar, however, was determined that my captivity should not end just then. He removed me to a different part of the town, mounting me on a horse which was unmanageable, and I was thrown off in at-tempting to go through a doorway. It was rather low, so that I struck my head against it and fell, narrowly escaping being trampled to death. As it was, the animal put his foot on mine, making me scream with pain. My captor, lifting me on to the horse, told me to turn round and look. Conceive my feelings on beholding our soldiers, who were but a short distance from me! I could have cried . . .

The body of rebels . . . did not take the same course. Some went to Furrukhabad, while others swelled the army of the boy-king. A few others, who were tired of fighting, resolved upon retiring to their homes. Among the last was my captor, who took me along with him.

The country was now so surrounded by our forces that a journey of four days took twenty to accomplish, and I had to walk all the way. My feet were perfectly lacerated, and so weak was I from constant fever, ague, and privation, that every moment I thought I should have sunk; but He who had filled my cup to the brim helped me to drink it . . .[37]

After a long and dangerous march, Amy arrived with Ismail Khan at Goothnee, on the outskirts of Allahabad.

I had been in this outlandish village for about a month, when constant reports of the success of the British troops on every side were brought to my captor, throwing him into a great fear. It was also rumoured that every district was to be searched for Christian captives, and it was proclaimed that the Government would grant free pardons to all those rebels who delivered up their prisoners. Now was the time for the sowar to save his life by delivering me up. I watched him closely, and found that he seemed considerably perplexed. On the one hand he appeared distrustful of the *bona fides* of the Proclamation, as, treachery being the breath of his nostrils, how could he abstain from suspecting the British of being guilty of a ruse to reclaim their white brethren? On the other hand, if he were found in the possession of a white captive, his life would pay the penalty. Of the two evils he decided to choose the first, the second being stamped with too great an element of certainty to be pleasant to contemplate. He at last informed me that he would release me, provided I gave him a solemn undertaking to act as his advocate, and obtain for him a free and full pardon for the part he had played in the rising.

Oh, the joy of living once more, free and unfettered, and among

civilised and refined surroundings! I felt like a soul who had so-
journed in hell, and was now about to leave the abode of the
damned! I could have leaped and danced and cried, and hugged my
captor for very joy . . . I was ready to promise [him] anything and
everything, and to do all that a woman's wit and ingenuity could
suggest in effecting my release. Still suspicious, he made me reduce
my verbal promises to writing, and even himself dictated what I
should write. To make doubly certain, he enlisted the services of an
English-speaking Munshi to translate to him, word for word, all that
I had written.

Fully restored to confidence, he released me, and I proceeded, as
quickly as my enfeebled condition would permit, to journey to the
nearest village, called Synee, that part of the province being more or
less restored to quiet and order. To reach Synee I had to cross a river,
and found, to my vexation, that the native boatmen were unwilling to
carry me over, thinking I was a native and perhaps connected with
some rebel party. On assuring them, however, that I was a white
woman in disguise, they consented.[38]

And so Amy's story comes to a close. She was reunited with her
relatives the Flouests, a family of indigo-planters in Allahabad,
and in 1858 settled in a suburb of Calcutta, a 'mental and physical
wreck'. There she met and married William Bennett, a railway
engineer, and spent the rest of her life making a meagre income
by giving piano lessons and resurrecting ever-more sour memories
of Cawnpore.

She was still there at the age of seventy-four, long after William
Bennett's death, alone and almost destitute: a Mutiny victim to
the end.

8

The Siege of Lucknow

———

Never . . . has the noble character of Englishwomen
shone with more real brightness . . . Far from being in our way,
they were ever a source of comfort and help to us; ready to tend the sick,
to soothe and comfort the dying, and to cheer and sustain the living
by all those numberless offices of love and affection
which woman only understands.[1]

It was known as the City of Gardens, and one of the richest and loveliest in the land. Lucknow was the fairy-tale gem of Oudh, and when *The Times* correspondent William Howard Russell first saw it in November 1858 he was quite addled by the splendour: it was like a fabulous vision, he said, of

palaces, minars, domes azure and golden . . . long facades of fair perspective in pillar and column, terraced roofs – all rising up amid a calm, still ocean of the brightest verdure. Look for miles and miles away, and still the ocean spreads, and the towers of the fairy-city gleam in its midst. Spires of gold glitter in the sun. Turrets and gilded spheres shine like constellations. There is nothing mean or squalid to be seen. There is a city more vast than Paris, as it seems, and more brilliant. Is this a city in Oudh? Is this the capital of a semi-barbarous race, erected by a corrupt, effete and degraded dynasty? I confess I felt inclined to rub my eyes again and again.[2]

It was hard to believe, given the look of the place, that in the middle of all this civilized magnificence some two thousand people (of whom 237 were European women and 260 – at the beginning – their children) had just undergone 139 days of hell, incarcerated in what was essentially an elegant but hopelessly over- crowded prison surrounded by low mud walls, a few fortified trenches, and a surreal assortment of such impromptu barricades as packing cases, petticoat hoops, bedsteads, books, and the odd harmonium. Over two-thirds of the besieged had died (to say nothing of the thousands of sepoys killed outside), picked off by four voracious enemies: the rebels, the heat, disease, and malnutrition.

It all sounds pretty miserable, and it would be crass to pretend it was not. But the retrospective story of Lucknow is as different in tone from that of Cawnpore as were the two cities themselves – and there are far more voices left to tell it, too, for it is essentially a story of survival.

Because Oudh was such a recent and grand addition to the provinces of British India (it had been annexed only in 1856), its military and civil population was full of proud new arrivals. Gar- risoned in its capital city at the beginning of May were 900-odd European soldiers, mostly of Her Majesty's 32nd Regiment (but including the officers in command of several units of over 2,000 sepoys). The administration of the area called for hundreds of civil functionaries, too, from the gravest of diplomats down to the most assiduous clerk; they all lived either in cantonments and lines beyond the city walls or (as in the case of the various Commission- ers, doctors, and so on) in the leafy grounds of the handsome Residency compound in the city itself. Lucknow was a fashionable place to be.

The figurehead of the European population was Sir Henry Lawrence, who had arrived to take up his appointment as Chief Commissioner in March. Admired, respected, almost revered, he was the brother of John Lawrence of the Punjab (who later went on to become Viceroy) and widower of Honoria, one of the most enthusiastic and unprejudiced memsahibs of the age.[3] After her death in 1854 he is said to have devoted himself austerely to duty, merely biding his time in as efficient a way as possible until their reunion. He was a little, withered old man of only fifty-one who had just been ordered to take leave for his poor health's sake when, on 15 May, the news of the Mutiny's first outbreak came through to Lucknow. Whether he would ever have succumbed to his doctor's wishes is doubtful and, anyway, immaterial: as soon as he heard what had happened he started on the preparations which eventually saved his garrison from annihilation.

Along with several other British dignitaries,[4] Sir Henry had long been aware of the possibility of unrest in this rich and smarting kingdom of Oudh, and had already discussed with the government what strategic precautions should be taken to combat it. Such precautions did not at first include disarming the native troops (although he did decide to move out of the city Residency into a bungalow in the military cantonments at Muraion, three miles to the north, in order to be closer to whatever action there might be) and to those not directly involved with these matters – the memsahibs of Lucknow, for example – it was the same old charmed city it had always been: Meerut and Delhi must have been tragically cursed by a rotten vein of disloyalty amongst their troops. British Oudh, on the other hand, was new, brave, and staunch. There was none of the panic here that seized Cawnpore and other stations. Dinner-party gossip had it that Sir Henry had been seen directing the digging of trenches around the city Residency, while gargantuan stores were being delivered to its gates. What is more, it seemed the native huts and mud-walled buildings that rambled closely around its perimeter slopes were being systematically demolished. Leave the holy places, Sir Henry had apparently said, but get rid of the rest:[5] he was an endearingly eccentric man.

The officious Mr Gubbins, Financial Commissioner, was also said to be strutting round the Residency compound issuing orders for his own house's fortification and insults to Sir Henry with equal vigour. Vain and jealous (although still sensible enough to foresee the likelihood of a siege), he considered Lawrence dangerously arrogant and muddle-headed; the fact that the feeling was mutual added a tension to the next few weeks that could well have been done without.

The mechanics of the mutiny itself at Lucknow are, by now, depressingly familiar. There had been trouble there as far back as April, when one of the European doctors had been seen sipping medicine from a bottle in the hospital stores, thereby contaminating it for all his Hindu patients. What had been a careless blunder was immediately transformed by the sepoys' indignation into a deliberate insult to their caste. The unfortunate doctor's wife bore the brunt of their revenge:

We were in bed and sound asleep when the women came screaming that the house was on fire, and on rushing out [we found] the thatch was in flames. Never shall I forget the horror I experienced. I tore my children out of bed and in my *nightgown* ran over to the Dashwoods' house, but had I not met one of the officers who relieved me of the children I think I should have fainted by the way. At 12 o'clock the whole of the roof fell in and there is nothing left of our house but the walls . . . it makes me tremble to think of it.[6]

Sir Henry's calm air of authority must have been exceptionally convincing: Dr and Mrs Wells' experience was put down amongst the other memsahibs to an isolated excess of native volatility, and even after the massacre at Delhi there continued to be a strong sense of confidence in Lucknow. Maria Germon's husband, Charlie, was a Captain in the 13th Bengal Native Infantry and away from home on 'city duty' the night the news of the massacre came (armed, incidentally, with his lovingly prepared and customary snack of 'bread and butter, Mango Fool, quail and a few vegetables'). But even though she was on her own, Maria politely refused offers of company from her solicitous neighbours, preferring instead to keep a dagger under her pillow, a dressing-gown by her bed, and her two beloved and faithful 'doggies' on guard by the door. 'I don't think I ever slept sounder in my life,' she said.

It was not to last: Lucknow was fast becoming the rallying point for rebels and mutineers who were counting on the disaffection of its vast native population to swell their numbers, and by 21 May, the day Sir Henry was appointed Brigadier-General in Oudh and given absolute power over its entire military and civil population, fourteen frightened ladies were seeking refuge in his Residency bungalow in the cantonments every night while the rest shivered in the heat at home to the sound of fires and shouting in the distance. The mutiny proper broke out at precisely nine o'clock on the evening of Saturday 30 May, and by the next morning most of the European garrison had gathered within the confines of the Residency compound up in the city, together with whatever belongings and servants they could muster and squeeze in.

The compound is still there amongst the towers and domes and trees of Lucknow. It has been turned into a park and the dozen or so buildings remaining within, set in about a thirty-seven acre site on raised ground by the side of the sacred river Gomti, have been preserved in the same state in which they were left by the British at the end of the Mutiny. It is terribly beautiful, this place: I went one evening, just as the sun was beginning to sink and the last of the Indian picnickers was leaving. There were roses and scarlet cannas everywhere, and verbena and bougainvillaea amongst the palms and colonnades. A path winds through the sturdy Baillie Guard Gate, past Dr Fayrer's house and the fine old Banqueting Hall to the Residency building itself, which at that time of day glows mellow and red with the tiny, neat slices of brick of which each ruined building is made. Everything still standing is savagely scabbed and mutilated by the almost continuous bombardment of the siege, and the churchyard is full of wide, mass graves with reams of names on its stones; but now, given a smiling chowkidar and the thought of a good meal and comfortable bed to go to, there is a definite air of tranquil nobility about it – 'a feeling of quiet power', as one of Sir Henry's descendants put it[7] – which is dangerously alluring. It is easy to forget, in such reveries, that the land on which it stands is Indian, not British.

Maria Germon was astonished at the change in its usual relaxed atmosphere on her slightly indignant arrival there on the morning of Monday 25 May.

At 3 a.m. came a message for Charlie to go over to Sir Henry's – he went and I lay on till gunfire [about five a.m.] when I got up and went into the garden to arrange my flowers – little thinking what was coming. C. came back about half-past five when to my astonishment he told me it was Sir Henry's express orders that all ladies should leave cantonments and go down to the Residency in the City – so I suspected he had heard bad news and I afterwards heard that they considered the Cawnpore troops would rise for certain and then we had but little chance, so I set to work to collect what I thought valuable and all I should want, not knowing how long I should be kept from home. I got in such a heat packing, for Charlie had had an offer of a seat in the Herns' gharree for me for half-past seven as he was Captain of the week and could not take me down himself – he made me take some coffee and packed up what he could of eatables and drinkables not knowing how we should get on at the Residency. I dressed and packed up what I could and at half-past seven the Harris[es] and Mrs Barwell came for me and we drove down to the City, passing on our way innumerable carriages and buggies all off to the Residency with ladies and children – such a scene – when we drove up to the Residency everything looked so warlike – guns pointed in all directions, barricades and European troops everywhere – such a scene of bustle and confusion – we then heard there was hardly a room to be got – ladies had been arriving ever since gunfire, so Mr Harris went over to see if Dr Fayrer could take us in – he came back saying yes, and away we went, thankful to get into such good quarters – two ladies were there already and five came after us with three children, so that every room was full. This house as well as Mr Gubbins' and Mr Ommaney's (both also full) are within the Residency compound and are barricaded all round – still, in case of disturbance we have orders to assemble at the Residency. Of course, there were all sorts of reports and alarms going about consequent on our flights. The heat is intense, I never experienced anything like it . . . I cannot sleep at nights for it. Our beds are all under one punkah. I and Mrs Fayrer and Mrs Anderson – the others are as thick but it is nothing to the Residency – our party here is a very agreeable one – we meet at chota hazree [an early-morning snack] and then after dressing, breakfast at ten – then have working, reading and music (there are some good performers amongst our party), tiffin [luncheon] at two, dine at half-past seven and then the Padre [Mr Harris] reads a chapter and prayers and we retire.

Tuesday, May 26th. The day passed quietly – several husbands and fathers visited their beloveds, but mine could not leave his station duty – in the evening I went to the Residency to see Mrs B[ruere][8] who had a child dying. I never witnessed such a scene – a perfect barrack – every room filled with six or eight ladies, beds all round and perhaps even a dining-table laid for dinner in the centre, servants thick in all the verandahs. Lots of the 32nd soldiers and their officers, and underneath [in the tykhana, or cellar] all the women and children of the 32nd barracks – such a hubbub and commotion. It is an upper storied house – the upper storey not nearly so large as the under one and yet in that, including servants and children, there are ninety-six people living – poor Mrs B[ruere] was in great distress. She and another lady had a small room to themselves, only her five children. I was so thankful I was not there – it is just like a rabbit warren.[9]

Each building within the Residency compound was now considered a separate garrison, with its own share of fighting men (both professional and hastily conscripted amateurs) and arms. Some garrisons were decidedly more comfortable than others. The Gubbinses', for example:

Our regular meals had . . . been diminished from three to two. A cold luncheon only was served, and we made an early dinner at four . . . One glass of sherry and two of champagne or of claret was served to the gentlemen, and less to the ladies, at dinner. One glass of light wine, Sauterne, was provided at luncheon . . . By these timely precautions the supplies which we had were husbanded, and the wants of our numerous guests [which at one point numbered nineteen adults and thirteen children] were provided for during the whole siege. Besides, we were often able to render assistance to persons in other garrisons who urgently needed aid, and to the wounded in hospital. After the siege had begun, and the commissariat arrangements got into train, rations were issued of beef or mutton, with flour or rice, and salt, to Europeans, according to a fixed scale. These were made over to my servants and cooked by them, such additions being made to the meal as our store-room afforded. These, however, besides the daily addition of spices, and sugar, were limited to a few canisters of preserved salmon, and a few of carrots, which were produced whenever we invited a friend from any of the other garrisons to dinner . . .

At dinner, our chief luxury were rice puddings, of which two daily appeared on table. The eggs for these were derived from a few poultry which we had managed to preserve; and the milk [so sorely in want for children elsewhere] from goats and two cows belonging to our guests, which were half-starved during the siege . . . One cup of tea was made for each person at six in the morning, our English maid, Chivers, presiding at the tea-table.[10]

Before the siege proper began, there tended to be a gentle

exodus of an early morning when those memsahibs who could would leave for their old neighbourhood to check on both their houses and their husbands. Maria was amongst them:

Friday, May 29th. I drove with Miss Helford down to cantonments about five o'clock and had the inexpressible delight of seeing my old Charlie – the doggies I thought would have eaten me up.[11] I had chota hazree with him and sat chatting till seven when the Helfords' gharree came for me again – the day passed quietly, some drove out in the evening with Dr and Mrs Fayrer, I did not. Dr F.'s elephant is always brought in the evening to the verandah to have his dinner, we are generally all sitting there – he has sixteen seers [about two and a half stone] of attah [ground wheat] made into immense chupattees – this evening he performed all kinds of feats – took the Mahout up on his back by his trunk, then put out his fore-paw and the Mahout climbed up that way, roared whenever he was told to speak and at length salaamed and went off.[12]

There were few such amusements elsewhere. In the Begum Kothi (literally, the Begum's Mansion), a self-contained complex (complete with its own mosque) which had once housed the fine and lofty apartments of a lady of Lucknow's royal family, life was already extremely grim. Katherine (or Kate) Bartrum was billeted there, and described it on her arrival on 9 June as a dirty and uninviting place, with neither a stick of furniture for her comfort nor even a punkah to stir the stagnant air. It reeked.

Kate's story is one of the most affecting of all the tales of Lucknow. She was a Somerset girl of twenty-three,[13] and had been living in the remote station of Gonda since September 1856, as the wife of an Assistant Surgeon, Robert Bartrum, and the mother of what was by all accounts a particularly chubby and bonny toddler, Bobbie. Kate's diaries and letters show with un-common candour just how deeply and completely she loved both husband and son: she considered herself a fortunate and happy woman. Even when the astounding rumours of the Mutiny's outbreak at Meerut were proven true, Kate was calm and almost serene: like Helena Angelo in Cawnpore she believed the most important thing in life (other than God, of course) to be family solidarity, on which physical closeness depended as much as emotional support. Come what may, she asked nothing but to live or die with those she loved the best. So she was appalled when an order came through from Sir Henry that the ladies of outlying stations like Gonda should be sent in to the relative safety of Lucknow. For her, the Mutiny's greatest catastrophe happened the moment she lost sight of Robert Bartrum.

The journey was horrific: there was only just enough time to gather a few of Bobbie's bits and pieces together before leaving (at six in the evening) on elephant-back for the sixteen-mile trek to Secrora. There Kate and the only other memsahib in Gonda, a Mrs Clark, were supposed to meet up with another party of refugees and travel on together to Lucknow under a native escort. But they were too late: the Secrora party had already left, and Kate and her companion were forced to set straight off again, at midnight, in the hopes of catching up during the sixty-odd miles they had still to go. Neither had more clothes than those she had been wearing when the orders from Sir Henry had arrived, and – even more uncomfortable – they could not trust their guides:

Our spirits were by no means cheered at hearing the threatening language of our escort during the whole of that fearful night, and feeling our own perilous position – two helpless women and two little children, entirely in the power of these men . . . Sometimes they made our elephant stand still whilst they lay upon the ground laughing and talking; but whenever I asked them for water for baby to drink, they would give it me. Once when they were loading their guns, I asked them what they were going to do. 'Oh,' they said, 'there are so many bad people about, we are going to fight for you.' And so we journeyed on . . .'[14]

Early the next morning they managed to overtake the Secrora party, and after another sleepless, terrified night, they arrived 'weary and exhausted with hot winds, dust, and scorching sun, and worn out' to face the confusion of the Residency. The two women from Gonda were separated once inside the Baillie Guard Gate, and Kate was shown into a stifling little chamber in the Begum Kothi, which she was told she was sharing with thirteen other refugees. Each family appropriated a portion of it, which was tactfully looked upon by the others as private property, and there they ate, slept, and did their daily duties. Kate's time, she said, was fully occupied 'in nursing, and washing our clothes, together with cups and saucers, and fanning away the flies which have become a fearful nuisance. Sometimes when the food is placed on the table, we cannot tell what it is, for it only looks like a black and living mass.'[15]

Even in the comparative comfort of Dr Fayrer's house, the novelty of the situation was almost wearing off for Maria Germon.

Sunday, May 31st. Charlie came over and breakfasted with us – we all went into Dr Fayrer's room and had prayers, Mr Harris reading them. Charlie then went to see if Sir Henry had arrived and I wrote my overland letters and was just finishing when an order came for all ladies to go over to the Residency as they expected a rise in the City – we collected our bundles and under the burning sun walked over to the Residency where we were told not to congregate too many in one part as it was not safe – every room in the upper storey was crammed, we could hardly get room to put down our bundles. At last Miss Nepean offered me a corner in one room – but the perfect babel it was with the number of children and the heat being fearful

up to then with no punkah going, it was enough to drive one wild –
we set down in this miserable state the whole day. There was tiffin
going on and we were invited to partake but Mrs Fayrer sent over
for a tiffin for us afterwards from her house. I saw my husband every
now and then but he was under Major Anderson. In the evening the
two Padres tried to have prayers but we could scarcely hear anything
from the babel of tongues and the sound of the screams of so many
children [Charlie and Maria, incidentally, had none] – it was perfect
misery. I was dying with thirst and had nothing of my own to drink –
at last a lady took pity on me and gave me a cup of tea – a perfect
luxury – we heard firing going on all evening . . . but the rebels were
repulsed – several shot and others taken prisoners and these were
afterwards hanged. Martial Law is proclaimed in Oude so they are
hanging several, night and morning . . . About seven Sir Henry came
down from cantonments with a large escort – he was received with
great cheering. Four more guns had come down with him . . . and
every preparation was made expecting an attack that night. Every
man was at his gun and the post fires lighted in readiness – there was
no chance of sleeping down in this hot babel so I and several other
ladies took our bedding up on the roof and slept there – it was a
lovely moonlight night and never shall I forget the scene. The pano-
rama of Lucknow from the top of the Residency is splendid and
down immediately below us in the compound we could see the great
guns and all the military preparations, all every instant expecting an
attack and firing going on in the distance. However, I was so worn
out with the previous night that I lay down and was asleep in a
second – of course, I did not undress – nor had I done so the night
before. I started frequently, fancying I heard the tramp of the mob
coming. We had the two Padres up with us and they determined to
watch by turns. Mr Polehampton began: he had a double-barrelled
gun, pistol and sword – he walked round and round for two hours
and then woke Mr Harris, but we could not help laughing, Mr H.
was so sleepy that [Mr Polehampton] told him he did not think there

was any necessity for stretching up then. I shall never forget the night, looking so peaceful in contrast to the scene below. I put up an umbrella over my head to keep off the ill effects of the moon. Every hour the sentinels were calling out, 'All's well' – it was certainly more a scene from a romance than real life.[16]

Kate Bartrum, meanwhile, spent the nights cradling Bobbie and gazing at the stars in the hope that Robert was looking that very moment at the same ones, and confessed to feeling condemned, like a caged bird. Her friends pitied her, so desperately lonely was she and anxious and in love: Maria and several other Lucknow lady diarists[17] mention her with tears (they say) in their eyes.

Especially when they consider what happened to her later on.

There was no such sympathy for the unfortunate Mrs Bruere, whose devotion to her husband evinced quite another response from Mrs Germon:

Friday, June 5th. Rose at gunfire as usual for the heat is almost unbearable. I am glad to leave my bed – several of the 32nd officers [joined us] while we were all sitting in the garden discussing why the hanging is stopped – there has been none the last two days – before that they were hanging six or eight morning and evening . . . In the evening I went over to see Mrs B[ruere] who is in great distress having just lost her baby – she told me of her narrow escape the night of the mutiny in cantonments – she was down there with all the children although Sir H. Lawrence had forbidden ladies to go there – she says she and the Major were in bed when a Havildar came rushing in begging her to fly for the sepoys were up in the Lines – and immediately after the mutineers came into the house and asked for the Sahib and Mem Sahib. She flew with her five children escorted by three friendly sepoys first into the servants' quarters but the bullets came whistling round so thick that the sepoys cut a hole in the mud wall for her to escape at the back and they fled to a village but the villagers came out and threatened to take their lives if they remained so they went and took refuge in a dry nullah – it was about fifteen or twenty feet deep so that they had to sit and slide down the bank – the sepoys lay down in the bank and watched. Her poor baby had dysentery and had nothing on but his nightdress – no wonder it died a day or two after – but then it was her own fault, she ought not to have been in cantonments. She drove up to the city next day but Sir Henry was so angry with her for having disobeyed his orders that he would not allow her an escort.[18]

Poor woman. Her servants must have admired her, at least.

As June progressed, with the pre-monsoon air growing clotted and more rank by the day, there began to appear outbreaks of disease amongst the Residency's swarming population. It severely curtailed the already rather attenuated social life of Maria and her companions at the doctor's house by limiting their evening visits – but soon, it would be too dangerous to wander about the compound anyway.

Saturday, June 20th. I got up early and Charlie came about half-past seven and stayed nearly an hour – after breakfast Dr Partridge read *Guy Mannering*[19] to us while we worked. I cut out and made a flannel shirt for Charlie . . . We are forbidden now to go over to the Residency or the Begum Kotee as there is small-pox in both, in the former Mrs Bird had it and one of Mrs B[ruere]'s children. Mrs B[ird] is removed into a tent in all this heat. Today a letter came from General Wheeler at Cawnpore saying they still held out and had provisions and ammunition for one fortnight more, that no reinforcement had reached them, but that their greatest enemy was the sun – more had died from sunstroke than by the enemy and that their greatest consolation was that they were keeping the enemy from us . . .

Tuesday, June 30th. As soon as I got up I found Dr Partridge all booted up and spurred for service and I then heard a detachment had been ordered off to meet the enemy who were five miles off . . . I sat out till seven and then went in to bathe to be ready for Charlie; however, he never came, to my surprise, and I sent off a note . . . asking what kept [him]. While the man was gone with it, some came flying in saying our party had been surrounded by the mutineers who were in great numbers and that several of our officers had been killed and just then to my horror came back the note I had sent with a message from Captain Francis that my husband had gone out with the detachment. I never shall forget the dreadful suspense, as the news was brought in that Colonel Case, Captain Stevens, Mr Thomson and Mr Brackenbury of the 32nd were killed, the latter always paid us a visit in the mornings and evenings. At last came Dr Partridge saying they were sorely pressed by the enemy but that he had seen my husband all right – soon after came a sepoy saying Charlie had sent him to say he was all safe and immediately after a sepoy came to tell me Charlie was coming in on a gun as he was very faint and that Major B[ruere] was wounded – of course I was frightened thinking Charlie had got a sunstroke. He told me afterwards he had had a very narrow escape as he was far back in the retreat. It had proved far different to the glorious expectations that had been excited on first starting, for the Native Artillery proved faithless and the enemy being in far greater numbers than the spies had led us to expect, our little party was surrounded and it was only a wonder any escaped to tell the tale. The sun also was so overpowering that many fell down from sheer faintness without a wound and were cut to pieces by the enemy – for few had any horses to return with – they, the officers, had dismounted to fall in with their men and the horses disappeared – either the enemy or the servants made away with them – poor Charlie's charger amongst them (the poor old horse that was shot in the nose on the night of the mutiny). It was a fearful morning never to be forgotten, this affair of Chinhat – another wonderful escape for dear Charlie for which we cannot be sufficiently thankful. The enemy began firing on us as they followed the retreating party – our gates were closed and the siege commenced.

We got a cup of tea and something for breakfast as best we could sitting behind the walls to escape the balls, not that I fancy any of us had much appetite. At last the balls came so thick that we were all ordered down into the tyekhana and kept there – towards evening the firing ceased a little and we sat in the portico to get a little air – there were twenty-four of us in the house, eleven ladies, six gentlemen and seven children. Captain Weston was the Commandant of our garrison which consisted of an officer and some twenty of the 82nd Queens with some native pensioners and a mixed party of men to work the eighteen- and nine-pounder guns in the compound. At night we proposed sleeping in our own rooms, but Dr Fayrer considering it not safe to do so we all stretched our bedding on the floor of the tyekhana – those in the centre getting the benefit of the punkah – we took it by turns to watch for one hour.[20]

'This affair of Chinhat' was no mere misfortune. It was a rout. Sir Henry seriously misjudged the number of rebel forces he was engaging, and his band of 700 fighting men (half of them Europeans and half Indians), with their ten guns and an eight-inch howitzer, were completely overwhelmed. His Indian troops found the so-called battle of Chinhat an appropriate moment to mutiny, thus depleting an army already enfeebled by its customary morning hangover and the lack of anything to eat or drink for breakfast; what followed was an ignominious retreat, with the loss of over 300 officers and men (and the precious howitzer) together with any last vestige of British morale.

The rebels were quick to capitalize on their victory by following the British back into the city and beginning the onslaught on the Residency compound – of almost anything from conventional shot and shell to nails, flaming arrows, bullock horns, and offal – that was to last for the next five months.

Thursday, July 2nd. The attack at the Bailey Guard gate and our compound [just within the gate] was tremendous and while we were at breakfast we were all inexpressibly touched and grieved to hear poor Sir Henry [Lawrence] had been mortally wounded – a shell from the very eight-inch howitzer the enemy had taken from us at Chinhat had burst in his room in the Residency and given him a fearful wound in his thigh[21] – he was brought over to our verandah and Mr Harris administered the Sacrament to him. Sir Henry then sent for several whom he fancied he had spoken to harshly in their duty and begged their forgiveness and many shed tears to think the good old man would so soon be taken from us, our only earthly help in this awful crisis. Sir Henry then appointed Major Banks his successor. The firing was fearful – the enemy must have discovered from some spies that Sir Henry was at our house . . . we all gave ourselves up for lost for we did not know then the cowards they were and we expected every moment they would be over our garden wall – there was no escape for us if they were once in the garden. We asked Mr Harris to read prayers and I think every one of us prepared for the worst – the shots were now coming so thick into the verandah where Sir Henry was lying that several officers were wounded and Sir Henry was obliged to be removed into the drawing-room. We gave out an immense quantity of rags to the poor soldiers as they passed up and down from the roof of the house wounded. Toward evening the fire slackened but we were not allowed to leave the tyekhana – at night Mr Harris came and read prayers again and then we all lay down on the floor without undressing.[22]

Lawrence's impending demise rather cut the besieged population of the Residency compound adrift. With his death they would lose not just their patriarch but, as one officer put it, 'a prop in the world . . . He was a rare specimen of God's handiwork.'[23] It seems to have made them all a little lonelier. And he was not the only one to be leaving for a better place:

Friday, July 3rd. When we awoke we found all our servants had bolted excepting my kitmagur and Mrs Barwell's and one or two ayahs – the Fayrers had not one servant left, so we were obliged to get up and act as servants ourselves and do everything except the cooking – even to wash up plates and dishes, etc., and perhaps it was a good thing, it kept our thoughts from dwelling on our misery. Dear Charlie came to see me in the afternoon and brought a jug of milk for the poor children . . . We happened to be at dinner and I gave him a piece of meat but he seemed too much done up to eat and actually carried it away in a piece of paper to some other gentlemen who could get none – no arrangements had been made for messing as yet and no one knew where to get anything.

Saturday, July 4th. Firing had been going on all night and it continued all day, but we were so engaged in kitchen duties we scarcely noticed it. Poor Sir Henry died in the morning – he had been in great agony from his wound – he was buried with the rest at night but even he did not have a separate grave, each corpse was sewn up in its own bedding and those who had died during the day were put into the same grave.[24]

The hours of darkness were the two chaplains' busiest times: only then was it safe enough to risk a hurried procession to the churchyard to bury the dead (although snipers were always on the lookout and there were a number of funeral casualties). On one occasion five babies were laden into the grave at once, and on another one of the chaplains, Mr Harris, had to bury the other, Mr Polehampton; throughout the whole of the siege there was only a single night's respite.

Like Maria Germon, Kate Bartrum was having problems with kitchen duties, too. The few pots and pans she and her friends in the Begum Kothi could find were rapidly assuming an immovable sheen of verdigris which turned all their food a lustrous green; there was not enough water both to cook with and to wash every day, and so turns had to be taken. A ration system was started soon after the siege began which provided a barely adequate diet for the fit and healthy (although the implements with which to cook it – and the knowledge – were sadly lacking, blunt nail-scissors not being terribly effective for cutting elderly buffalo steaks). But the fit and healthy were diminishing fast. Babies were being born into disease-filled rooms to weak and hungry mothers who could not feed them; Julia Inglis, the wife of the colonel of the 32nd and as such the garrison's Burra Mem, had a goat whose milk she used for her own three boys. Julia was one of the most compassionate and sensible women around, but even she could not bring herself to prejudice her children's lives by sharing this most precious of commodities. There were one or two cows to be found in private hands, but otherwise the youngest children had to make do with whatever their mothers could find. They faded fast – unless they had influential (and babyless) friends like the Gubbinses, that is, or knew some generous soul like Monsieur Deprat, a French merchant, who as long as his stocks lasted would dispense his stores of *saucissons-aux-truffes* and cigars with cheerful generosity to whomsoever asked.

Deprat had a good cellar, too, and there never seems to have been any serious shortage of alcohol. When anyone of property died within the compound, his goods were usually put up for auction to raise money for his dependents; as the settlement of the auction accounts was not usually due until next payday, by which time the buyer might well be dead himself, the prices paid for popular lots were astronomical. But alcohol rarely fetched high prices. Indeed, champagne was so plentiful that the doctors in the hospital were using it (for the lack of any opium or chloroform) as an anaesthetic: the usual dose for the amputation of a limb was a single bottle, taken at one draught immediately before the operation began.

Inevitably, as time went on, blisters of personal animosity

began erupting amongst the closely quartered thousands in the compound. These were usually containable: when permission was denied by one officer for Maria's piano to be delivered from cantonments, she simply declared him a mean-minded misery and applied to another and friendlier authority (and goodness knows where they put it – on the barricades, probably). She seems to have been particularly irritated, too, by one of the refugees from Secrora, a Mrs Boileau and her children, with whom she was sharing her room. She takes their restlessness at night and lingering, undramatic illnesses as a personal slight and there are frequent rather tight-lipped entries in her diary about their general droopiness of spirit.[25] Others indulged their waspishness on rather more obvious targets: strange Mrs Ogilvie, for instance, a Scottish doctor's wife, who insisted on 'cleaning her teeth before us all' and 'dressing transparently',[26] or whoever was hogging the services of the boys from the Martinière boarding school in Lucknow who had been sent into the compound with everyone else and were doing sterling work as choirboys, military auxiliaries and (more helpfully to the memsahibs) particularly well-bred washers-up. And there was always that Gubbins man with his English maid and afternoon tea.

Anger was a luxury that could not be afforded for long, though: one's thoughts were too often concentrated on the fine and arbitrary line that divided death from life in Lucknow. The most casual discussion amongst the ladies of the garrison would always turn to the after-life – indeed Julia Inglis and her friend Adelaide Case, whose husband fell at Chinhat, declared that they never spoke seriously of anything else. It is hardly surprising: death had become an extremely public affair, with both the sick and the wounded, from brave Sir Henry to the newborn baby, taking perhaps several days to sink into an anonymous grave, and the collective fear that the final reward for those who survived the siege might well be worse than dying here amongst one's own people.

Some said they would prefer suicide to dishonour, and begged Dr Fayrer to provide them with phials of prussic acid just in case, while others, like Mrs Case, simply declared that 'all we have to do is to endeavour, as far as we can, to be prepared for our death, and leave the rest in the hands of Him who knows what is best for us.'[27] Most of the Lucknow diarists noted the deaths of such victims as Colonel Halford of the 71st Native Infantry, who suffered a 'complete break-up' and killed himself, or those shot in ignorance whilst on various reconnoitres by their own men. Perhaps the most pathetic circumstance of all was the case of Messrs Eldridge and Keogh, remembered by the chaplain's wife, Mrs Harris:

Such an awful thing happened here yesterday! Because there are not murders enough done by the heathen, two Christian Englishmen quarrelled, and, in the heat of passion, one of them seized a pistol and shot the other through the body. James buried the murdered man [Eldridge] this morning. He was the riding-master of the 7th. Cavalry; so respectable a man that he was to have had a commission given him. His murderer [Keogh], the Serjeant-Major of the same regiment, also bore the highest character, and was liked and respected by every one who knew him, and the two were bosom friends. It seems the quarrel began with the wives disputing about the drawing up of a curtain; this trivial matter led to words between the two husbands, and in an instant the dreadful deed was done.[28]

It seemed to Maria Germon that no one dare take being alive for a moment longer for granted: on the evening of Wednesday 15 July her party 'sat in the verandah singing songs and glees and it made me quite melancholy for the round shots were whizzing overhead and no-one could tell but that the next might bring death with it.'

The dismal spirit of Cawnpore seems to be descending upon us, but there were lighter moments, enjoyed by those still robust enough (as Maria was) for a sense of humour – and even the odd unexpected treat.

Friday, August 21st. We had had a most disturbed night – an attack about twelve – I heard 'turn out' called out from the gentlemen's room and being half-asleep and half-awake I and Mrs Anderson rushed from our beds over two other ladies in our haste and much to our amusement several of the ladies abused us for making a rush, for surely we might leave our beds when we chose especially as we had been put in the most dangerous corner of the room – this amused us much and we lay down again in a fit of laughter. I heard almost every hour strike during the night. At daybreak . . . washed tea things, made chota-hazree, gave out stores, bathed, washed clothes, then made breakfast and arranged stores' room . . . Charlie came as usual – dinner today was roast mutton but as there was very little we opened a tin of salmon and Mrs Need (an Englishwoman who cooks for us) made us a roly pudding of attah and suet – to us a perfect luxury . . .

Wednesday, August 26th. Dearest Mother's birthday. We had had a wretched night with Mrs Boileau's children and the firing, I actually lay till seven. Dear Charlie sent me a beautiful bouquet of roses, myrtle and tuberoses. I went down and got my mug of tea without sugar and milk (I use Charlie's silver mug as cups are scarce) and a chupattee, then went and sat at the door for a little air, went and had a wash of clothes. Today our rations are reduced – gentlemen get twelve instead of sixteen ounces of meat and we six instead of twelve – with rather less *dal*. A sentry was shot through the leg in our verandah in the night and Dr Fayrer was hit by a spent ball. After breakfast I mended a pair of Charlie's unmentionables with a piece of Mr Harris's habit presented for the purpose. Charlie came for a little chat but a note from the Brigadier called him away. A little milk punch is doled out to us every day about one and I drank dear Mother's health in mine. I afterwards sat at the door making a flannel waistcoat for myself – at four we had dinner, after dinner the invalids came out and took the air on their couches at the door – at seven I went down and made tea for all, then sat at the door till half-past eight when we had prayers – then to bed and I had a good night's rest, though the children were rather squabbly.[29]

It was those Boileaus again. There were some other unwelcome guests beginning to annoy Maria and her friends by now, too, along with the rats and flies and stink-bugs: lice. Or, as the mem-sahibs preferred to call them, their little legions of 'light infantry'.

Friday, September 18th. We had a slight attack in the night. While dressing this morning a bullet came into the outer room with such force that it struck off one side of the frame of a picture, leaving the glass whole. My labours increased every morning by my having to wash my hair and a greater number of clothes than formerly. An eclipse of the sun visible between nine and eleven. A tolerably quiet day spent by me in making night-caps to keep my head from contamination as all lie so close together at night, fifteen under our punkah. As we were talking in the evening I ventured to say I thought we had never passed a single hour day or night since the siege began without some firing. I was immediately laughed at and told not *five minutes* even. If this ever reaches my dear ones at home they will wonder when I tell them that my bed is not fifty yards from the eighteen-pounder in our compound – only one room between us and yet I lie as quietly when it goes off without shutting my ears as if I had been used to it all my life. Eighty days of siege life does wonders.[30]

To Kate Bartrum, who had nursed her dwindling infant through cholera and been dangerously ill herself, the eclipse of the sun was just one more portent of unhappiness: 'the natives foretell a famine', she reported. 'To many of our weary hearts, sunshine has been eclipsed for a long, long time . . .' But then she adds something which seems uncharacteristically optimistic: 'who knows how soon it may appear again?' she asks. For by now, as the end of September approached and Maria Germon was on her last bar of soap, the rumours which had plagued the garrison's peace of mind all through the siege of the imminent arrival of help from Henry Havelock (which was generally supposed to be 'five or six days away', whatever the date of the rumour) really did appear to have some substance. Kate was eager to believe it, anyway:

September 23 – Such joyful news! A letter is come from Sir J. Outram, in which he says we shall be relieved in a few days: everyone is wild with excitement and joy. Can it really be true? Is relief coming at last? And oh! more than all, will dear Robert come . . .?[31]

In fact, the relieving army, under the command of Henry Havelock, had been on its way from Cawnpore ever since the end of July; each time it sortied out, however, it was savagely beaten back and it was not until General James Outram's reinforcements arrived six weeks later that the column could march for Lucknow with success. Their distant guns could be heard from the Residency compound on Thursday 24 September, by which time the suspense of waiting was almost intolerable: everyone was remembering Chinhat – and Cawnpore.

It was all going to be all right, though: Jessie Brown said so. Jessie was a corporal's wife of the 32nd, who had spent the siege in a haze of candlelight and camphor in the rat-infested tykhana of the Residency building, and her celebrated story provides a fittingly heroic end to this particular chapter of the Mutiny's history. With its central elements of faith vindicated and innocent self-confidence, and its oh, so happy ending, it became a sort of symbol of all that made the siege and its endurance so popular a story back at home. Here, assumed from the testament of Julia Inglis herself, is the version from *The Jersey Times*, which enterprising newspaper was one of the first to publish what soon became a legend:

Poor Jessie had been in a state of restless excitement all through the siege, and had fallen away visibly within the last few days. A constant fever consumed her, and her mind wandered occasionally, especially that day, when the recollections of home seemed powerfully present to her. At last, overcome with fatigue, she lay down on the ground, wrapped up in her plaid. I sat beside her, promising to awaken her when, as she said, 'her father should return from the ploughing.' She fell at length into a profound slumber, motionless, and apparently breathless, her head resting in my lap. I myself could no longer resist the inclination to sleep, in spite of the continual roar of the cannon. Suddenly I was aroused by a wild unearthly scream close to my ear; my companion stood upright beside me, her arms raised, and her head bent forward in the attitude of listening. A look of intense delight broke over her countenance, she grasped my hand, drew me towards her, and exclaimed, 'Dinna ye hear it? dinna ye hear it? Ay, I'm no dreamin', it's the slogan o' the Highlanders! We're saved, we're saved!' Then, flinging herself on her knees, she thanked God with passionate fervour. I felt utterly bewildered; my English ears heard only the roar of artillery, and I thought my poor Jessie was still raving; but she darted to the batteries, and I heard her cry incessantly to the men, 'Courage! courage! hark to the slogan, – to the Macgregor, the grandest o' them a'. Here's help at last!' To describe the effect of these words upon the soldiers would be impossible. For a moment they ceased firing, and every soul listened in intense anxiety. Gradually, however, there arose a murmur of bitter disappointment, and the wailing of the women who had flocked to the spot burst out anew as the colonel shook his head. Our dull lowland ears heard nothing but the rattle of the musketry. A few moments more of this death-like suspense, of this agonizing hope, and Jessie, who had again sunk on the ground, sprang to her feet, and cried, in a voice so clear and piercing that it was heard along the whole line – 'Will ye no believe it noo? The slogan has ceased indeed, but the Campbells are comin'! D'ye hear, d'ye hear?' At that moment we seemed indeed to hear the voice of God in the distance, when the pibroch of the Highlanders brought us tidings of deliverance, for now there was no longer any doubt of the fact. That shrill, penetrating, ceaseless sound, which rose above all other sounds, could come neither from the advance of the enemy, nor from the work of the Sappers. No, it was indeed the blast of the Scottish bagpipes . . . Never, surely, was there such a scene as that which followed. Not a heart in the Residency of Lucknow but bowed itself before God. All, by one simultaneous impulse, fell upon their knees, and nothing was heard but bursting sobs and the murmured voice of prayer. Then all arose, and there rang out from a thousand lips a great shout of joy which resounded far and wide, and lent new vigour to that blessed pibroch . . . To our cheer of 'God save the Queen,' they replied by the well-known strain that moves every Scot to tears, 'Should auld acquaintance be forgot,' &c. After that, nothing else made any impression on me.[32]

There are just two things one should note about this story. The first is that it is generally considered to be entirely apocryphal, and the second is that despite all the euphoria at the time, 25 September was *not* the day the siege of Lucknow ended.

Far from it.

9

Meanwhile and Elsewhere

———

*Poor Mrs Currie's nerves are very shaky. As she sat down to dinner,
she said to her cavalier, 'I hope we shall rise safely from dinner.'*[1]

Eighty-seven days had passed since the beginning proper of the
siege of Lucknow, and considerably more since the fey Jessie
Brown and other women (and ladies) of the garrison first entered
the Residency compound on 21 May. Meanwhile, 'the Devil's
Wind' (which many Indians believed inspired the Mutiny) was
blowing hot and strong throughout the region. There were porten-
tous dreams being dreamt by real Celtic memsahibs, too: by Mrs
Hunter, for example, in the Punjabi station of Sialkot. She was the
wife of a Church of Scotland missionary, the mother of a small
child and foundress of the first 'female school' in Sialkot: a busy
lady. Unlike many memsahibs, she could ill afford the time for idle
fancies. Yet, on the night of 7 July, she had a dream so real and
terrifying that it resulted in her leaving Sialkot with her family
(and nowhere in particular to go) the following day. What she had
seen in her sleep was her own murder, and the killing of her
husband and child. After keeping vigil the next night with friends
just outside the city, the Hunters set out for Lahore – which meant
turning back through Sialkot – on the morning of 9 July.

It was too late.

Mrs Hunter was the only memsahib killed at Sialkot. The

carriage in which the family was trying to escape was surrounded by sepoys busy trying to free convicts as it passed the city gaol, and one of them shot both man and wife with the same ball. They were then dragged out with their child and massacred in the street. It was said that she might have been spared, as the other memsahibs were, had she not been guilty of deliberately insulting the Moslem faith by setting up that blasphemous school for girls.[2]

For a first-hand account of the uprising in Sialkot, and an immediate impression of the chaos involved, the breathless Mary Gilliland does well. Most of the witnesses of the siege of Lucknow were able to tidy up their diaries and correspondence for the sake of publication; Mrs Gilliland, on the other hand, wrote wildly and spontaneously into the blue, not sure whether her letters would ever reach her mother in England nor even whether they would be read when they got there, so indifferent did her parent seem to this distant daughter. 'I've got no letter from you since last January', complains Mary at one point, 'which surprises me very much. I am always asking myself what can it be that prevents your writing to me but cannot think of any excuse . . .'[3] Still, she felt it her duty to keep in touch, and once she started on the story of the mutiny, it proved rather difficult to stop.

I must tell you half our 9th Cavalry were ordered off with the other troops in May and a Major Baker a great friend of ours went in command his wife went with him and they wanted us to go live in their Bungalow which is next the Brigadier's and a magnificent one which we did we only brought our Piano and clothes over as the House was left splendidly fitted up for us . . . well all went on with [us] as pleasant as a summer's dream till the morning of the 9th July when first about ½ 4 oc James got up as usual to prepare for going to practise he was in the bathroom when I heard Gun shots close to me I jumped up and looked towards where I heard them but could see nothing I then saw our 2 servants in the Garden and went to the door to call one of them [. I think we deserve a full-stop.] I enquired what was the matter he answered cooly [sic] the Cavalry are up and killing all Sahibs I ran to James and we began dressing ourselves as fast as we could we thought of nothing but our lives and left all behind us, we ran over to a Convent close to us where we heard the people were hiding but it was not the case we found only the Nuns the School Children and a poor Italian Priest there . . . we begged to stay with them which they agreed to and we all went into a little hut at the back of the house we numbered 28 – 20 of whom were children[. W]e remained there for about 15 or 20 minutes with the doors wide open to avoid suspicion when one of the convent servants came to say the Mutineers were taking away the Carriages we all said 'very well let them take everything but don't tell our hiding place' however this was useless for the servants are all quite as pleased to see us English killed as the Rebels are to do it so in a few minutes . . . 3 or 4 of our Cavalry fellows came to the house we were in with pistol and Julween (or sword) drawn in either hand.

The poor priest stood up from where he was sitting near a little window and as he did so a Pistol muzzle was p[l]aced there and fired now we thought our slaughter had begun and the agony of mind we all endured I cannot describe however God was merciful and the Ball by a miracle hit no one altho the place was so crowded, the Priest drew near to the door for the Rebels wanted him there to shoot him he had the Chalice in his hand and as the man nearest him pointed his pistol to shoot him he put it closely up to his face and as if the Good Lord made him powerless he let his pistol drop to his side three times this happened the same way and with the same effect and the only way we can account for the man's acting so is that they are all fearfully superstitious and he must have thought the Chalice was some spell which would destroy him if he injured the Priest, well but I must tell you now about ourselves . . .[4]

Draw breath.

Mary goes on to describe (in a single sentence) how she and James were hidden and left behind in the house when the nuns and children were led away by the rebels, and how the convent gardener offered, for 'about four or five pounds in Rupees', to bring them a disguise so that they could escape to the guard house and join the rest of the European garrison there.

. . . so we dressed up poor James as a Native in one of [the] Servant's clothes and I put on a large thing which covered me nearly all down . . . also fortunately James had a sheet which concealed him all but his eyes and this being a common fashion of Dress with the people here excited no remark then we set out . . . Some of the Christian Bandsmen . . . galloped out quickly to [us] and escorted [us] in safety to the Guard, our Colonel [Lorne Campbell] and wife were there the Rebels for some reason of their own brought them there without injuring them in the Morning we also saw Miss Graham whose father [a doctor] they shot beside her in the carriage a few hours before . . . also another poor lady [the wife of a different Dr Graham] whose husband they murdered as he sat between her and another lady [Mrs Gray] in the carriage and flying for their lives . . .[5]

Eventually, while the rebels were occupied in looting the treasury, Mary and her friends managed to steal to the fort ('I can tell you no joke . . . under a frightful sun and great excitement') where they stayed until the rebels, having virtually destroyed the cantonments, rode off towards Delhi.

My dearest Mother you will naturally ask what has become of our house and property all this time, I will tell you: they first plundered the houses of everything even to the chairs and tables then they smashed to atoms the Glass, Doors, and everything which was too heavy to carry away our poor piano was pounded into morsels, every article of clothing carried off and in fact nothing left but the 4 bare

walls of the house and the heap of ruins which our things are reduced to[. T]his is the case with everyone in the Station so we are no
exception all my lovely dresses are gone everything but what we
escaped in and to end the matter my cook when coming out of the
hut got my money to carry and the villain has walked off with it
too . . .[6]

Once the immediate panic of any particular outbreak was over,
and once the memsahibs had ceased to fear for their lives, anger
was the usual (and natural) reaction. But one memsahib stands out
amongst the Mutiny's annalists as never having been afraid at all –
never mind terrified – and she seems to have managed to be
furious right from the start. She was Annie Durand, Burra Mem
of Indore, south-west of Bhopal. Her husband, Colonel Henry,
had recently been appointed the Governor-General's acting Agent
for Central India, and considered himself a prudent and dignified
individual. When the general air of unrest which seemed to char-
acterize late May in British India reached Indore, he gathered the
Europeans into his Residency building and used a contingent of
the local loyal Maratha Prince Holkar's troops to defend it. It was
that guard, under the leadership of someone who had up till now
been completely supportive of Durand, which mutinied on the
morning of 1 July, and opened fire on the astonished inhabitants
of the Residency.

Annie was outraged – not so much with Holkar and his men
(such mean-spirited treachery was only to be expected from 'the
Asiatic', after all) as with her own countrypeople:

. . . what *disgusted* me beyond measure was the dastardly conduct of
our troops, *soldiers* they did not deserve the name of, and I was almost
equally provoked at two of the officers, whose one idea seemed
not to hold out to the last but to be off and save their wives and
themselves with all possible speed – long before the attack or the

probability of danger . . . and when danger came all they appeared to think of was an immediate retreat . . . I was more anxious to remain than go, and really did not at all contemplate our being driven to retreat by the miserable cowardice of our own troops, but so it was . . .

We had, unluckily, one or two terrible alarmists; among the worst was a Captain Magniac and his wife. They both bored me beyond expression with daily and hourly histories of what was going to happen . . . Mrs M. was a perfect torment till at last I almost ceased either listening or speaking to her . . . You would almost have laughed had you seen Mrs Magniac (whose name should have been spelt without a g) rush up from her own room below, when first Holkar's artillery opened fire upon us. She was half dressed, with her hair streaming about her face . . . the image of despair and terror. I cannot comprehend any woman with half a grain of sense exhibiting such desperate alarm – but she had been living for five or six weeks in continual panics, consequently, when real danger came, she was unfit to bear it decently, and, really, she was quite a nuisance in the house.[7]

Just as the Cavalry (under its British officers) was about to concede an ignominious and very dangerous defeat, the ladies and children who had survived the outbreak were ordered into ammunition wagons, given an escort of 150 sowars and two guns, and sent off towards Bhopal.

We had no time to think of saving anything and left the house by the back verandah while Holkar's artillery were raking the front . . . [O]ne lady . . . was furious with me because I expressed unqualified indignation at the cowardice that had forced us to retreat. She thought I ought to be so grateful to the men for saving our lives . . . I would willingly have remained if Henry could have got rid of the other ladies, rather than have seen him exposed to the distress and mortification of retreating.[8]

If any female had been allowed to stay, I am sure it would have been this self-styled 'worthy daughter and wife of soldiers',[9] but, alas, her life was forcibly saved and after several perilous days and nights on the road, she and the other refugees reached Bhopal. There they were given a change of clothes and some food before moving down to Mhow at the end of July.

Annie Durand was still writing acid letters home from Mhow a month later, but by the middle of September she was dead. No doubt she would have wished to go in the staunch defence of her own person/country; in fact, she is described as having failed merely 'of exhaustion'. Charlotte Canning noted regretfully in her diary that Annie would be sorely missed by Colonel Henry: 'she was a good, useful wife and worked for her husband like a secretary'.[10] What more could any gentleman ask?

The mutiny at Indore, like that up at Sialkot a week or so later, was over and done with in days. Elsewhere, it tended to spread itself over a series of episodes, confusing in their chronology and each a little cataclysm of its own. Such was the case at Fatehgarh, the British station attached to the Indian city (three miles away) of Farrukhabad.

The position of Farrukhabad, standing stately on the Ganges between Shahjehanpur and Cawnpore, and the colourful court of its Nawab Taffazzul Hussain Khan, both helped justify its loosely translated name of 'the fortunate town'. Neighbouring Fatehgarh was a thriving garrison with a well-settled British community complete with all the necessary accoutrements of a civilized life, including church, culture, and scandal.

One of its most outrageous residents was beautiful Bonny Byrne (née de Fountain), who had arrived a few months before the Mutiny as the nineteen-year-old wife of Ensign Reginald Byrne – and was responsible, said some, for the notorious 'Parade-ground Massacre' of 23 July 1857, when thirty-two men, women and children were released from squalid captivity, and killed.

These Christians were the survivors of an escape attempt from the besieged fort of Fatehgarh in boats down the Ganges. Before the siege began, back at the beginning of June, the European population had fled the station in two boats, hoping to get to the supposed safety of Cawnpore. One boat – with Amy Sutherland aboard – did reach Bithoor, and you will remember the fate of its passengers. The other, having separated from the first, landed near Dhurumpore and its cargo of forty refugees (including Amy's mother and sister) was sheltered by the local zemindar, Hurdeo Buksh, before they decided, most of them, to return to the fort at Fatehgarh. Within days of their return, however, the 10th Native Infantry, of whose certain loyalty they had previously been per-suaded by Hurdeo Buksh, disbanded itself and on 28 June a rebel attack on the fort began. The embattled Europeans – now numbering around one hundred, including only thirty-three able-bodied men – made their second escape attempt on the rain-swelled Ganges during the early morning of 4 July, but one of their vessels was seen at Rampur and fired upon, and those who survived were captured and taken to the palace of the Nawab.

Which is where Bonny Byrne comes in.

Amelia Eliza Byrne, otherwise known as Bonny, was particu-larly delighted to find herself in Fatehgarh. She had lived there as a child with her widowed mother Adolphine de Fountain, and enjoyed the status accorded a long-established Eurasian family with good connections. At least, her mother thought they were good connections: from the age of fourteen Bonny was playing hostess to the Nawab of Farrukhabad himself. He used to come and visit her, and Adolphine was thrilled.

When the time came for Bonny to be educated, she was sent to the Kidderpoor Girls' School in Calcutta; there she did just what was expected of a young lady like her by marrying an eligible young ensign she had met at a ball. Reginald Byrne's first posting on their marriage in October 1856 happened to be to Fatehgarh, whereupon he and Bonny moved in with her mother again and soon (at the express invitation of Adolphine) the Nawab was renewing his respects.

Bonny's husband was apparently unaware of what was going on until apprised by a friend, and is said to have arrived home unannounced one afternoon to find his wife and the Nawab embroiled 'in close and earnest conversation'. Reginald literally kicked the Nawab out of the house, and was cursed with an enraged vow of vengeance for his pains.

What followed is a little uncertain: Byrne is recorded as having been killed at Cawnpore, so presumably he was amongst the successful (thus far) refugees of Fatehgarh. But Bonny and her mother were not: on the contrary, they were taken into Taffazzul Hussain Khan's zenana at the palace, where Bonny aroused the fiercest jealousy on account of her youth, her beauty, and – most significantly – her obvious pregnancy. And this is why she was later supposed to have played such a decisive part in the Parade-ground Massacre. When the captive survivors of Manpur were dragged back from the river to be shut up in the palace stables, the Nawab did not intend at first to kill them. But thanks to the arguments of his senior wife, who was all too eager to include Bonny and her unborn baby amongst the condemned feringhee to maintain her own heirs' position, the Nawab was persuaded to dispose of them and, on 23 July, all twenty-two women and children (including the remaining Sutherlands) were led on to the parade-ground, sat against a wall, and shot.

It was the fact that Bonny and Adolphine were not amongst their number that persuaded the newly appointed British Magistrate in Fatehgarh after the Mutiny that they must have played some part in the massacre themselves. He applied to the Governor-General for permission to hang them both, but it was denied. 'There has been enough bloodshed of this kind,' said

Canning, by which I assume he meant the fruitless exchange of one person's life for another.

So Bonny survived. Her gravestone lies in the European Kutcheri cemetery in Cawnpore, lovingly and elaborately inscribed; the death of Amelia Eliza, 'the lamented wife of Edward John Chandler, Sub-Collector' whom she married soon after the birth of her son, left 'her Mother, Husband and other Members to bemoan her loss. She was a sincere friend and truly attached Wife' who lived certain in the knowledge that Christ 'forgiveth all my sins and healeth my infirmities'. The date on the stone is 3 February 1859.[11]

One of the few refugees who fled Fatehgarh at the first alarm back at the beginning of June was the Collector's wife, Charlotte Probyn. She was amongst the forty whom Hurdeo Buksh sheltered at Dhurumpore, but instead of returning to the garrison with the others to trust in the avowed loyalty of the sepoys there, she decided with her husband to stay in hiding – even though this meant living secretly for two months in a village cowshed, before moving to a tiny and isolated jungle hut where her baby died. His wet-nurse had run away before the first British exodus from Fatehgarh; since then Charlotte had been trying to sustain him on whatever fluids she could find, supplemented by doses of opium. The next child up, a 'dear pet' of a girl who was just beginning to walk and talk, would have coped well with the heat and squalor of the Probyns' temporary home if she had not had to endure the suffering of teething. According to her mother, she 'had not strength [enough] to get her eye ones, and wasted away to a shadow so that all her little bones were visible, and on the 21st of August I held another loved but lifeless child in my arms.'[12] By this time, the Probyns and their two surviving children were on the way to Cawnpore: this perilous voyage lasted three weeks, and involved their constantly being undercover by day, and dressed as natives. When they arrived at Cawnpore on 31 August, Mrs

Probyn being now 'the only lady there', they were more dead than alive – but they survived. Later, whenever the Collector was asked to recall the escape, he refused. 'I cannot write on this subject – vengeance! Vengeance!'[13] was all he could say.

Maria Mill was another woman who chose to follow her own instincts rather than the general plan. When mutiny broke out in Fyzabad, the European population was offered shelter straight away by the local Rajah Maun Singh, and all but Maria took it. She preferred, however, to entrust her own life and that of her three children to a 'respectable native' who promised her officer husband that the family would be safer in his care. But once Major Mill had deposited them and left, the native shut them in 'a miserable mud hut' and started muttering about rupees. Soon he turned them out, and led them back to their old home. The major was nowhere to be found (in fact he was killed in the uprising) and, while Maria was trying to gather her wits, 'Sepoys began intruding themselves into every part of the house, even into the room in which I was sitting, where they sat down upon chairs, had the drawers and boxes opened before them, and began to take away whatever they fancied.'[14]

Maria was at last offered passage down the River Gogra to Dinapore, but after an hour on the water her boatmen abandoned her. When a band of rebels took the boatmen's place, informing her that she must 'leave the boat immediately or they would cut off my head', she decided that they were only trying to frighen her (which no doubt they were), and refused to move. In the end she was forced off, but still had the determination to hire another boat and demand to be taken on to Dinapore. After negotiating a price, she and the children were swathed in a cloth, like cargo, and the boat moved off. Before it got to its destination, though, Maria was told that there was a rebel boat closing on hers in pursuit, and again she was ordered off.

What followed was a delirious three-week journey from village to village, with baby Charlie on one arm, the young lad Johnny on the other, and her eldest child, Alice, at her side. 'I told Alice the fate I anticipated', she said, 'and the child seemed strengthened from above, for her answer was "Dear Mamma, if they do kill us we shall go to Jesus and be happy – I am not afraid." '[15] Indeed, Maria remembered begging one lot of curious villagers they met to put them all out of their misery.

Charlie, the baby, did not survive the journey to eventual safety at Gorruckpore. No one could quite understand how his mother and the other two did: she had spent most of the time, according to the reports Charlotte Canning heard, wandering about 'quite mad', and 'no human beings had ever been seen so thin'.[16]

Charlotte Canning, in her letters and diaries, made a point of tempering the grim news reaching Calcutta during July and August 1857 with inspiring stories of survival. Especially women's survival.

July 9. Mrs Talbot went to Howrah to see a poor Mrs Block, who came with Mrs Goldney and another from Sultanpore. They had wandered about more than a fortnight, sometimes kindly treated, sometimes sent back from place to place to avoid dangers, and at last they got to Allahabad. She and her child were in clothes they found in a field amongst all the smashed and battered furniture and things turned out of the houses . . .

Sunday, August 2 . . . We had a dinner of a few refugees in the evening – the Lennoxes from Fyzabad, and a Mrs Webster from Banda, a very pretty young woman, who had travelled for a fortnight in a buggy, which was upset at the first start and broke her collar-bone. But on they went, sleeping under trees by the roadsides at night, and flying from place to place. They had twenty-five gentlemen with them fully armed, and only one other lady and a few half-castes. Their adventures were not so bad, but they saw villages burning on all sides, and knew that the people who had not got away as soon as they did were

killed. Mrs Currie ... gave me a piteous account of the refugee
people in the house she looks after – children with careworn anxious
faces, who were obliged to lie in bed the first day [after their arrival],
whilst their only garment was washed. Almost every one, in all their
dreadful histories, has to tell of some kind Rajah or faithful servant,
and now and then even of a Sepoy. One followed an Officer and his
wife all the way to Calcutta. Poor Mrs Currie's nerves are very shaky.
As she sat down to dinner, she said to her cavalier, '*I hope we shall rise
safely from dinner.*'[17]

There was one story more remarkable than all the rest. It involved Mrs Leeson, whom last we met in Delhi left for dead by
the mutineers who killed her children. The sole memsahib to
witness the Siege of Delhi from first to last, doughty Harriet
Tytler, was there when the story was first told. Some time around
the middle of August, she remembers, 'two Afghans came into
camp with a scrap of paper on which a message was written in
charcoal from a Mrs Leeson, saying she had been rescued by these
two men and wished to be brought into camp.'[18] The men were
immediately offered 1,000 rupees to deliver her, but refused the
money, 'saying they had not saved her life for money, but for
humanity's sake ... At last the poor woman was brought in by one
of the men ... and immediately was sent over to me, as the only
other English woman in camp.'

God only knows what that poor woman must have suffered on that
burning 12th of May with an anguished heart, a wounded body,
lying in the blazing sun, without a drop of water to quench her cruel
thirst, made doubly worse by the fear of moving lest it be seen she
was still alive. Her rescuers and women of the priest's family were
most good to her. Once only they begged of her to become a
Mohammedan. She said she could not. They had saved her life,
and it was in their power at any time to take it, but never could she

renounce her religion. She begged of them to find her a Bible out of all the books that were daily being burnt in the city; however, not knowing English, they could not distinguish one book from another and brought her many, but no Bible. She was so unnerved and terrified by the horrors of the 11th and 12th of May that nothing could induce her to come down from the room she occupied. It was a small isolated one at the top of the house and supposed to be uninhabited. It had no windows or opening but the one leading to the women's apartments below.

After her two deliverers had communicated with Hodson and received his permission to bring her into camp, there was some delay in carrying out their plans, on account of which she became impatient. They tried to convince her of the great danger, both to her and to themselves, in doing anything hurriedly. However, to please her, they resolved at last to make the attempt. Mrs Leeson was naturally slightly dark, but they darkened her still more, until she looked like themselves, and, having hired a country bullock-cart, they put their own women in along with her and got a trusty friend to drive, while the two Afghans themselves walked on either side of the conveyance. On reaching the Lahore Gate of the city, the guard stopped them and insisted on seeing who were inside, being greatly suspicious of Europeans being concealed. The two men begged hard, saying they were only their 'Zenana' or female relatives, going to Kudam Shareef to worship at the shrine, upon which the guard made them put out their hands and arms from under the cloth covering of the cart. Seeing those, as they supposed, of native women only, they allowed the cart to pass out beyond the walls of Delhi. After the party had gone some considerable distance, they took Mrs Leeson out, dressed her as an Afghan boy, and sent the cart with the other women back to the city through another of the gates.

The little Kandahari, for one was an Afghan from Kandahar, went on ahead to see if the road was clear, while the other, an Afghan from Peshawar, and Mrs Leeson waited with anxiety for his return.

Not seeing him come back, they felt sure something untoward had happened and started off by themselves, taking a circuitous way to avoid detection. Mrs Leeson, in her terror, fell down a 'nullah,' or dry bed of a rivulet, and grazed herself from her shoulder to her foot on one side. She must have suffered greatly from the abrasion, but I never heard her murmur or make the least complaint. At last, very early on the 10th of August, after hairbreadth escapes, they reached our picket and, on presenting Major Hodson's permit, were allowed to enter camp.[19]

Mrs Leeson was allowed to stay in Delhi only for as long as it took to organize her journey to the comparative safety of Umballa, and there she remained until Delhi was retaken by the British in the middle of September.

On our entering Delhi after its capture [writes Harriet Tytler] and taking up our quarters in Kamuran Shah's palace, Mrs Leeson returned from Umballa and stayed with us until the arrival of her husband, who had escaped . . . to Agra, where he had been shut up with the rest of the Europeans, all that time in ignorance of the fate of his family. Their meeting, as may be imagined, was very sad. They went off almost at once to the college grounds, the scene of the tragedy, to search, but in vain, for the bones of their murdered children.[20]

The siege and eventual recovery of Delhi formed the military core of the Mutiny. After the outbreak on 11 May, and European evacuation of the city itself, the British marched back to occupy the great ridge overlooking Delhi from the north-west. Meanwhile, within the city walls, the rebels were mustering far greater numbers of fighting men, and equipping themselves with far heavier arms, than the British could ever hope for. But they lacked the definitive leadership (despite the symbolic presence of the king) and military artistry to take advantage. The British held on to the ridge for three-and-a-half months, until enough momentum had been built up to attempt the assault on the city that would determine the future of the Raj.

And Harriet Tytler saw it all. She had escaped the initial outbreak eight months pregnant, with her husband, a Captain in the 38th Native Infantry, her children of four and two, and their French maid Marie. After a (by now) predictably alarming journey they managed to get as far as Umballa, over a hundred miles away, where they stayed until the hastily mustered Delhi Field Force was ready to march back for the city. When it did, Robert Tytler went with it as the troops' Paymaster, taking his weary family with him, and by the time they got to Alipore (a few miles to the north of Delhi) on 7 June, Harriet was utterly exhausted. As preparations were being made for the Field Force to occupy the ridge (and so begin the so-called siege), the memsahibs were ordered out of the way. Their numbers had been gradually swelling over the last few days as refugees from various hiding-places around sought safety in the British camp, and their presence in this potential battlefield was considered at best distracting and at worst a military liability.

General Barnard, the C. in C., directed that all women and children should hold themselves in readiness to leave the camp on a certain day for Meerut, and that we should travel seated on the backs of pad elephants. Perhaps my readers may like to know that a pad elephant means an elephant with a thick straw mattress fixed over the back, on which riders sit as best they can, holding on somehow, though with difficulty owing to the peculiar rocking motion of an elephant's walk . . .

When I heard of the mode of travelling decided upon for us, I was truly appalled, as it meant certain death in my case. So I asked my husband to interview the General and beg of him to allow me to remain a short while longer, after which I should be glad to go wherever he desired. When the good old man, known for his kindness to all, heard of the state of mind I was in, he at once said, 'Poor lady! poor lady! let her stay,' and thus it was that I was allowed to stay throughout the whole siege, the only lady in the camp, for no one later on could be spared to escort me safely away. This was the evening of the 19th, and my baby was born at two in the morning of the 21st, two days, or rather just thirty-two hours, later!²¹

Harriet and the children were at this stage living on an old bullock cart. 'It was an immense long thing, about twelve feet long and four feet broad, and had been used as a crockery van to take goods up to the foot of the Hills, and so had springs and a railing all round. My husband had the two end railings removed and a thick thatch put on, with the sides all enclosed with matting except two places for windows.' The baby was born in some old straw strewn on the floor.

My baby was born with dysentery and was not expected to live for nearly a week. When the child was out of immediate danger, the kind-hearted doctor said, 'Now, Mrs Tytler, you may think of giving him a name.' Poor child, his advent into this troublous world, a pauper to begin with, was not a promising one. There he lay, near the opening of the van, with only a small square piece of flannel thrown over him, the setting moon shining brightly on his little face and nothing but the sound of alarms, calls, and shot and shell as lullabies, both then and till the end of the siege. Unfortunately for me, Marie was strangely inexperienced as to the treatment of new-born babes, so that when I saw her seize him by his right leg to wash him, I cried out, 'Oh, leave him, leave him! I will do it myself.' A brass *chillumchi* (washing-pan) was brought to me, and I gave my poor baby his first bath, just six hours after he was born.

A week after the birth of the child, the monsoon, or summer rains, broke with great force. Till then we had comforted ourselves with the thought that the thatched roof of the van would prove watertight; instead of which it leaked like a sieve, and in a few moments we were drenched, baby and all, to the skin. My husband, coming at that moment to see how we were getting on, said, 'This will never do,' and at once searched for a better shelter. Fortunately the bell of arms[22] near which our cart stood was empty, and he obtained permission to put us into it. This being secured, he took our native man-servant, Jamalka, along with him to Scott's battery and brought back fresh straw to spread on the ground for us to lie on. When this refuge was ready for us, I walked with a drenched sheet wrapped around the infant and myself to the bell of arms, which was now to be our home till the 20th of September ... I was able to nurse my child without the aid of bottles or cow's milk, and this was providential, for neither bottles nor milk could have been procured for love or money.

We slept on the floor with only two wadded razais, or native quilts, under us, no pillows or sheets, till the sale by auction of the effects of an unfortunate officer who had been killed, when my husband bought his sheets, and these we supplemented with our few clothes rolled up as pillows. The want of sufficient clothes was felt by us severely during the siege. No native vendors were in camp, and with great difficulty I got sufficient coarse stuff to make two little petticoats for the baby, which brought his wardrobe up to about the standard of the rest of us. The other two children, Frank and Edie, had little else but what they had escaped in. I could only boast of two cotton petticoats, bought from my native ayah, and the clothes I had escaped in. While these were being washed and dried there was nothing for it but to remain *perdue*, wrapped in a sheet.

My life in that bell of arms was chiefly spent in darning, from morning to night, the few clothes we possessed to keep them from falling to pieces. I also had a small shawl that a lady had kindly sent me from Meerut. My husband was somewhat better off, for some soldiers he had brought out in a troop-ship round the Cape of Good Hope, hearing how we had lost everything on the 11th of May, got a few white clothes together, and one of them brought the small bundle and placed it quietly under my husband's chair. Was it not an act of real kindness and sympathy on their part? The donor merely said, 'You will excuse us, sir, but some of us thought they might be acceptable,' and disappeared before my husband could recognise who had done the most kind deed or thank the givers.

The heat was terrible and the flies were worse. Delhi had always been noted for its pest of flies, now many times worse, owing to the carcasses of animals and also to the presence of dead bodies lying about everwhere . . .

I could not keep my small boy Frank out of the sun for even an hour in the day, either in the van or in the bell of arms. He would amuse himself running about in the scorching heat, hatless, for the sufficient reason that he did not possess one, now playing with one soldier, now with another – they were all so fond of and good to the boy. How the child survived the heat and sun is a mystery. As to little Edith, I had to keep her in somehow, for, having only recently recovered from a serious illness, exposure to the sun might have killed her. As it was, the little thing used to faint once or twice every day, saying, '*Mama, burra durram hai*,' or 'Mother, it is very hot.' I used to reply, 'Yes, darling, go to the door; it will be cooler there,' but she would be off in a dead faint before she could reach it. Poor child, if she escaped the above she would faint in her bath, but never did a day go by without her fainting, while to keep her under shelter was almost an impossibility, so that I was in despair what to do.[23] At last a bright idea entered my head. It was rather a unique one, which was to scratch holes in my feet and tell her she must be my doctor and stop their bleeding. The process went on daily and for hours. No sooner did my wounds heal, when she used to make them bleed again for the simple pleasure of stopping the blood with my handkerchief. But it had the desired effect of amusing her for hours.[24]

Time went on and the baby, wonderfully, thrived. By the middle of September it became clear that the recapture of Delhi must at least be attempted, and the day of the great assault was named. It was 14 September – just ten days before Havelock rode in to relieve Lucknow, 200 miles away. 'All eyes of both friends and foes were waiting for the result of that fearful day,' says Harriet, 'for had we lost Delhi, every European in India would have had to die.'

My brother, Lieut. E. L. Earle, of the Artillery, had the most dangerous post allotted to him, and while laying his gun to fire on the Cashmere Gate on the 13th, the morning before the assault, was seriously wounded by a shell taking a piece out his right elbow and side, and was picked up for dead. The carabineer soldier who took his place was killed half an hour later, and the man who followed met the same fate. The rebels had that day caught one of our poor soldiers and crucified him on the Cashmere Gate. Thank God, the poor fellow was not long suffering, for he was killed almost immediately by a round of shot and bullets. The enemy had been very brutal even to their own countrymen, for, on our entering the city, many were found near the Cashmere Gate dying of wounds inflicted by red-hot ramrods being thrust through and through their flesh, this being because they had been suspected of being spies. Such is war with all its horrors.

As soon as my husband heard of my brother being wounded, he had him brought over to his office tent, and there I attended to his wounds. They were awful to behold, especially the one in his side – it made me shudder to look at it. He would not allow anyone but myself to dress his wounds. There were no Red Cross nurses in those days and his one cry every morning was, 'Harrie, when will you come to me? Why don't you come?' I was in the bell of arms and he in the office tent. The truth was that I could not come sooner than I did, for I had to bathe three children every morning in a brass *chillumchee* or basin, a process which was necessarily a slow one . . .

The 13th, as may be imagined, was a day of great anxiety to us all, for we knew the morrow was to bring us either total failure and death or victory. Two breaches had been effected in the wall near the Cashmere and Water bastions, and four engineer officers examined them during the night of the 13th and reported them practicable. Orders were promptly issued for the assault to take place at daybreak on the following morning. The morning of the 14th rose to see the day of revenge on that doomed city, and alas! it was to be the last sunrise for many a brave soldier, both European and native.

I knew from the fierce booming of the guns that terrible fighting was taking place; and how earnestly we few left in camp prayed for victory and deliverance! The agonising suspense of not knowing how things were going was almost unbearable. It was a morning never to be forgotten. At last the glad tidings of a great victory reached us, and we could offer up prayers and thanksgiving for God's mercy to our brave men.[25]

A week or so of fighting followed the assault on Delhi, punctuated by riotous looting and drunkenness on the part of these noble victors, until the streets of the city fell quiet. There were well over a thousand casualties amongst the British, and untold numbers of Indians killed (including the deliberately murdered sons of the king himself), and by the time it was all finished, the Indian Mutiny, Freedom Struggle, call it what you will, was all but over.

Harriet stayed on.

As soon as we were settled in our new home, known as Kamuran Shah's palace (he was an uncle of the old king and had been dead some time), I felt it was time to have our baby boy christened, for he was over three months old. So Jamalkha, our faithful cook (a baker by profession), made a fine cake, and we invited all the officers still in Delhi to see the child baptised. Of course, before this, the question arose as to what his name should be. The soldiers suggested that we call him 'Battlefield Tytler,' but I felt that would be too dreadful a name, and not one he would be thankful for later on; so, much to their disgust and annoyance, for they quite considered the infant their own particular property, we compromised the matter by naming him 'Stanley Delhi-Force Tytler.' My husband had been reading *Marmion* to me just before the outbreak of the Mutiny, and recollecting Marmion's last words, 'On, Stanley, on!' it struck me as being pretty and appropriate.[26]

Harriet mentions little of the faithful French Marie's life during the siege. She does make an appearance as her mistress's memoir draws to an end, though. She had apparently been inconsolable at the loss of her traditional national dress in the flight from Delhi back in May, so as soon as the road to Meerut was clear again, Harriet determined to redress poor Marie's misfortune by going there to get her 'the necessary materials' to make a splendid new Breton cap. But strangely, Marie seemed reluctant to wear it, 'which I could not understand, for though a plain woman she looked really nice in it.'

After wearing it only twice when she went out with the children on our elephant, she came into my room and threw her cap on the floor saying, 'I will never wear the horrid thing again.' I was so astounded and asked her what she meant by doing so. She replied, 'All the soldiers laughed at me.'

But later on we found out the real facts, when she took me by surprise saying she was going to be married to a sergeant, a widower in the 60th Rifles. I was indeed very sorry to hear it, for she was such a faithful servant and so devoted to all the children . . .

After a short time the marriage took place. We gave her a silk dress and she wore the most antiquated old straw bonnet she had picked up as loot in the city and in which she looked the plainest old bride I have ever seen in my life.[27]

10

The Relief of Lucknow

---

*God bless you, Missus. We're glad we've come in time
to save you and the youngsters.*[1]

While Delhi celebrated its freedom (or, from another point of view, its return to subjugation), Lucknow remained a city still very much involved in the Mutiny. General Havelock had led his men through the perilous wilderness outside – with the loss of seven horses shot from under him the while – and negotiated the lethal city streets like some latter-day liege with his knights to rescue maiden England in distress. He braved the heathen guard at her gate, pushed down her prison doors, and clasped the swooning heroine to his heart. A cheer went up (God save the Queen!) and prayers were said in gratitude for deliverance. This oft-pictured scene is from the same chivalrous canon as Cawnpore – and bears about as little relevance to the truth.

The force sent by Generals Havelock and Outram, with the sweaty, kilted Highlanders as vanguard and Sikhs following on behind, did indeed fulfil Jessie Brown's dream by breaking through to the Residency on 25 September (with the loss of hundreds of British and Indian lives) and for a brief period it did seem as though the siege, at last, was over. But within hours of its arrival it became patently clear that what had been designed as a relief operation was in reality only a matter of reinforcement. The

Lucknow rebels' numbers were rapidly being swelled by fugitives from Delhi and elsewhere, until it was reckoned there must be about one hundred thousand of them in the city. The British were making the odd sortie from the Residency and the occupied Alambagh, a splendid complex a few miles outside the city in the direction of Cawnpore which used to be the queen mother of Oudh's country residence, and gently building up a strategy which might finally lead to real relief. But it was obvious such relief must still be weeks away.

To Kate Bartrum, it hardly mattered. She was entirely taken up with the imminent arrival of Robert.

September 25. – Firing heard in the city all day, and at six in the evening the relieving force entered the Residency, and at that moment the noise, confusion, and cheering, were almost overwhelming. My first thought was of my husband, whether he had accompanied the reinforcement, and I was not long left in suspense, for the first officer I spoke to told me he was come up with them, and that they had shared the same doolie on the previous night. My first impulse was to thank God that he had come; and then I ran out with baby amongst the crowd to see if I could find him, and walked up and down the road to the Baillie guard gate, watching the face of every one that came in; but I looked in vain for the one that I wanted to see, and then I was told that my husband was with the heavy artillery and would not be in till the next morning, so I went back to my own room. I could not sleep that night for joy at the thought of seeing him so soon, and how thankful I was that our Heavenly Father had spared us to meet again. The joy was almost too great, after four such weary months of separation, and I could hush my child to sleep with a glad and happy heart – a feeling I had not experienced for many a long night.

September 26. – Was up with the daylight, and dressed myself and baby in the one clean dress which I had kept for him throughout the siege until his papa should come. I took him out and met Mr Freeling who told me that dear Robert was just coming in, that they had been sharing the same tent on the march, and that he was in high spirits at the thought of meeting his wife and child again. I waited, expecting to see him, but he did not come, so I gave baby his breakfast and sat at the door to watch for him again full of happiness. I felt he was so near me that at any moment we might be together again: and here I watched for him nearly all day. In the evening I took baby up to the top of the Residency, to look down the road, but I could not see him coming and returned back to my room disappointed.

September 27. – Still watching for my husband, and still he came not, and my heart was growing very sick with anxiety. This afternoon Dr Darby came to me: he looked so kindly and so sadly in my face, and I said to him 'How strange it is my husband has not come in!' 'Yes,' he said, 'it *is* strange!' and turned and went out of the room. Then the thought struck me: Something has happened which they do not like to tell me! But this was agony too great almost to endure, to hear that he had been struck down at our very gates. Of this first hour of bitter woe I cannot speak ... My poor little fatherless boy! Who is to care for us now, baby?[2]

Kate was comforted by the chaplain's widow Emmie Polehampton. She felt God had 'forgotten to be gracious' and wrote in her diary that she would put her whole trust now in baby Bobbie instead: 'Now he was doubly dear to me: all I had to make life endurable.'

The next day, the two servants who had travelled with Dr Bartrum arrived to tell Kate what had happened.

They brought in his horse, my own black horse that I had had so many happy rides upon; he had carried my husband safely down the country, when he escaped from Gonda and had come up with him again to Lucknow. Oh! it was so sad to see him come in without his

17. Nana Sahib, always cast by
the British as the Mutiny's arch villain,
was the rebel leader supposed to have
ordered the two massacres at Cawnpore
during which over 200 women
and children perished.

18. The Rani of Jhansi, warrior queen
and Indian Mutiny heroine, who many
believe was forced into rebellion
by British treachery.

19. An apocryphal but not entirely unlikely view of the
massacre at Jhansi, where British families were taken to a garden
outside the city walls and killed.

20. Inside the Bibigarh after the second massacre at Cawnpore: a popular picture of the pathetic chaos that remained after the building's dead inhabitants were dumped in a well outside.

21. The well itself with the Bibigarh in the background by Vincent Brookes.

22. The most popular version of Ulrica Wheeler's fabled fate
after her capture at Cawnpore by a sepoy. In fact she lived relatively
peacefully with her rescuer until his death.

23. Fugitive officers with their families escaping through
the jungle. The trek to safety could take weeks, with many lives lost –
as well as the odd baby born.

24. The ruins of the Baillie Guard Gate in Lucknow, where
Robert Bartrum was killed, and the Banqueting Hall, which served
as the besieged Residency's hospital.

25. The Residency building still comparatively whole
in the early days of the siege of Lucknow.

26. The Begum Kothi, where
Kate Bartrum spent most of the siege
of Lucknow in a small, dark room with
thirteen others, photographed
in 1858.

27. The Bartrums (*left*), who
arrived in the 'peaceful security' of Gonda
in September 1856. Little more than a year
later both Kate's husband and
her baby were dead.

28. *Jessie's Dream* by Frederick Goodall, in which legendary Scots lass
Jessie Brown swears, while everyone else is sinking into despair, that she hears
bagpipes skirling in the distance, and sure enough (but quite some time later),
along come the Highlanders to relieve the siege of Lucknow.

29. Julia Inglis, looking uncharacteristically stern, with Colonel John and two of
their three children. A plaque on the Residency walls records Julia's 'heroic
and self-sacrificing devotion to duty' during the siege.

30. Harriet and Robert Tytler. Harriet was the only British woman to witness the siege of Delhi from first to last.

31. The Begum Zenat Mahal of Delhi, whose glowering presence in her crumbling palace became a post-Mutiny tourist attraction until her exile to Burma in October 1858.

32. *An Incident in the Indian Mutiny* by Edward Hopley. His besieged British family looks suitably soulful whilst awaiting rescue, obviously little cheered by the music on the stand ('The Campbells are Coming').

33. The massacre well, Cawnpore, *c.*1880, tranquil at last. The memorial screen and the white marble angel it surrounds were both transferred to All Souls Church, Cawnpore, on Independence in 1947.

34. The track leading down to the Satichowra Ghat at Cawnpore has changed little during the years since the Mutiny. It remains a strangely still and melancholy place.

master. The servants brought in a few things belonging to him: his sword, pistol, and intrument case had all been taken from him.

September 29. – Dr Darby came to see me again today, and brought with him Dr Bradshaw of the 90th, who was with dear Robert at the time he fell. It made me almost forget my own sorrow to hear him spoken of in such high terms of praise. His was a glorious death: coming to the rescue of his wife and child, he fell at his post doing his duty. Dr B. told me that as he was going across the courtyard with my husband, he said to him, 'Bartrum, you are exposing yourself too much!' 'Oh,' he answered, 'there is no danger;' when he was immediately struck in the temple and fell across his companion, saying, 'It is all up with me,' and died instantly. They laid him in a doolie, but whether he was ever brought into the Residency, which is not probable, or buried in the courtyard, or never buried at all, I could not ascertain . . .[3]

Bartrum's body was never found.

There were now more than a thousand extra people in the Residency compound: all mouths to be fed. But the rather surreal chance discovery of an underground swimming bath packed full of grain soon after their arrival, and the artillery wagon bullocks they had brought with them, were enough to stave off famine. There was more room now, too, because the reinforcements had managed to push the rebels back a thousand yards or so from the muddy barricades beside the Baillie Guard Gate and Dr Fayrer's house, which brought a number of fresh buildings into the Residency's fold. For the first time since the siege began some of the ladies (Maria Germon amongst them) found the courage to take the occasional little constitutional walk: those horribly accurate snipers who had accounted for so many deaths during the past months were thought far too far away to pick them off now. Paradoxically, though, the number of direct hits on particular posts and garrisons increased during this second part of the siege.

Before, the rebels had been firing their weaponry at too close a range to be accurate, and often shells would sail right over their intended targets. But now, they were far enough away to take sight and aim, with deadly result.

At least the stagnant old routine had changed with the arrival of what became known as the 'first relief', even if the immediate circumstances of the besieged remained much the same, and to Maria, for one, there was an air – however faint – of optimism about the place. To counter the bleak news of Cawnpore brought in by the reinforcements (indeed, the same Dr Darby who was comforting Kate had just heard of his own wife's and baby's deaths in Wheeler's entrenchment) there was the enormous excitement of British Lucknow's newest entertainment: looting.

Thursday, October 1st. No news [writes Maria Germon] . . . Dear Charlie came quite lame (the Doctors say we must all get scurvy living on the same food so long and without any vegetables). He brought me some beautiful china and a splendid punch bowl, his own looting.

Saturday, October 3rd. They say our troops are still gaining ground in the City – several of the enemy's guns were blown up today. Miss Nepean came over in the evening and dear Charlie bringing some more china.

Sunday, October 4th. We all came out in clean or new dresses that we had kept for the Relief. Mrs Harris and Mrs Barwell went to the Brigade Mess to Church. We had service in our own [Dr Fayrer's] house at 3 p.m. – several gentlemen came and Charlie amongst them . . . I enjoyed a cup of tea with him – of course without milk and sugar but it seemed Paradise to be alone with him again. He gave me a beautiful manuscript worked in small green and white beads on pink and gold paper – Dr Fayrer said, no doubt, by the ladies of the Court.[4]

Even the chaplain's wife herself, Georgina Harris, was delighted to be presented with some 'plated dishes' her husband had bought: 'they will be very useful to us if we ever set up house again in India.'[5]

The Times correspondent William Howard Russell was less sanguine about this looting (as an outsider), and later described it with uncomfortable candour.

It was one of the strangest and most distressing sights that could be seen; but it was also most exciting. Discipline may hold soldiers together till the fight is won; but it assuredly does not hold for a moment after an assault has been delivered, or a storm has taken place. Imagine courts . . . surrounded with ranges of palaces, or at least of buildings well stuccoed and gilded, with fresco-paintings here and there on the blind-windows, and with green jalousies and Venetian blinds closing the apertures which pierce the walls in double rows. In the body of the court are statues, lines of lamp-posts, fountains, orange-groves, aqueducts, and kiosks with burnished domes of metal . . . At every door there is an eager crowd, smashing the panels with the stocks of their firelocks, or breaking the fastenings by discharges of their weapons . . . Here and there the invaders have forced their way into the long corridors, and you hear the musketry rattling inside; the crash of glass, the shouts and yells of the combatants, and little jets of smoke curl out of the closed lattices. Lying amid the orange groves are dead and dying sepoys; and the white statues are reddened with blood. Leaning against a smiling Venus is a British soldier shot through the neck, gasping, and at every gasp bleeding to death. Here and there officers are running to and fro after their men, persuading or threatening in vain. From the broken portals issue soldiers laden with loot or plunder: shawls, rich tapestry, gold and silver brocade, caskets of jewels, splendid dresses. The men are wild with fury and lust of gold – literally drunk with plunder. Some come out with China vases or mirrors, dash them to pieces on the ground, and return to seek more valuable booty. Others are busy gouging out the precious stones from the stems of pipes, from saddle clothes, or the hilts of swords, or butts of pistols and fire-arms. Some swathe their bodies in stuffs crusted with precious metals and gems; others carry off useless lumber, brass pots, pictures, or vases of jade and China.

Court after court the scene is still the same. These courts open one to the other by lofty gateways ornamented with the double fish of the Royal Family of Oude, or by arched passages, in which lie the dead sepoys, their clothes smouldering on their flesh.[6]

Ethics aside, this new diversion could hardly fail to be welcome to the benighted memsahibs of the Residency. One of Maria Germon's favourite days was ornamented by the fruit of such spoils as these. She remembers 26 October was the date set for 'the prize auctions' of the property that had been collected from the ransacked palaces. 'I knew Charlie was going but had no idea he meant to purchase; however, while I was in my room Mrs Clarke came running in to tell me he had arrived with a most beautiful Cashmere shawl for me – I ran out and Charlie threw it into my arms',[7] and she was, quite simply, happy.

Maria was somewhat busier after the first relief than she had been before: at the beginning of October she was appointed *maîtresse* of the commissariat, in charge of weighing and apportioning the garrison's rations. These were reduced twice during the next six weeks or so. 'We were obliged to be most prudent,' noted the colonel's wife, Julia Inglis, 'and only eat just enough to satisfy hunger. I cannot say I ever suffered from actual hunger, but I very often felt I should like to eat more than I had, and an extra piece of chappattie was a great treat to us all.'[8] Some people – like Julia's companion Adelaide Case – had the mixed pleasure of being beneficiaries of provisions under a deceased friend's will, while auctions of food and tobacco continued sporadically. There was not the great heat to deal with now, of course

(Maria needed that shawl in the evenings) and the incidence of
disease began to abate as the weeks of the siege wore on, but
otherwise this little, concentrated world functioned much as it had
done since June:

I had an escape this evening [wrote Mrs Harris on 23 October]: a
bullet went through the leg of the chair I was sitting on; it just
glanced upwards and struck me on the side, but having expended its
force on the chair I was not hurt . . .

This morning an 18-pounder came through our unfortunate room
again, which we flattered ourselves was so safe, and which we had
made so comfortable. It broke the panel of the door, and knocked
the whole of the barricade down, upsetting everything. My dressing-
table was sent flying through the door, and if the shot had come a
little earlier, my head would have gone with it . . .[9]

There was much more military activity going on outside the
Residency boundary, too: more or less distant firing could be
heard on most days as the British defence of Lucknow evolved
slowly into an attack. Signals and secret letters brought news of
progress to the besieged regularly now, and there was even the
odd English newspaper to be found – months old, usually – getting more and more tattered and precious as it made its rounds
amongst the eager readers of each garrison.

On 31 October, a letter arrived purporting to have been written
by some European prisoners in one of the palaces in Lucknow. It
was certainly signed by them, but was uncharacteristically terse
and formal in address. The undersigned were being kindly
treated, it said, but as Julia Inglis remarked, 'of course they might
have been forced to write it, so it did not give us much comfort on
their account.'

One of those whose signature was on the letter was Madeline
Jackson, she who had managed to escape from Sitapur and found

her way to Rajah Loni Singh's palace at Mithowlie with her
brother Mountstuart, two of his colleagues (Lieutenant Burnes
and Sergeant Morton), and the three year-old orphan Sophy
Christian.

Once Madeline and her ragged and worn-out party had
reached Mithowlie, it had seemed for a while they were safe.

[W]e began to talk – and the Rajah who looked in a tremendous
fright, assured us, he would do what he could for us, and they got us
charpoys to sit on, and brought water and fruit, and after a time,
took us to a kind of long hut (we heard afterwards it was the head
gardener's) in the garden – one side was partitioned off for Sophy
and me, we were all so exhausted we lay down and slept.

M[ountstuart] called me later and they brought us something to eat –
and the sergeant got butter or ghee and plantain leaves, and dressed
our feet – which were in a dreadful state with blisters and cuts – we all
wobbled and could hardly put our feet to the ground . . .

Well, [Rajah Loni Singh] fed us, and had white sheeting clothes
made for us, and told us all the news he heard, keeping us carefully
hidden – but always denied knowing anything of Capt. and Mrs Orr
– who we had heard, he was protecting. After a few days he sent us to
a small fort in the jungle – belonging to him – it looked deserted –
and no food was brought us till quite late – and that we found out
afterwards was sent by Capt. Orr who was hidden in the jungle with
his wife and child.[10]

Patrick and Annie Orr had been stationed at Mohumdee,
where she was the only memsahib, when mutiny broke out at
nearby Shahjehanpur.[11] The subsequent massacre there had made
it imperative for Annie to be smuggled out to safety, and on 31
May she and her seven-year-old daughter, Louisa, made a twenty-
six mile march, by night, to the supposed sanctuary of sympathetic Loni Singh. Once at Mithowlie, she and the child were

consigned to a dreary, desolate and utterly empty building in the grounds; they were refused food by the wary Rajah but allowed to get their own from the village, and subsist as best they might. Astonishingly, they were joined by Patrick Orr soon after the massacre of all the Shahjehanpur and local refugees (but one) at Arungabad on 7 June: he was the sole survivor.

Despite the privation of their hiding-place, Madeline considered the Orrs to be a fortunate and generous couple:

They had their servants – and a tent – and money and a few plates and things – and we heard all their experiences . . . both Capt. Orr and Mrs Orr spoke the native language well – and managed to hear of all that was going on. They sent letters by their servants – and at last we heard Capt. Hearsey and some others had got away from Seetapore and that my poor sister [Georgiana] was with them – also Mrs Greene – and at last we got a letter from her – how grateful we were – her letter was full of hope and courage – and Capt. Hearsey wrote she was so brave and so good, she was a great help to them all. She told us she got through the river with many others and that Mrs Greene pulled her up the bank, and that they hid in the jungle, till found by some men whom they begged to save their lives. They were some of Capt. Hearsey's sowars, he had sent to try and save fugitives – so they took them to Capt. Hearsey who was hidden with a sergeant, his wife and son – they got away on elephants I think, and joined some other fugitives from another station, and were then hidden in [a] Raja's palace and were trying to get sent to Calcutta – we had several letters from Capt. Hearsey – they sent us some books, in which [Georgiana] had done little sketches of the places they were in – they were somewhere near Nynethal [Naini Tal] and sent us some quinine – Capt. H. said that she kept up all their courage – poor Mrs Greene had lost her husband. The last letter we got from them said they feared they were betrayed. Then we heard from natives that they were trying to escape in the jungles – I think that was in August. [In fact, Georgiana and her companions were captured again and eventually killed by the Moulvee of Lucknow on the day of the first relief, in revenge of British success.]

We also heard at that time that Lone Singh was suspected and would have to give us up to the rebels. We never went out of the Fort [where the Orrs by now had joined them], which was a high stone building with a kind of verandah room around three sides, a gate on the 4th and a court in the middle – we could walk on the roof without being seen from the outside and could see the top of one tree over us. We had native string beds – charpoys to sleep on – and native dishes and food – for the Orrs had only about two plates and cups – the Rajah sent some food – but the Orrs sent a servant to buy more and their servants cooked and kept the place tidy and took letters – in quills – or in the soles of their shoes – and were most faithful.[12]

These letters made the Orrs' and Jacksons' captivity well known. They received answers not only from Captain Hearsey's party (as long as it was at leisure to write) but also from Patrick's brothers in Lucknow, and even on one occasion from Sir Henry Lawrence, who included another to Loni Singh 'offering rewards if we were safely taken to the English'.

[S]omeone sent me a pair of boots – from Lucknow I think [where they could ill be spared, no doubt]. We had leather shoes made for us by a native – at least for the men and the children – Mrs Orr shared her things with me – as she had some – we all kept fairly well while in the Fort – tho the heat was dreadful – we fanned ourselves with little native fans. I used to fan myself and little Sophy most of the night – in my sleep I think – the mosquitoes were very bad too – I had a lump on my hand for a long while from those fans. Mrs Orr's Ayah used to fan her and her little girl.

We were very lucky to be with the Orrs – as we had neither money or servants and could none of us speak the language well. The children were a great comfort – little Sophy called me Mama and was a very bright, clever little girl – imitated the natives most amusingly and was a great pet – she had grown quite strong from being always in the open air. There were no doors or windows, except the Gateway which was always shut – the servants going thro the usual small one – there were arches in the verandah, in which we hung purdahs, to make our rooms. Mrs Orr, I and the children had one side, the gentlemen another, and the servants the other. I think we ate in the shady side of the Court – we had a table and a couple of chairs and stools – the poor men used to walk up and down for exercise like tigers in a den . . .

While we were in the jungle – there was a beautiful total eclipse of the sun [the same one watched so wistfully by Kate Bartrum on 18 September] – we watched it thro smoked glass or reflected in tubs of water. The effect in the forest was lovely – every leaf threw a strong shadow – like moonlight – birds twittered and went to sleep – and woke up again when the sun shone out again – and all the time the natives blew conches and beat tom toms.

Another event was a chase after a big tree lizard – about 5 feet long – it looked like a small alligator up in the tree. The natives said it was poisonous and would have killed us.

We also often had alarms of snakes – from frogs which cried like children – snakes chase them for food, poor things. We used to jump up on chairs, Mrs Orr and I and the children. There were also scares of wolves and we heard of native children being carried off by them – little Sophy was hardly ever out of my sight – she and little [Louisa] Orr both had fever badly – Capt. Orr shot peacocks and Mrs Orr made soup for little Sophy . . . The gentlemen made draughtsmen and used to have long games on the ground – marked out – we still got letters and wrote – but rescue seemed far – and the natives used to say our 'raj' was over . . .[13]

It was none the less a time of comparative comfort, this sojourn in the jungle near Mithowlie. During it the captives grew calm and almost strong; the wounds on their feet healed and, thanks to the influence of the Orrs, they were able to enjoy a degree of independence. But all this came to an end on 20 October, when Rajah Loni Singh was persuaded by lobbying rebels that as the British were losing the war (they said), hostages such as his would have little value in the end. And if he wished to preserve himself, it would be prudent to hand the sahibs and memsahibs over to them. Which he did.

[M]en came who took Capt. Orr's gun – said we were to go – would not let us take anything – Mrs Orr tried to . . . get money and her jewels and was pushed back – I tried to go for her – but was pushed back too. We thought they would cut off our heads and send them into Lucknow – but at the edge of the forest they took us to, they had two native carts – drawn by two bullocks – in which they told us to get – and a lot of soldiers marched along – M. and I and Sophy and Sergeant Morton in the 1st – Capt. and Mrs Orr and Loui and Mr Burne[s] in the other. They were only big eno. for 2 – and had no springs. They had top covers and side curtains to keep the sun out. They stopped at a village and got a smith and brought out irons – Mrs Orr and I begged them on our knees not to put them on – uselessly – they had some for Mrs Orr and me – but Capt. Orr and M. said they would take 2 sets each – so after a talk those were taken away. Those horrid irons were soldered round each ankle – and had two chains which they tied by a string round their waists – we tore our clothing in strips to wrap round them – but even then they made sore places. The poor serjeant [Morton] fainted when his were put on. All day we went on – and at every village stopped and crowds came and looked at us . . .

I woke one night, and heard them talking whether it would not be less trouble only to take our heads into Lucknow – I was frightened –

tho we knew we might be killed at any minute – and woke M. He did not fear – and wanted me to drink water and get quiet I refused and said pray for me – and we did – till quiet and courage came again to me – and ready for anything we lay down and slept again.[14]

After a few more days and nights of uncertainty, Madeline and her companions were led to the gates of Lucknow, and on towards the Kaiserbagh, the palace of deposed King Wajid Ali Shah of Oudh. Their arrival nearly caused a riot, so incensed were the rebels (daily being driven towards defeat by the British) to see such a cravenly complacent sight.

When near the palace – the soldiers seemed afraid the people would kill us and made us get out of the carts, which could not stir for the crowd – we were first and I went to Mrs Orr's cart and saw a man with a big knife make a rush at her – the soldiers stopped him and made us walk on between them – M. could hardly stand [for the fetters] and had to be supported between 2 men – Mr Burne[s] was out of his mind – Capt. Orr carried his little girl and helped his wife – I managed to lift up little Sophy – tho I could hardly do it, as she was a big child – and made the men keep off the press – the sepoys were doing their best to get us in safe . . .

[N]ear the gate, my fingers got jammed between a soldier's gun and the wall – I suppose I got very white – the blood came out under my nails – the soldier who couldn't help doing it – he was squashed against the wall – looked so very sorry – I had to smile and pretend it didn't hurt – and then we were in and the door shut against the horrid crowd.[15]

Within the palace the prisoners were treated to 'piles of different curries and kowabs [kebabs] – and yellow and white rice' and housed in 'nice big rooms with English furniture'. Their irons were taken off and medicines, when needed, administered fast and efficiently. But the suspense of waiting to hear, hourly, what was to become of them was almost intolerable: 'poor Mr Burnes and the Serjeant were both half mad, and little Sophy had a kind of falling fits – fainting quite suddenly . . .' This luxurious limbo went on for about a month until, on Monday 16 November, the sound of English voices shouting outside 'and the natives yelling and groaning and all the horrid noises of fighting' brought the news of the second – and this time successful – relief of Lucknow.

[We] just longed to be able to tell them to come at once and take the palace and the head people – they could have done it as there were no soldiers in it and they were all in dismay at this new army getting in so quickly – and they had no leader. [But] of course we should all have got killed first – and as it was, they were so infuriated, they came in saying the men must go with them. They would not take Mrs Orr and I. They wanted to take little Sophy, but left her hearing she was a girl. We were all stunned – M. kissed me and we all said goodbye.

The last I saw – they were trying to tie their hands and M. refused and tried to shake them off – I rushed to help him, but they pushed me back and pulled a curtain – and I don't know what happened – I suppose I fainted for I woke and found myself laid on a sofa and Mrs Orr pouring water over me – and I told her I saw them shooting [the men] in the Court and [they] were coming for us.

I remember her staring at me.[16]

The arrival of the second relief force, under the leadership of Sir Colin Campbell, was not the occasion for elation the first had been. Everyone was too tired. And in any case, there was such a lot to do, and so far still to go, before the safety of the besieged could be guaranteed. The women and children had to be evacuated from the Residency and somehow sent on to Calcutta, while those men who were able were needed to join forces against the failing rebels.

Sir Colin took Lucknow on 16 November; he wasted no time in issuing orders for all non-combatants to leave the compound, expecting them to be ready, with only 'what can be carried in the hand', at whatever time of the day he thought fit on 18 November. This threw Maria Germon and her companions into a frenzy of organization, hardly relieved at all by the subsequent news that an extra day was being allowed for preparations. 'Several of the ladies sat up all night stitching things of value into their petticoats', she remembers, and those who, like her, were lucky enough to have more possessions than could be carried in the hand were hard put to devise some system of smuggling them out.

Charlie Germon came up trumps again: he managed to procure for his wife 'two old men', one of whom undertook to carry a bundle of bedding for Maria and the other her dressing-case; he also petitioned for leave to accompany her part of the way through the city when the time came, there being no carriage available to take her. Such machinations were going on in every garrison of the Residency, and its population sank to sleep on the night of 18 November thoroughly exhausted by all this unaccustomed action, and 'all worn out'.

Thursday, November 19th. Charlie came over the first thing and said Captain Waterman had lent him a coolie so I had to pack another box and as Herar Singh [a loyal Sikh sepoy] had invested 35 Rupees in a pony (without orders) for me to ride, I got a side-saddle from Mrs Fayrer and then came news that the Brigadier had cancelled Charlie's leave as so many had been applying for the same – it came like a blow for this may be our parting in India. However, it was no time to give way, so I dressed in all the clothes I could, fearing I might not be able to get the others carried . . . I put on four flannel waistcoats, three pairs of stockings, three chemises, three drawers, one flannel and four white petticoats, my pink flannel dressing-gown skirt, plaid jacket and over all my cloth dress and jacket that I had made out of my habit – then tied my Cashmere shawl sash-fashion round my waist and also Charlie's silver mug and put on a worsted cap and hat and had my drab cloak put on the saddle. I forgot to say I had sewed dear Mother's fish-knife and fork in my pink skirt and had put a lot of things in the pocket of it. I had also two under-pockets, one filled with jewellery and cardcase, the other with my journal and valuable papers. I then filled my cloth skirt pocket with pencil, knife, pin-cushion, handkerchief, etc. – all my lace was sown up in a bag which I wore also.

At half-past ten Charlie and Captain Weston, with great difficulty, got me up on my pony which was no joke dressed and laden as I was and with no spring in me. Captain W. and a large party were in fits of laughter. At last I succeeded and Charlie took me out to the Baillie Guard gate and there we parted with a shake of the hands not knowing when we should meet again.[17]

Maria was lucky. She had survived, her husband had survived, she had lost no children and even seems to have gained a fair amount of property during her time under siege. Julia Inglis's family was kept intact, too, and the childless chaplain James Harris and his wife still had each other. This was unusual, though: there were very few women making their way out of the Baillie Guard Gate that Thursday who had not lost a husband, brother, sister or child – and many men who had lost their wives. There are various commemorative plaques posted around the Residency buildings and gardens today: one marking the spot where poor Miss Palmer's leg was blown off with a round-shot on the second day of the siege; another thanking Julia Inglis for her part in trying to brighten the meagre lot of the women of the 32nd Regiment who spent the 139 days of the siege amongst the rats and cockroaches of the dim tykhana; more dotted around the churchyard, remembering the names (but not the graves) of those who died. But the most affecting of all must be the huge tablet which briefly tells the story and records the statistics of those five dismal months: less than a third of those who entered the compound at the beginning of the siege lived to leave it at the end.

The evacuation of the Residency was a hazardous business. It involved a four-mile-long caravan of heavily guarded women, children, sick and wounded making their way (on a bewildering array of animals and wheels) first to the gardens of the Sikunderbagh, the scene, two days previously, of the massacre of over two thousand sepoys by the British, and then on to the Dilkusha Palace. The Dilkusha – or 'heart's delight' – was set in a park on the south-eastern outskirts of the city, near the magnificent Martinière college; here the refugees were to set up camp before staging on to Allahabad and Calcutta, by way of Cawnpore.

It was hardly a joyful affair for Kate Bartrum, this journey towards salvation. She could not celebrate her own survival after Robert's death; all that mattered was the safety of little Bobbie. At least she was spared the frenzied needlework with which Maria Germon greeted the order to abandon the Residency: 'Well! I can only carry my baby, and my worldly effects can be put into a very small compass, since they consist merely of a few old clothes.' Now that she had lost her faith (and I wonder how many more secretly suffered that particularly shameful and desolate bereavement during the course of the siege?), the long trek ahead quite terrified her.

My heart fails me at the thought of the terrible march, with no one to look after me or care for me but God. I have lost my kind friend Dr Darby, who has been wounded; and they say he will not recover. He promised to take care of me on the journey to Calcutta, but now I am utterly friendless . . .

November 20. – Camp [at the Dilkusha], five miles from Lucknow. We are at last released from our captivity. At six last evening I left the entrenchments in a doolie, with baby, passing through the Bailey Guard gate, the Furhut Buksh Palace, the Court of the Motee Munzil, and on to Secundra Bagh. In many places the road was very dangerous, and it would have been safer perhaps to have walked; but the doolie bearers ran as fast as they could, and we all reached Secundra Bagh in safety, where we were regaled with tea and bread and butter, a luxury indeed, after siege fare . . .[18] When it became dark the order was given for us to march, so we got into the doolies again, and then we heard that we were not to go on until eleven that night, so we remained in our doolies in the road. I saw Mrs Polehampton at a short distance from me: she was in distress, for her buggy-horse had fallen down and she could not get on. She came and sat on the ground by my side, and then returned . . . to try and get a doolie, so I was again left alone; the night was so cold, and poor baby could not get to sleep amid such confusion. At eleven p.m. we were ordered to move on as quietly as possible. We had been going on for a long time, when I thought it was remarkably quiet, for I could not hear the tramp of the doolie bearers behind, and I looked out and found I was quite alone in an open plain. I asked the bearers whither they were taking me, when they said they had lost their way. It immediately occurred to me that they were taking me to the sepoys: I sprung out of the doolie, and ran with my child in my arms, screaming across the plain until I heard voices answering. I knew not whether they were friends or foes: but still I ran on and met a party of our own men. 'Why,' they exclaimed, 'how did you come to be here? We, too, have lost our way, and only know that we are close to the enemy's pickets. However,' they said, 'do not get into the doolie again, and we will do our best for you, poor girl.' They were so kind, and helped me on, for the sand was very heavy, so that with baby in my arms I could scarcely walk.

After walking some distance we heard a noise amongst the trees, when the men exclaimed, 'Oh God, it is all up with us; we are done for now.' They placed me in the middle of them and whispered, 'Don't scream, and we may be able to creep on presently.' I was paralyzed with terror, and pressed my baby closer to me . . . We presently moved quietly on, hearing nothing more, and at three the next morning reached our own camp, where, wearied and exhausted with fatigue and terror I sat upon the ground to indulge in a burst of tears . . .[19]

They all stayed some days at the Dilkusha, sleeping on the ground in tents, reading the letters which had been saved for them (which in Kate's case included several from Robert on his way to Lucknow) and preparing for the dangerous expedition to Calcutta. Kate's reserves of courage were sinking fast as they neared Cawnpore:

November 28. – Heard heavy firing today . . . and had to make a forced march of thirty-eight miles. A most weary and fatiguing day: the camp was pitched within two miles of the river. We did not reach it until three the next morning. I had no tent, and sat on the wet ground until daylight, with my baby in my lap. It was a lovely night; the stars were shining so brightly; but it was bitterly cold: no one came to speak to me . . . I felt that night as though I was forsaken by God and man.[20]

Kate's party eventually reached Calcutta on 30 January (having spent Christmas in transit at Allahabad) and her passage home in the *Himalaya* was fixed for 12 February. Emmie Polehampton was to accompany her, and once she had actually been aboard and seen the cabin in which they would sail for home, Kate's battered spirits began to recover. Bobbie had been sent some pretty new clothes by his grandmother in England, and these, together with all her hopes for his future, tempered his mother's nagging fears for his health. He was looking terribly tired and pale, and no wonder, but Kate was sure that the sea voyage would 'renovate his strength, and that before he reaches England he will be quite a different child.'

On 18 February, Mrs Fayrer and Julia Inglis called to wish the Bartrums *bon voyage*.

They were grieved to see my little darling looking so unwell: he seems very weak, but I take him out every evening for a drive, and he is so quiet I do not think he is in pain . . .

February 11. – My dear child seemed so weak this morning, and I could not get him to take any food. Mrs Polehampton told me that Dr Goodeve thought my baby very ill. I knew what she meant, but I *cannot* spare him, and I do not think God will take away my little lamb when I have nothing else left. He slept nearly all day and was very quiet: he did not appear to be suffering. In the evening I laid him on the bed and he seemed to be sleeping comfortably. At one a.m. he got restless, but when I spoke to him he looked up and smiled; then I walked about with him till he began to struggle, and I was frightened and called Mrs Polehampton. She told me to lay him in my lap: he was gasping for breath, when I turned away my head, for I *could* not see my child die. She said, 'Look, how bright his eyes are growing! . . . too bright for ours to look upon' . . .

When the morning came, we gathered some orange blossoms and placed them round him, who was 'no longer babe but angel', and when his little coffin came we laid him in it . . . At five p.m., Dr Fayrer came and fastened down the lid, when I had given him his last kiss . . . We carried him in the mourning coach to the cemetery, where many met us, and showed by their silent sympathy that they had learned to weep with those who wept . . .

Now I could realise that he was gone from me for evermore, when I went back and found no joyous baby welcome, no little arms to clasp my neck; but there lay the dress he last had worn, the little hat and shoes, and the toys about the room; but where was baby? 'All Thy waves and Thy storms have gone over me.'

February 12. – Sailed from Calcutta and bade farewell to the land where all I best loved had found a resting place.[21]

11

The Memsahibs Depart

Quit this country. Now it is no place for women.[1]

After half a year shut inside, it was decided the denizens of the fort at Agra might leave. Come December 1857 more and more troops were arriving from England to form sweeping columns meant to cleanse the whole Mutiny arena of any last trace of insurrection. The unpredictable and disparate nature of the uprising had changed: by now it had hardened into a full-scale British military campaign against a series of organized rebel armies fighting under the leadership (too late) of a zealous, charismatic and accomplished company of native heroes and heroines. The opportunists, the bandits and badmashes who had been happy to jump on the bandwagon before, were largely silent now. It was safe for the memsahibs to come out of hiding and time, at last, to go home.

Before Ruth Coopland and her companions embarked on their various journeys from Agra, however, a 'grand fête' was held in their honour. It was arranged on 9 December by those soldiers who had been nursed by the ladies of the fort as a thank-you for their care, and although everyone was invited, only those memsahibs who had done their duty in the hospital were allowed to wear the huge red and white satin rosettes the grateful 9th Lancers had made them. One such nurse, Mary Vansittart, remembered the moment that rosette was pinned to her dress as one of the proudest of her life.[2]

The fête, or picnic party, was held in what must be the most beautiful (and most unsuitable) setting for such an occasion on earth: the Taj Mahal. Mrs Coopland relished the implied insult:

It was a very gay scene. In one of the mosques of the Taj, all the ladies, children, officers, and soldiers were gathered; and here and there might be seen a native, looking green with rage at their sacred building being thus desecrated. The mosque was beautifully decorated with flowers, and a table was spread with all the dainties that could be procured. Almost every one looked happy and cheerful, and the ladies went from one soldier to another saying kind words, and congratulating them on their recovery . . .[3]

There was a dance after tiffin, and promenades through the gardens to the banks of the Jumna where one could gaze at the huge red fort in the distance and begin to think of the future.

The arrangements for evacuating the fort depended on the imminent arrival of a column of troops (fifteen miles long, it was said) marching from Delhi to Cawnpore. It had left the capital during the first week of December and was expected at Agra within days. The idea was for it to gather up the Agra fugitives on its way through and escort them to Cawnpore, whereupon they would travel on to Calcutta either by steamer or overland. But the column was waylaid by rebels and, what with this and the reports coming through of heavy fighting between the British and the so-called Gwalior Contingent of mutineers at Cawnpore, it seemed sensible to abandon the plan. This meant that those who were able to make their own way safely out of Agra were free to do so and, along with several other memsahibs of the fort, Ruth Coopland decided to head for Simla. She had an aunt there, with whom she and the baby might stay until it was possible to travel down to Bombay and get home that way instead.

They left on 12 December, Ruth armed with some new pillows made for her by a friend ('as we were to take our bedding with us') and an early Christmas present of a plum cake baked in a biscuit tin. She went almost reluctantly:

I now reflected on the past, and thought what a good thing it was, that we [widows], who had been so heavily afflicted, were thrown together amongst others all more or less afflicted by the same cause, instead of being left selfishly to brood over and cherish our sorrows; in which case we might have succumbed, and perhaps lost our reason. But living in a constant state of anxiety, we were compelled to mix with others and sympathise with them; which opened our hearts, and made us feel less desolate.[4]

Poor Kate Bartrum could have done with a little of what another sufferer[5] called this 'beautiful brotherhood' amongst the memsahibs of the Mutiny. It was healing.

Ruth's trek to Simla took her through both Meerut and Delhi. She spent Christmas in Delhi, and indulged with most other British visitors there in its peculiar sightseeing attractions. She saw the room, for example, in which Annie Jennings and Mary Clifford were killed on the morning of 11 May – 'the stains of blood on the wall are yet to be seen' – and for a special seasonal treat, was taken on Christmas afternoon with friends to see the cracked old puppet king of Delhi himself. He looked suitably degraded, thought Ruth, surrounded by slovenry and filth.

We ladies, after gazing at the king and his son . . . were allowed to see the queen, Zeenat Mahal, – a favour not granted to the gentlemen. It seemed absurd to humour thus their silly prejudices, when they had spared no European in their power any indignity or insult. However, we raised the 'chick' which separated the queen's room from the king's, and entered a very small bare, shabby room. Seated on a charpoy we beheld a large, bold-looking woman, with not the least sign of royalty or dignity about her. She seemed about forty; her complexion was tawny, and her face large and coarsely featured, with darting black eyes and wide mouth, and dark hair partially concealed under her white cotton chudda . . . Judging by her looks, she seemed capable of inciting the king to deeds of blood, which she was accused of having done. She began asking Mrs Garstone [Ruth's companion] and the other lady about their husbands, and why Mrs Garstone had not brought her children, as she wished to see them; then, looking at my black dress, she sneeringly asked me what had become of my 'sahib.' I was so angry at her look and tone of heartless contempt, that I said 'Chupero' (silence), and walked out of her presence.[6]

After deciding that Delhi should be 'rased to the ground' in memory of 'all the victims of the mutinies' (by which, of course, she means the British), Ruth left the city for the foothills of the Himalaya, arriving in Simla at the beginning of January.

My aunt's house was . . . three or four miles from the entrance of the station. After ascending a steep path . . . the bright lights gleamed, and I was soon joyfully welcomed by my aunt and cousins . . . I was delighted to find myself in an English-looking, brightly-lighted drawing-room, and actually to go upstairs into a homelike bed-room, papered, carpeted, and curtained, warmed with a glowing fire, and having a little cot for my baby, and then to descend into a comfortable dining-room, where a Christmas dinner was spread . . .

All the houses have names, which is very unusual in India: my aunt's was 'Closeburn,' and another 'The Rookery.' Simla is the Cheltenham of India.[7]

– and nearly as welcoming, in its comforting familiarity, as Surrey-like Gwalior had been to Ruth almost exactly a year ago, when she first set foot in India.

It was a very busy place, Simla, during these closing stages of the Mutiny. Up until now it had been considered a place of comparative safety, a refuge to which memsahibs still at large at the beginning of the troubles might be dispatched by preoccupied husbands. Its role changed into a sort of *poste restante* station, where wives would go to wait for forwarding instructions, or widows to recoup their strength before facing the journey home (whether that home be elsewhere in India, or back in the mother-country). And slowly, the burden of those memsahibs' writings home from Simla and its neighbouring stations changed too, from the immediate horrors of the Mutiny to more pressing, mundane matters.

Augusta Becher – she whose hair had turned grey overnight during that rather shame-faced scare at Simla back in May – was aggrieved not to have been allowed to follow her husband Sep's column when it left for duty in November. Now her complaints were not of the general direness of circumstances, but of a very particular and personal kind: Sep's being passed over for promotion, and the debts they had incurred through not having been paid for three months, for example. This lack of money – just when it was most needed – was a common problem. Minnie Wood, who spent the Mutiny in Jhelum growing steadily more and more disillusioned by her husband and disgusted by India, could think of little else. Archie declared himself too ill in December 1857 to resume his rather tedious captaincy (and so start earning a tolerable salary again): he preferred rather to sit around moping about the family's imminent penury and whining at his mother-in-law's meanness in refusing to bail him out. Minnie was terrified lest their lack of funds might prevent them from escaping this ghastly country, whose only gifts to her had been a climate hot enough to blast the skin from her face, and piles. There was not even enough money to pay a doctor to attend the baby, who distressed his mother vastly by noisily teething and constantly wetting himself all over everyone. What was more, Minnie had discovered herself to be pregnant again ('It sickens me to hear people talk of Merry Christmas . . .'). Never mind history in the making: Minnie wanted out.

At least she had her liberty: there were those at the beginning of the new year who still dared not – or could not – escape from hiding. Reports were seeping through to Calcutta of a Mrs Phillips, formerly (like Madeline Jackson) of Sitapur, who was kept concealed in a native village for a total of ten months before finally being persuaded the war was over.[8] The Gowan and Belcham families had only just emerged from their covert near Allyghur, where they had been disguised under the protection of a local police officer for five months. Their people at home had supposed them dead, massacred at Bareilly during the mutiny there on 31 May. In fact, a Belcham baby had been *born* during their disappearance, and all seven refugees declared themselves for ever in debt to Mithoo Lal, the policeman, and the kind and faithful Hindus of his village.[9]

And what about Madeline Jackson and Annie Orr in Lucknow? Their incarceration was the longest of all (except, perhaps, for the life-long affair of Ulrica Wheeler). They heard the second relief arrive from their palace prison, and Madeline saw the murder of her brother Mountstuart, Patrick Orr, and Messrs Burnes and Morton – but nothing else happened. No dramatic liberation by the British, no sordid little back-room execution: just blankness.

No one came near us or brought us food that day [16 November, the day the men were killed] or the next. We had all had breakfast and the remains had not been taken away and luckily there were bits of chupatties and rice left which we gave the children . . . Mrs Orr and I had none for about 36 hours – 2 days and a night – I got light-headed very soon. I think we both hoped we were dying . . .

Then the Residency began to shell the Palace – (the place we were in was getting knocked to pieces) so the soldiers took us to another . . . We were then taken to the little room and verandah where we were for a long time. I heard the Residency people going past at night . . . [The tiny room] was high eno' – tho' only about 7 or 8 feet high – but it was only long eno' for us to lie down in and not broad eno' for us to lie flat side by side in – so the children laid with their heads on our arms, lower down – there was a door we shut at night, and it was winter and cold – there was a raised ledge on one side, we sat on. We had no chairs – or tables . . . In the covered verandah the guard sat night and day – about 12 or 20 who took turns – they sat with their matchlocks loaded and fuses lighted – they were to take care of us and also to prevent our getting away – I amused myself sometimes walking close up to their guns – seeing them clutch them and their lighted match – I suppose they thought I should shoot them – I laughed . . .

Then little Sophy got worse – and one day went on fainting and sleeping – I did not understand but Mrs Orr saw at once she was going and laid her on a rezai in the open air – the natives bought one of their priests to say prayers over her and to bless some water in a cup which they gave her and said she would be well – but she only breathed hard a little and then just went to sleep – poor little darling – I had no idea she was so ill, and was heart-broken – Mrs Orr sent word to [Wajid] Ali, who was the head man, who took care of all the women in the Palace – and was taking care of us – and he came and ordered people to bury her and at night they took her away. We had wrapped her in a rezai and Mrs Orr gave another to the man, for fear he should take that. Mrs O. said afterwards she must have had water on the brain, which comes from much fever – I think it was the 22nd November that she died.

I had now no one to do anything for – and couldn't eat – and one day Mrs Orr told me the men must see me eat – or would make me – I said give me anything but don't let them come near me. So the chief sat in front and I ate – rice – which seemed like dry hay – the wretch encouraging me – and my tears streaming at my misery . . .

We heard we were to have been killed . . . but a Moulvie said no success attended them because they killed women and children and we were the only ones left and must be kept for hostages. Soon after Mrs Orr showed me a little scrap of the Bible she had kept – it had wrapped up some quinine for little Sophy – Isaiah 51 – verses 11, 12, 13, 14 and 23 . . . [The captive exile hasteneth that he may be loosed, and that he should not die in the pit, nor that his bread should fail.] I was very wretched, and did not take its comfort then tho' I did later – I gave it back to her saying – 'it is yours.'[10]

There were rumours soon after Sophy's death that Madeline and Annie were to be separated, and each assigned to one of the rebel chiefs as his own particular prize, but these evaporated in the panic surrounding reports of an imminent British attack on the women's hiding-place. Dressed in the silks and bangles of Lucknow ladies, they were evacuated to another house, which Madeline heard had been her sister Georgiana's last home before she and her companions were killed at the approach of the second relief. 'I looked all round the walls to see if they had by chance written on them – but there was nothing.'

I got very ill with dysentery and used to faint – now I think of it, it was just what little Sophy had – 'Sophes', she called herself, poor little darling. One day I fell flat on my face in the court[yard] – my shoes flew over my head and a candlestick I had also – the guard opposite rushed across and I had such a horror of anyone touching me – I managed to spring straight up, stand, and say 'stop' (which they did) – then I said 'give me my shoes' – and crept back to Mrs

Orr – she and the Ayah made me smoke opium, I fancy in a hookah, after eating, which did me good . . .

We took turns to cook our dinners – Mrs Orr taught me to make excellent curries and kowabs – the monkeys used to be very troublesome – once I was cooking and a lot came jabbering round me – I rapped their fingers with a stick for some time – but so many came – and began pulling my clothes and my hair – so I ran away – banging a door against them – they instantly seized the sauce pan – and upset it – as there was oil in it, there was a blaze, which frightened them away – and I had to cut more vegetables and get more dinner ready.

We heard the English troops were close to Lucknow and would soon storm the place – letters were sent and received and Wazid Ali knew the rewards offered for us – but seemed very hopeless. Then he arranged to send little Louie Orr to the E[nglish] Camp. She was dressed like a native, her feet and hands stained – and was carried out of the house like a bundle of clothes on the Ayah's back – she was a very slight child – could speak the language perfectly and knew she was to pretend to be the Ayah's child – then the Ayah was to make her over to a Sowar who was to say she had small pox – and he rode off with her to the E. Camp – he was stopped several times by natives – but at the word small pox they left him – and she was got safely in – but those 2 or 3 days were dreadful for the poor mother.

Wazid Ali was always changing our guard or bribing them. He gave us stuff to dye our hands and feet to be ready if they could get us away – at last the English shells began to fall and our house was suffering. I saw a cannon ball hit the wall but it only knocked a bit of plaster off – the shells seemed to do more damage.

Then he got a dhoolie for us – we were known [by the natives] to be hidden somewhere so all dhoolies were stopped and hands had to be shown – so I had to be ready to show mine as mine were smallest – they were stained but my nails were too pink for natives' hands – we were stopped once, but the people with us said we were court ladies and could not show our hands – and we were allowed to go on. I looked thro' the chinks in the curtains and saw groups of natives sitting talking – till the range of the shells came nearer – and then move farther and sit down again in the calmest way. We were taken to a beautifully carved wooden house – Hindoo – nobody saw us, as we were treated as court ladies . . . They brought us some very delicious cream to eat . . . We were given a long upper room with peep holes which looked into a big covered court where the native ladies were. They looked so pretty with long satin trousers and gauze veils and coats and their hair turned back and braded in one long tail with strands of gold and colours nearly to the ground. Eunuchs went in and out among them . . .

We were getting very anxious that news of where we were should be got to the English – but our messengers [Mrs Orr's trusty servants] came back saying they could not get near. Shells and cannon ball came overhead with such a noise – almost touching the roof – we used to watch the shells which looked lovely – a ball of smoke by day and of fire by night. W. Ali was very anxious by now – as it had been found out that he had carried us off as hostages and troops were coming to kill him and us too – so he had got men and fighting was going on – when we heard a rush below and a rush up our stairs and I flew out to see what was happening and there was a tall Englishman! We were saved! I called out and ran back to Mrs Orr. He came in and another Englishman ran up – Capt. [Macneil] and Mr Bogle – they said 'Are you Miss Jackson and Mrs Orr? Come at once.' Wazid Ali came, and a number of those we had thought were native ladies but were writers' [clerks'] wives – half castes – and a palkee was got. Mr Bogle stopped to look after the rest – and a lot of little Ghoorkas carried us off – up and down ravines like cats – Capt. [Macneil] with us – and we were in the English Camp, saved. It seemed such an impossible thing – English soldiers rushed out to greet us – and Sir Colin Campbell and the Ghoorka Chief and a lot of others – telegrams were sent to England at once – and Calcutta – they asked me who I wanted sent to in India and I burst into tears and said all mine were killed. They took us to some tent some officers gave us – Mrs Orr's brothers were sent and next day her little girl was in her arms."

It was the beginning of March, 1858.

Most fugitive memsahibs from the Mutiny ended up, sooner or later, at Calcutta. For Madeline that is where the journey home ended: she married her cousin Elphinstone Jackson, who was Judge of the High Court there, and settled to bring up a family and write – some twenty years after the event – her memoirs of what went on during those long weeks between the outbreak at Sitapur and the fortunate arrival of Messrs Macneil and Bogle. For others it acted as a far-flung outpost of home: a place where sympathy, practical support and convivial – refreshingly elective – company were offered and accepted with equal gratification. Charlotte Canning was a natural axis for the various relief operations that were swiftly set up as soon as the refugees started arriving in Calcutta. She was able to collate and disseminate news of various survivors, making countless visits to congratulate or comfort them and bestowing on an extraordinary number of new-born babies what appeared to be a peculiarly popular favour: Godmotherhood. When Helena Angelo had been so indignantly forced to leave Cawnpore by her husband last May, she failed to mention that she was pregnant; her son, born on 21 September to a father now dead, was one of Charlotte's first spiritual charges – even though she did not actually see the baby until Helena brought him, with his sisters, to show her just before embarking for England on 4 December. The family made a deep impression. 'Poor woman,' wrote Charlotte afterwards. 'I cannot describe the feeling of seeing those little innocent sweet-looking children, who so very narrowly escaped being murdered, or, as they say, thrown up into the air and caught on bayonets!'[12] She was cheered to hear that the government had promised to pay Helena a year of her husband's salary, as well as a pension, and the Relief Fund was paying for an outfit of clothes and her passage home.

This Relief Fund was financed largely by the public subscriptions that had been pouring into Calcutta from Britain at the rate of £800 to £1,000 per day since July 1857.[13] Its official objectives, noted in a memorandum sent by the Relief Committee to the Lord Mayor of London on 22 October, were pretty well all-embracing, providing

1. Board and lodging on arrival in Calcutta for refugees who are without homes or friends to receive them;
2. Clothing for refugees;
3. Monthly allowances for the support of families who are not boarded and lodged by the Sub-Committee;
4. Loans to sufferers to provide furniture, clothing, &c.;
5. Free grants to sufferers for the same purpose;
6. Passage and diet-money on board river steamers to all who have not been provided with the same by the Government;
7. Loans to officers and others to pay for the passage of their families to England;
8. Free passage to England for the widows and families of officers and other sufferers, including travelling expenses to Bombay and Calcutta;
9. Education of the children of sufferers.[14]

Not everyone took advantage of all that was on offer, however: perhaps there was nothing to go home to in England. Charlotte Canning heard of one officer's wife who, having been granted her passage and £50 for clothes, was desperate to find a soldier's widow to accompany her and help with the children. There was none 'of any sort or kind' to be found: 'They like to stay in a regiment and marry again. It does not sound very feeling, but I believe the practice is common. I am told of a Bengal Artillery widow who was such a good cook and menagere that she was snapped up directly and had four husbands in succession, and those chosen out of many aspirants.'[15]

From November onwards Calcutta, amongst other ports, began to welcome arrivals from England, as well as waving off its re-lieved emigrants. These were the troops sent out to help mop up the mess in the aftermath of the Mutiny proper. Charlotte Can-ning had heard of some officers being allowed to bring out their wives, which was madness.

No one can imagine how wretched they will be in the crowded hotels, with all sorts of people passing through . . . They never will see their husbands [as Augusta Becher found] until the country is com-pletely settled, and they will not hear from them much oftener than in England, and it is most improbable that they will have a chance of nursing them if wounded, for in all this time hardly any wounded officers have come down.[16]

Even Florence Nightingale herself had been advised not to travel out to India: Charlotte refused her offer of help, saying there was nothing at all for her to do 'in her line of business'.[17]

Nevertheless, there were fresh memsahibs arriving and ex-pecting to be able to follow their husbands through camp and cantonment together. They hoped to join the likes of our old friend Mrs Muter of Meerut, who succeeded in staying with her venerable colonel until he was sent home sick in February 1859. She was not a great favourite amongst the other ladies staying on – through design or default – after the Mutiny's end. The unchisarit-able Minnie Wood came across her in the convalescent station of Murree (where the hapless Archie was engaged in trying to recoup his strength and some money): 'Mrs Muter is very prim, wears awfully shabby, old-fashioned clothes, and her back looks as if it had a poker down it. She never pronounces her 'r's, and talks of 'webels' and 'wifles', which nearly kills me with laughter.' The colonel, on the other hand, was 'a brick', tall and good-looking. A shame, really.

One new arrival who did manage to flout expectations and accompany her officer husband on (almost) the whole of his eight-month, 2000-mile tour of duty in northern India was Mrs Fanny Duberly.

Fanny's was a sensational name already: in 1855 her book describing the hefty part she had played in the Crimean War was published,[18] with its centre-piece eye-witness account of the Charge of the Light Brigade. She had ridden with her husband at the head of the Eighth Hussars, honey-blonde and beautiful in a habit of sky-blue and gold, and become their elegant and spirited doyenne, as daring and eager as the rest. Perhaps it was her own mutinous spirit that impelled her to accompany Captain Henry Duberly again on his posting as Regimental Paymaster to join the Rajputana Column in December 1857. No one seems to have questioned her (non-existent) right to be there on horseback amongst the combatants, and it was only the comparative tedium of the whole exercise that stopped her second book, *Campaigning Experiences ... during the Suppression of the Mutiny*, becoming as fascinating a success as the first.

No doubt the unfeminine exploits of Fanny met with a sour response from her sister memsahibs in India. Why should she be allowed in camp and on the march when they were expressly forbidden even to see their serving husbands? One officer's wife, Charlotte Dampier, was so incensed at the official order against ladies travelling 'up country' to be with their spouses that she planned her own small insurrection in defiance. She and husband Henry secretly arranged that she should come anyway, from Calcutta to Bhagalpore, some 200 miles to the north, with her two sisters and their children for moral support, and it was not until Charlotte's party had been a week on the road that Henry

changed his mind. He had heard that officers were being sus-
pended for encouraging the memsahibs: it was too great a risk.
And so the women were left stranded for two months until the
order (which had been expected at one time to extend for a year or
more)[19] was lifted. Fanny, through sheer bravado (or arrogance?),
got away with it.

Another thing about Fanny that annoyed her peers was her
professed admiration for some of the Indian women she met
during the expedition of 1858–9 – and with one in particular, the
chief Rani of Bhuj:

One thing struck me: when in conversation with the ranee, she asked
rather eagerly if I had ever been actually present at a battle. On
being answered in the affirmative, she fell back in her chair and
sighed. A whole lifetime of suppressed emotion seemed to be compre-
hended in that short sigh![20]

There is much to be said about the part played by Indian
women during what they would term the First War of Independence. Far more than I can say here. Unlike any of the Mutiny's
memsahibs, several of these women were active fighters for their
cause, and in the opinion of *The Times*, at least, showed 'more
sense and nerve' than all the so-called leaders of the rebellion put
together. They are regarded as heroines of the new India even
now, and their stamping-ground is dotted with flamboyant mem-
orials to their physical and spiritual bravery, refreshing antidotes to
the rather pompous and lugubriously gothic inscriptions com-
memorating all those who died for their country (i.e. all the British
who died for England) still to be seen almost everywhere else.

The 'ordinary' women of India we know disappointingly little
about. There is a series of alternately heart-warming and disturbing vignettes running through the chronicles of the Mutiny of
native women risking their lives for the memsahibs of the house-

hold (think of Emma Larkins's Ayah, for example),[21] or being surrounded in their villages and indiscriminately burned to death; of shadowy figures in tattered saris nursing and sheltering fugitives in their own homes, and being killed and thrown down wells by their husbands to avoid the dishonour of being raped by the British.[22] There must have been countless sacrifices made in loyalty to the rebel ideal – for the women must have responded more to an ideal of freedom for their sons than the badmash rabble amongst those doing the fighting – but they remain unrecorded. Only the glamorous few made it into Indian folklore and their legends are as colourful as any the Mutiny produced.

Azizun of Cawnpore is one of the gaudiest of these heroines. She was a prostitute – like Hosainee Khanum, chatelaine of the Bibigarh – who seems to have been particularly attached to the sowars of the 2nd Cavalry, on whom she would bestow her favours in return not for money but a vow of heart-felt patriotism. During the siege of Cawnpore she set up the headquarters of what became known as the Comfort Brigade in a gun battery to the north of Wheeler's entrenchment, whence she and a group of her sister courtesans would tour the various rebel positions, armed and dressed in cavalry uniform, distributing food, drink, and other blandishments to the men. They nursed the wounded, relayed information from one post to another, and generally made themselves an indispensable part of Nana Sahib's forces. 'Azizun the Brave' is even credited by some (as, you will remember, was Hosainee Khanum) with responsibility for the Bibigarh massacre. It was Azizun, they say,[23] who persuaded the Nana that the people wanted these women and children dead, and that unless he ordered their slaughter his position as rebel leader would be politically untenable.

Azizun was interviewed by the thorough Colonel Williams along with everyone else he could find after Cawnpore was taken back by the British; her deposition is, understandably, unilluminating.[24]

She was accused by others interrogated by Williams of having been promised unimaginable riches – 'a houseful of gold coins' – for her part in mustering anti-British feeling during the Mutiny, but it was the stated general policy of the government not to punish mere women, and Azizun the Brave soon melted into the bustling anonymity of bazaar life, and disappeared.

So did the un-named heroine of the Sikunderbagh massacre in Lucknow, the episode during which some 2,000 sepoys were killed by the British at the time of the second relief. But if you look carefully in a little railed-off courtyard opposite what is now the Botanical Museum you will see an unlovely statue – a plinth with the crumbling bust of a severe-looking lady on top – which commemorates her moment of glory during the Struggle for Freedom in 1857. The legend on the side tells her story.

The Unknown Heroine. In the centre of the court was a tree. When the slaughter was almost over and a number of British soldiers lay dead [under it] the Colonel asked an officer to look at [the] tree. The officer couldn't see so he fired and down fell a body. The person he had shot was a woman whereupon he bursts into tears with regret saying I would rather have died . . . than have harmed her.

Even though she had quietly been picking off those of his comrades who were feckless enough to be resting in the shade? They all seemed to meet with some British admiration, these Indian Mutiny heroines. The attitude is a little like Viscount Canning's when congratulating the Begum of Bhopal for her constancy against the rebels: she had been an unswerving ally, he said, and a staunch friend. 'And you a woman, too!' A staunch enemy, if female, was just as fascinating. They were Amazons (foils to the memsahib angels) and awfully good value. Especially the Rani Lakshmibai of Jhansi, whom her greatest adversary on the battle-field (General Sir Hugh Rose) could not but compliment as 'the bravest and the best military leader of the rebels' and – the greatest accolade, this – 'a man among the mutineers'.

The Rani's story elicits the same sort of controversy as her comrade-in-arms Nana Sahib. The wholesale massacre of Jhansi's European population on 8 June,[25] of which the Eurasian Mrs Mutlow and her children were sole survivors – may or may not have been the Rani's fault. She certainly had justification, in the rebels' eyes, for wanting the British not only out but gone, and she was blamed, accordingly, as the 'Jezebel of India'. But her attitude to the government afterwards suggests that she only ever intended loyalty to the British. She was celebrated now – as then – as her country's Joan of Arc, its Queen Boudicca, and she did fight most fiercely for Jhansi in the end. There is a famous and rousing statue of her in Gwalior and portraits of her on station walls all over the place depicting her as one of the four figureheads of the First War of Independence (the other three being the Nana Sahib and his fellow rebel leaders, Tantia Topi and Rao Sahib). And yet at one stage, even during the revolt itself, she was officially entrusted with the local government of Jhansi as proxy for the very authorities who had denied her inheritance.

Rani Lakshmibai was the widow of Jhansi's former ruler. The Maharajah had died in 1853, just two days after adopting a boy whom he named as his heir. This practice of adoption was a common one and never (up until now) open to dispute: if there were no natural successor, a legally-chosen one would do. Lakshmibai was entrusted by her husband with the upbringing and training of her new son, and with the management of his inheritance – Jhansi – for as long as she should live.

However, Lord Dalhousie, Governor-General at the time of the Maharajah's demise, was not inclined to honour such traditions, and proclaimed instead that although the Rani and her 'son' would receive a generous pension, and be allowed to keep their personal possessions, Jhansi itself would be annexed by the British. The Maharajah's line was finished.

Just as Nana Sahib had done in similar circumstances, Lakshmibai appealed first to the government in India and then, by representative, to London. Especially when it transpired that all her husband's debts were to be paid out of the promised pension. Nothing changed, though, and she and the boy settled down in their redundant palace to wait. Eventually justice would be done.

When the Mutiny broke out, it seemed natural for the rebels to seek the Rani's support, and they did. She was granted a personal bodyguard by the British to protect her from them, and promised loyalty in return. But the small force she had been assigned was not enough to discourage the massing mutineers from demanding her patronage, and she asked for more help. It was not forthcoming. So her argument, when she failed to do anything to save the Europeans in Jhansi, was that she could not: she was under siege herself. Anarchy ensued. After the massacre, she sent desperate and repeated messages to the British still pleading for help not only against the rebels but against rival factions emerging to claim Jhansi for themselves. Other than being requested to manage as best she might until the arrival of a new resident Superintendent, she was ignored.

Lakshmibai never openly confessed herself an enemy of the British until the end of March 1858, when action against the Gwalior contingent of rebels was at its height. By now Rose's force had beaten its way from Indore to the titanic walls of Jhansi's ancient fort, which he held under siege for two weeks before the rebels inside were able to escape (with the loss of some 5,000 lives) and join Tantia Topi's troops at Kalpi, a hundred miles away. The Rani – *their* Rani – rode with them.

[She] must have been very handsome when she was younger . . . [noticed one British witness.] The eyes were particularly fine and the nose very delicately shaped. She was not very fair, though she was far from black [and had] . . . a remarkably fine figure . . .[26]

She used to dress like a man (with a turban) and rode like one . . . She is a wonderful woman, very brave and determined. It is fortunate for us that the men are not all like her.[27]

From now on, Lakshmibai was committed to the rebel cause, and fought vigorously in its defence. She was killed near Gwalior, shot while charging on horseback, with two women companions at her side; before she expired she insisted on sharing out amongst her fellow soldiers all her jewels, and when she had gone, the wailing hung over the place like a pall.

Thirty years later, an Englishman called Martin is reported to have made a visit to her son (in a letter now unfortunately lost) expressly to assure him that she had never been a real traitor at all. 'Your poor mother was very unjustly and cruelly dealt with – and no one knows her true case as I do. The poor thing took no part whatever in the massacre of the European residents of Jhansi in June 1857. On the contrary . . .'[28]

I wonder if the son was pleased. Or convinced. Because he had presumably heard, as others had, what his mother had replied when first told of Dalhousie's plans to annexe her home. Quiet and firm, she made a vow: 'I shall never surrender my Jhansi.'

A slightly less active kindred spirit of Rani Lakshmibai was the formidable Begum Hazrat Mahal, wife of King Wajid Ali of Oudh. Although she shared the prostitute Azizun's humble beginnings, the Begum rose to heights so dizzy that she counted herself the equal of Queen Victoria – and perhaps even her superior.

Hazrat Mahal was one of the king's youngest and most alluring wives. She had been talent-spotted as an ordinary dancing girl and, once married to her admirer, had become one of the zenana's most forceful residents. When Wajid Ali was deposed by the British on their annexation of Oudh in 1856, and sent into exile in Calcutta, Hazrat Mahal was left in the palace in Lucknow to tend to her twelve-year-old son and press his claim to the throne. This child appears, in fact, to have been illegitimate, and the offspring of the Begum's life-long lover (who must somehow have got past the palace eunuchs)[29] – but this in no way cooled her ardour in pursuing, through him, the position of the Kingdom of Oudh's Regent Queen Mother.

After the evacuation of the Lucknow Residency in November 1857, Generals Outram and Campbell, having failed to hold the city for the British, planted a stronghold of troops in the gardens of the Alumbagh, to the south of the city, and withdrew. This gave the Begum her chance to emerge as the people's warrior queen, their natural figurehead (given the absence of the king himself), and she seized the opportunity by staging a Grand Address, during which she ringingly exhorted the rebels to fight for their kingdom, their pride, and their self-respect. 'The whole army is in Lucknow,' she cried to the assembled thousands at the durbar, 'but is without courage. Why does it not attack the Alumbagh? Is it waiting for the English to be reinforced, and Lucknow to be surrounded? How much longer am I to pay the sepoys for doing nothing? Answer now, and if fight you won't, I shall negotiate with the English to spare my life.'[30]

It was one of the great rhetorical set pieces of the Mutiny campaign. But it did not avail the Begum much: the British were back in Lucknow as victors by March 1858 (when Madeline Jackson was finally freed) and on 1 November, another queen in what the rebels derisorily dubbed 'Far-off Englishstan' was staking her claim not only to Oudh, but to the whole of what in the good old bad old days had been British India. The proclamation published by Victoria that day was designed to re-establish the British Raj, and was full of incomprehensibly comforting formulae promising, essentially, the moral preservation of the status quo, except that the Queen and her government were India's rulers now, instead of that amiable but flawed old character John Company. It was hardly very reassuring in its protestations that, for example, '[w]e desire no extension of our present territorial possessions; and while we will permit no aggression upon our dominions or our rights to be attempted with impunity, we will sanction no encroachment upon those of others.' Her Majesty promised, however, that 'the natives of our Indian territories' would henceforth be treated no differently than all her other subjects. Their right to a religion, to ancestral property and every opportunity for advancement would be respected. As, of course, they always should have been.

The Begum was incensed. Her counter-proclamation, issued a week later, reads somewhat more directly than Victoria's:

At this time certain weak-minded, foolish people, have spread a report that the English have forgiven the faults and crimes of the people of Hindoostan. This appears very astonishing, for it is the unvarying custom of the English never to forgive a fault . . . The proclamation of 1st November, 1858, which has come before us, is perfectly clear; and as some foolish people, not understanding the real object of the proclamation, have been carried away, therefore we, the ever-abiding government, parents of the people of Oude, with great consideration, put forth the present proclamation in order that the real object of the chief points may be exposed, and our subjects placed on their guard . . .[31]

She lists these chief points one by one. Firstly, there is the supposed assurance that what was formerly 'held in trust' by the East India Company (i.e. British India) was now being resumed by the Queen. There is no advantage to India in this, says the Begum: nothing will change at all. Then there is the undertaking that all contracts and agreements made under the old pre-Mutiny regime will be honoured by the new. But what is such an under-taking worth, if the Queen insists on ignoring the wishes of all true Indians that their country be restored to them? The Queen's proclamation promises that there will be no sanctioned pro-grammes to convert non-Christians to what she states to be the 'true religion' of the Holy Trinity. 'That religion is true,' retorts the Begum, 'which acknowledges one God, and knows no other. Where there are 3 Gods in a religion, neither Mussalman nor Hindoo – nay, not even Jews, Sun-worshippers or Fire-worshippers can believe it true. To eat pigs and drink wine – to bite greased cartridges ... to destroy Hindoo and Mussalman temples on pretence of making roads to build churches – to send clergymen into the streets and alleys to preach the Christian reli-gion – to institute English schools, and to pay a monthly stipend for learning the English sciences ... with all this, how can the people believe that religion will not be interfered with?'

Where Queen Victoria offered justice to suspect rebels ('except those who have been or shall be convicted of having directly taken part in the murder of British subjects') the Begum predicted blanket punishments, and where the Queen promised a new infra-structure of roads and canals, the Begum demanded to know who were going to break their backs for a pittance to build them. 'If people cannot see clearly what this means,' she concluded bitterly, 'there is no help for them.'

There was not the spirit left in the rebellion to match the Begum's vigour, though, and as the British administration began to wax again in Oudh, she became an outlaw and fled to Nepal. She was promised her life and 'all the consideration which is due to her as a woman and a member of a Royal house' if she would give herself up to the government, but after rather tactlessly appealing to Queen Victoria (as one mighty queen to another) for political power as well, she preferred to stay in exile, where she died in 1879. After all, like the Rani of

Jhansi she too had promised never to surrender to the enemy. And victory or no victory in this great struggle for freedom, to her the British were still very much the enemy, the feringhee, the stealers of India's soul.

12

Towards Independence

*What would India be without England? And what would
the British Empire be without Englishwomen?*[1]

If the flying chuppatti heralded the Mutiny's outbreak, then the
flying chitty must have marked its demise. Earnest flocks of little
certificates started to emerge throughout the districts of British
India, issued and produced to prove the holder's loyalty to the
imperial cause during the recent unpleasantness. They were important documents: the gifts of Western civilization old Dalhousie
had deemed so exemplary for the Indians back in the 1840s did
not, it appeared, run to any sort of convention in respect of
human rights for the enemy. Despite 'Clemency' Canning's
worthy intention to refrain from the indiscriminate practice of
blood-revenge,[2] any Indian found (by the wrong person) without
proof of his fidelity was liable to be hanged for a 'nigger' (a
favourite post-Mutiny term) and a woman-killer.

While this sorting-out of the heroes from the villains was going
on, the British authorities were also keen to get as many of the
surviving women and their children home as possible. If the insurrection were to flare up again, there would at least be no need
next time to spend precious reserves of energy and manpower in
guarding the memsahibs. The outbreak would not have been half
so humiliating to the British had the women not been there in the

first place, restricting honourable officers and men both physically (in denying them an open theatre of war) and emotionally. It was time to leave it to the men.

Many memsahibs, of course, were only too eager to go. Now more than ever 'home' meant security (even if one's husband or brother or father must stay and finish his duties in India), and there was likely to be more comfort in familiarity now than any-thing. The mere sight of the homeward-bound vessel sent by a grateful government was enough to convince most of them that their troubles were over: to Ruth Coopland, finding herself aboard in 'a very pleasant party', the experience was in every way delightful.

We sailed in the evening, and the moon which had just risen, cast a soft flood of light over the clear blue sea, and the white houses and green trees of Bombay sloping down to the water. I had soon taken my last look of India, and its myriads of people, – most of whom are black at heart, – its burning sun, and all the scenes of horror I had witnessed.

We had a prosperous voyage . . . On the 26th of April, 1858, the 'Ripon' arrived at Southampton, where I was met by my father, and I again stood on the shore of dear old England; which, if I did not kiss, I embraced in my heart.[3]

For Mrs Muter, however, the voyage home on the *Eastern Monarch* was anything but prosperous. In fact it was more worrisome to her than anything that had happened since she had found herself waiting alone for that church service to begin in Meerut on 10 May 1857. All went well until the night before the ship was due to dock at Portsmouth, when she and her husband had gone to sleep in relieved anticipation.

Never while I live, and my senses remain, can I forget my next awakening. The whole ship seemed shattered into fragments . . . I was hurled from my bed and I stood in the darkness of death . . . stifled, I gasped for breath; the air was charged with sulphur, and the atmosphere such that it was death to remain . . . I found my hand on the door; by a great effort I pushed it open, and a rush of fresh air cleared away from my brain much of the shock from which I was suffering. Immediately my husband was standing by my side, and amidst the stillness that followed I heard his voice, as he called loudly to those on deck to raise the skylights . . .

At my feet an awful chasm yawned. Far down I could see a bright glare that told me the ship was on fire. The explosion had passed close to where we slept, torn up the decks, both this and that beneath, and blown away the after-companion ladder by which we gained the poop. Fragments of the brass balusters alone hung down, which my husband seizing, by a vigorous effort, he gained the poop; then stooping down he grasped my upraised hands, and in a few minutes I was lifted to the top . . . My mind was keenly active, though my body was powerless, and I was conscious it required the greatest exertion to raise me to the deck; yet I could do nothing to assist myself, although vividly aware of the awful fiery chasm down which I would be precipitated if my husband failed in his effort.[4]

Colonel Muter took command once they were safely out on deck and put his wife in a lifeboat while he stayed to organize the ship's evacuation. Astonishingly, only seven people were killed by the explosion on the steamer, despite the fact that it was carrying a 200-ton cargo of saltpetre, and was completely wrecked within half an hour. After spending the rest of the night in Portsmouth, the Muters went on to London, by now desperately in need of bodily and spiritual relief (and sure, at last, of getting it). But it was Epsom race week, and no one had a hotel bed to give them: for weary Mrs Muter, this was the end. 'There was something dreary and disheartening beyond expression in such a return to our country. It seemed as if the misfortune which entitled us to the hand of kindness caused us to be shunned where we had most expected to be met by a hearty reception . . . We lost everything but life in the wreck.'[5]

This depressing anticlimax must have been lightened a little for Mrs Muter by the air of celebrity attending the surviving Mutiny memsahibs once their books began to appear on the market. Hers – a rather dry tome, it must be said – was not published until 1911, three years before her death; but there were plenty of others available to an avid public, even as early as 1858. Most were about Lucknow: Kate Bartrum, Adelaide Case, Georgina Harris and Julia Inglis all published accounts within the year, while Ruth Coopland's *A Lady's Escape from Gwalior* came out in 1859. There was a steady trickle thereafter, in various periodicals and appendices as well as printed books, and in India as well as England; most were written ostensibly (according to their prefaces) for the benefit of the author's descendants, Kate Bartrum being one of the few to admit to another pressing and more mercenary concern. 'Most nobly did England respond to the cry of the widow and the orphan'[6] when she and little Bobbie arrived in Calcutta; no doubt it would manage even more generosity now that the widow was home, and alone. Actually, after living for a while with her family in Bath, Kate married again, and had three more babies (Katherine, Bradshaw, and Jane). But one suspects her story was never really meant to be a happy one, for she died only eight years after leaving India, in 1866, of tuberculosis.[7]

There is a jollier history of some of her companions: Emmie Polehampton, widow of one of the chaplains at Lucknow, went on to marry the husband of that stalwart of Indore, Annie Durand. She and Sir Henry were wed in 1859, and the first of Emmie's children was born the following year. Georgina Harris lost her husband in 1864 (and the dear dog Bustle at about the same time, after a delirious chance reunion with the officer who had offered to keep him during the siege); she lived on, however, until 1886. Julia Inglis (d. 1904) did not feel she could bring herself to write a full and calm account of what happened at Lucknow until thirty-five years after the event; nor did Madeline Jackson record her story until 1880, Sarah Fagan of Jullundur until 1883, and seventy-five-year-old Harriet Tytler until 1903. At least one of the Mutiny's diarists never quite calmed down: Mrs Gilliland, breathless survivor of Sialkot, lived to complete her century but, says her obituary in the local newspaper, she remained notably 'vivacious' and, one suspects, outspoken to the last.[8]

Not all the women chronicling the Mutiny and their part in what was after all the ultimate Victorian melodrama (with all the attendant blood and thunder and passion that might suggest) shared Ruth Coopland's conviction that a black skin meant a black heart. Many chose – or fairly readily acquiesced – to stay in India, or at least to return as soon as was practical, and lived there much as they had before the summer of 1857. Augusta Becher was amongst them. She had been ordered home without Sep, sailing in the hopelessly overcrowded old steamer *Southampton* (where for lack of space before his burial at sea the body of a man who died had to be stored in the grand piano) – but a year later she was back again with her husband, and the two eventually settled in Barrackpore with the seven of their ten children who survived infancy.

Although life as a post-Mutiny memsahib in India may have *seemed* the same as ever, I suspect Augusta was not alone in recognizing disturbing changes beneath the surface. They were most evident in her case in the nature of her relationship with Sep:

Till this time [i.e. 1857] I think my own inner life lay dormant, being so perfectly and entirely happy. I only gave thanks, for I more than idolised him, and we were truly one in tastes and feelings. But from this time of our separation I began to live a life to myself, and perhaps we have never again been so entirely 'one' as up to this time. It must be so when long separations come, as in all our Indian lives . . . Ah, well![9]

It must have been difficult to admit to these rumblings of womanly independence, especially when one's role had been so sensationally defined as one of Britannia's most graceful and dutiful daughters. Occasionally a diffident authoress would try to give a little dimension to this definition. 'I think that Englishmen ought to know what their countrywomen have endured,' wrote one in a sort of apologia for the inclusion in her memoirs of certain indelicate scenes:

Some men may think that women are weak and only fitted to do trivial things, and endure petty troubles; and there are women who deserve no higher opinion: such as faint at the sight of blood, are terrified at a harmless cow, or make themselves miserable by imagining terrors, and unreal sorrows; but there are many who can endure with fortitude and patience what even soldiers shrink from. Men are fitted by education and constitution to dare to do; yet they have been surpassed, in presence of mind and in the power of endurance, by weak women.[10]

We are back in the realms of the 'beautiful brotherhood' that so satisfied (and surprised) those memsahibs sensible enough to enjoy it. But I doubt if it survived the circumstances that engendered it, once the beautiful brothers were back with their menfolk in the camp and cantonments again.

Something else that would appear to have been lost with the resumption of British Indian life (for a while, at least) is the traditionally easy relationship between the memsahib and her staff. Easy for the memsahib, anyway: she had trusted them to do as she demanded. But now, however loyal they may have been personally, there was an air of suspicion around, which all too easily corrupted into dread. 'It is unfortunate,' wrote one Lucknowi historian, 'that Englishwomen since 1858 have always thought that every Indian has a knife in his hand.'[11] That might be a little extreme, but it was certainly the case that the trustworthiness of one's Indian acquaintances – who might once have even been friends – could no longer be taken for granted. One child of the Mutiny[12] remembered her mother continuing for years to dress the family in costumes of 'forest-green' for camouflage, just in case they should need to take to the jungle again at short notice: they could neither afford nor expect to rely on the help of Indians any more. And the immediate post-Mutiny period was not made any easier by the fact that now more than ever, after all that had happened at Cawnpore and elsewhere, the Empire was wearing the memsahib on its sleeve as an emblem of civilized and sentimental superiority – which meant, of course, a much lonelier and meaner way of life for her than might have been. Despite all this angels of Albion business, despite this putting of her on an impossibly lofty pedestal, it was promptly after the explosion the memsahib was supposed by so many to have ignited that she was most resented, both by traditional British Indians and by progressive native ones. The author William Buchan put this point best in his historical novel *Kumari* (1955):

The whole thing is and always has been a love affair. First and last that's been what mattered. And it's taken the course, worse luck, of most love affairs, beginning with persuasion – none too gentle in this case – followed by delighted discovery, mutual esteem, ravishing plans for the future, the first really frightful row, and a long, miserable cooling-off into polite bickering punctuated by sharp quarrels and joyless infidelities, each side withdrawing steadily and continually, more and more of its real self.

The first quarrel, the only one that mattered, was the Mutiny – that wound went deep and we've never ceased to suffer, in a way. By then we'd let our character change for the worse. We'd stopped wooing excitingly, violently, with real strength and a lot of poetry . . .'[13]

– and the reason for that was the memsahib. Having a spotless wife on the premises is no substitute to a red-blooded Briton for the exotic, inviting and fulfilling mistress India used to be.

So was no one taking any notice of what the women I have been writing about actually said? Was it not obvious by now that these were real people, individual personalities, and not the caricatures they had always been labelled? It seems not. Those books that I mentioned having been published on the first wave of sensationalism after the uprising were, in fact, drowned by the wave itself. They were treated as part of the whole Mutiny melodrama. Those that appeared later were more carefully considered, both in the writing and by those who read them, but being so they lacked the artless spontaneity of all those other women who were writing as the cataclysm happened. Their witness, in the desperately scribbled and cross-scribbled letters they smuggled home, in the grubby and tattered journals they cherished through every crisis and the heart-broken little notes they tied to the lock of a dead child's hair or the recovered medals of a fallen husband – their witness tells the real story. And most of it would only have been listened to by separate families, insulated by shock, before disappearing into bundles of other domestic jumble or, exceptionally, into the collections of libraries and museums: its influence was minimal.

Meanwhile, the moral respectability of British India was recovering to reach its self-proclaimed zenith nearly twenty years after the Mutiny began, when Queen Victoria was proclaimed Empress of India in 1876. The intervening period had seen the final departure of a number of Mutiny memsahibs who might have liked to be there for the vast celebrations. Charlotte Canning, for instance, frail and beautiful on her arrival in Calcutta in 1855, lasted no longer than six years, dying a gaunt old woman of forty-four. Minnie Wood would have enjoyed the spectacle (although one doubts her feelings of patriotism) had she not decided in 1861 that enough was enough, and left Archie and – perhaps surprisingly – her three children to come home and get a divorce. While all the junketings over the Queen-Empress were going on in India, Minnie was enjoying the second year of a new marriage. Harriet Tytler was there, though: she and Robert had settled in Simla in 1870; now she was a widow but still more at home in the foothills of the Himalaya than the softer folds of what she respectfully called the Mother Country. She and her daughter were in Delhi on their way back to Simla from a visit to England at the time of the great Durbar held by Viceroy Lord Lytton in December, 1876.

I believe it was the grandest sight ever seen in India since the start of our rule. I wish I had Kipling's pen to draw the scenes as I saw them. The Proclamation was indeed a wonderful sight, a sort of Arabian night and fairy scene. All the rajas were seated in a segment of a circle, each maharaja or raja or nawab vying with the others in grandeur of dress and jewels.

Lord Lytton was a very small man, but his Herald was immense in stature. He was chosen for his size to proclaim Her Majesty the Empress of India. This being done, all the regiments joined in a feu de joie, after which the bands played 'God Save the Queen' three times and a 101-gun royal salute was fired. Then the royalty left their boxes and mounted their elephants, everyone taking procedure according to his rank as a noble. It was both a lovely and a ludicrous sight. Lovely, because the elephants were so numerous, and as gorgeously dressed as their royal masters. They were followed by gaily attired horsemen, but they in turn were followed by the riff-raff, some even on donkeys. There was not a raja or prince of importance in the whole of India who was not present, by command, at that pro-

Towards Independence

clamation. I wonder what the effect was on the minds of those royalty to see the Viceroy's camp pitched on the very spot where the Delhi princes had been conquered by our army, which was only a fourth the size of the present one . . .'[14]

To Harriet, I am sure, it was a sight of great satisfaction, and a vindication of all she had endured just a mile or two away as the only memsahib present during the whole of the siege of Delhi. She was a proud woman. And this was a proud age, now, for the British Raj. Its high noon, its hey-day, had come at last. Enough time had passed since the horrors of '57 for the sahibs and their mems to be confident again, and in their beneficent relationship with the Indians, to congratulate themselves for a task well done. 'What would India be without England,' wrote an admiring German gentleman in a book published in 1909, 'and what would the British Empire be without Englishwomen? To these women [is] due the gratitude not only of their country but of the civilised world. Fearlessly the woman of British birth looks into the eye of danger. Faithfully and with willing sacrifice she upholds the standards . . . of culture and of service to humanity.'[15]

As independence slowly approached that standard began definitely, and very publicly, to waver again. And there was a horrible sense of familiarity about the atmosphere in 1919, when the British government sought to outlaw Gandhi's nationalists by forcefully extending wartime emergency powers. Despite the Mahatma's policy of passive resistance, this action provoked violence and rioting of an intensity unknown for over sixty years. It was not at Meerut this time that the crisis came, but at Amritsar, in the Punjab. On 10 April a mob of Indians – particularly Sikhs, this being their holy city – attacked various European establishments, killing three bank employees and, almost, a missionary memsahib. She was a Miss Frances Sherwood, who had been working with the Zenana Mission Society in the city for the past fifteen years.

Happening upon the mob whilst going about her business on her bicycle, she was pulled to the ground and beaten, only surviving (as did a lady doctor similarly attacked) thanks to the secret care of sympathetic Hindus. The British, of course, were enraged. Troops were quickly dispatched to quell the uprising, under the command of General Reginald Dyer, who declared 'we look upon women as sacred, or ought to',[16] and ordered all Indians who happened to pass the place of Miss Sherwood's assault to crawl along in the dirt on their hands and knees. Three days after the outbreak, he was responsible for the direct firing of his men into the huge crowd who had gathered in the Jallianwala Bagh for an illegal public meeting. Four hundred Indians were killed, and over a thousand wounded, there being nowhere to shelter from the gunfire, and no escape.

As soon as news of the Cawnpore massacres had reached Britain in the late summer of 1857, Lady Lucie Duff Gordon had distinguished herself by refusing to blame the Nana Sahib and his circle for what had happened. 'The real truth of the whole outbreak,' she wrote, 'I believe we shall never know – I mean the native side of the question.'[17] Few in England had been prepared to acknowledge that there *was* a native side to the question – or a question at all – before that. Now that it was obvious that Amritsar was part of the same question as Cawnpore, there were more voices ready to follow Lady Lucie's distant lead in deploring Dyer and those he represented for their blatant and dangerous racialism. The remarkable Annie Besant[18] especially resented such barbarity being cloaked, be it ever so thinly, in the name of chivalry. Old habits die hard, however. If they ever really die at all.

I think perhaps the Indians are more liberal in this respect (i.e. the changing of attitudes) than the British. I might have mentioned in my Introduction that I was wary of the guide in Agra who called me 'memsahib', assuming that it was as much a pejorative term there as it has historically become in Britain. It was ungenerous of me: although the memory of the Mutiny, the great Sepoy Rebellion, is kept fresh and strongly flavoured there, being an important part of the school syllabus and featuring regularly in books and videos, the response of the Indians I met towards the part the British played in it is calm and understanding. And when I mentioned to the more elderly of them that I was studying the memsahibs involved, I was smilingly encouraged. Ah yes, they said, the memsahibs: it is good you are remembering them.

But then the Indians are a very polite – and affectionate – people. So much so that even after independence they could not quite bring themselves to do away with all the monuments bequeathed them by the British of that most supreme memsahib of all, Queen-Empress Victoria. There are still bits, busts and figures of her littered all over the place (often literally) and in Lucknow, so significant during the Mutiny, is a particularly fine collection. There, round the back of a large municipal building, stand about a dozen statues, some of imperial gentlemen on horseback doffing their fine plumed hats, others of various dignitaries gazing with stern pomposity from crumbling plinths, but most versions of Victoria, slightly differing in age, style, medium and (a little disarming, this) in anatomical completeness. They are arranged in a rather crazy circle, facing inwards, and each seems carefully to be avoiding the others' eyes. It is as though they have found themselves there during some highfaluting social occasion but have not been formally introduced, and none dares break the ice.

One could draw some meaningful metaphor out of this, I suppose, all about the British turning their stiff, cold backs on India and refusing to communicate even with each other: several metaphors, probably. But there is no need. The Indians have said it all already by positioning these pillars of the old establishment where they have. The municipal building behind which they stand is, in fact, the entrance to Lucknow zoo.

The point is not maliciously made, and it is hard not to smile with the other visitors to the zoo as they pass from one strange lot of creatures to another. And though the very thought would no doubt have sent the typical (and imaginary) memsahib of days gone by into spluttering paroxysms of indignation, I suspect the real women who wrote this book might well – given time – have smiled too.

Glossary

This glossary is confined to words appearing in the text, and to the sense in which they are used. It includes those Indian place-names whose modern form is significantly different from that used by the British in 1857.

Attah	Ground wheat, or flour with the husks still present
Ayah	Native wet-nurse or nursery servant
Babalogue	Children
Badmash	Hooligan
Begum	A Moslem queen, or lady of exalted rank
Bhang	Hemp or cannabis
Bibi	Native mistress or, occasionally, wife
Burra Mem	First Lady, chief memsahib
Cantonments	The military station of a town or city
Cawnpore	Kanpur
Charpoy	A wooden bedstead with a string or webbing mattress

Chillumchee	A brass or copper water-bowl
Chota hazree	Literally, 'little breakfast', or an early-morning snack
Chowkidar	Watchman
Chuddur	A sheet or veil
Chupatti	Small round of unleavened bread
Dak gharry	Carriage used to carry passengers and mail long-distance in relays
Dhall / Dal	Split pulses
Dhoolie / Dooly	Covered litter
Durbar	Public meeting or audience
Feringhee	Europeans (it became, by implication, rather a contemptuous term)
Ghee	Clarified butter
Godown	Warehouse or storeroom
Gram	Pulse used for feeding horses
Griffin	A newcomer, endearingly gauche in the ways of British India
Havaldar	Native non-commissioned officer
Jamps	Bamboo-woven hurdles
Jemadar	An Indian officer of the rank of lieutenant
Jumna (River)	Yamuna
Karnaul	Kurnool
Khansamah	House steward
Khitmagar / Kitmagur	Butler
Koss	A measurement of about two miles

Lattiwallah	Someone armed with a steel-tipped bludgeon, or latti
Mahout	Elephant driver
Maidan	Open square, often grassed
Memsahib	Literally, 'lady-master' (Madam-Sahib)
Moulvee/Moulvie	Moslem scholar
Munshi	Secretary or tutor
Nabob	Successful merchant or entrepreneur
Nawab	Indian nobleman
Nullah	A ditch or river-bed
Palkee	Covered box-litter usually used by women
Pergunnah	A community or collection of villages
Pucca/Pukka	Proper, 'the real McCoy'
Pundit	Hindu lawyer or sage
Punkah-wallah	The native whose job it is to operate the household fans, or punkahs
Raj	Rule
Rajah	Ruler
Rani	A Hindu queen
Resai	Thin quilt
Sahib	Master: a European or generally superior gentleman
Sais/Syce	Groom
Sepoy	Native private infantryman
Simla	Shimla
Sowar	Native cavalryman
Subhadar	A sepoy officer

Tiffin	Luncheon
Tulwar	Native sword
Tykhana	Cellar
Umballa	Ambala
Velaitee	Stranger, from a long way away
Wuzeer	A minister
Zemindar	Indian landowner
Zenana	The secluded women's quarters of a household

Notes

For bibliographical details of sources quoted, please see pp. 280–90.

CHAPTER ONE: THE BIRTH OF BRITISH INDIA

1. Eden, *Up the Country*, 98.
2. Kindersley, *Letters*, 78.
3. The very first written account of a visit to India by a woman, according to the historian Rosemary Raza, appears to be Jane Smart's anonymously published *Letter from a Lady at Madrass* (1743).
4. Hibbert, *Great Mutiny*, 17.
5. The three 'Presidency-towns' of Madras, Bombay and Calcutta were founded as such in 1683, 1687 and 1699 respectively.
6. The 'Hole' was in fact the military gaol of British-built Fort William, a stifling space some eighteen by fifteen feet, where it is thought about 140 British defenders of the garrison were incarcerated by the local Nawab (acting with French support) in 1756. The morning after their imprisonment all but twenty-odd survivors were found to be asphyxiated.
7. *FSUP* I, 268–9.
8. Advice to the Royal Army (ms., Home Miscellaneous Series 727 (3), Oriental and India Office Collections).
9. *FSUP* I, 269.

10. ibid., 390.
11. *FSUP* V, 377.
12. MacMillan, *Women*, 110.
13. Fane, ed. Pemble, *Fane*, 165.
14. Eden, *Up the Country*, 98.
15. Kaye, *History* I, 258.

CHAPTER TWO: THE MEMSAHIBS ARRIVE

1. Thomas Hood, quoted in Kincaid, *Social Life*, 15.
2. MacMillan, *Women*, 16.
3. Hyam, *Empire and Sexuality*, 115.
4. This was the celebrated Colonel James Skinner, whose fond family insisted he never actually entertained more than seven wives at a time (Hyam, op. cit., 115).
5. Sneade Brown, *Letters*, 17.
6. Dated 18 December 1675 and 17 January 1676 (Kincaid, op. cit., 37).
7. Spear, *Nabobs*, 7.
8. Tytler, *Englishwoman*, 47.
9. *Tropical Trials: A Hand-book for Women in the Tropics* by S. Leigh-Hunt and Alexander Kenny.
10. Anon., *Englishwoman in India*, 202.
11. ibid., 96.
12. ibid., 14.
13. The 'Overland' was the alternative (pre-Suez Canal) route to India, and involved a trek from the Mediterranean coast of the Middle East to the coast of the Persian Gulf.
14. Maitland, *Letters*, 168–9.
15. Fane, ed. Pemble, *Fane*, 67, 64.
16. See Robinson, *Wayward Women*, 55.
17. See Taylor, *Star*, 123–42.

18. Advice to the Royal Army (ms., Home Miscellaneous Series 727 (3), Oriental and India Office Collections).
19. Kaye, *Golden Calm*, 126.
20. According to Emily Eden, who found herself 'rather oppressed' by Mrs Parks on more than one occasion.
21. Parks, *Wanderings*, II, 455.
22. Alfred, Lord Tennyson, *The Princess*, VI, 290.
23. Germon, *Journal*, 84–5.
24. Canning, *Glimpse*, 29.
25. Becher, *Reminiscences*, 142.
26. Coopland, *Lady's Escape*, 44–5.
27. ibid., 47.
28. The Mutton Club was a familiar institution in British India. Its members, or shareholders, kept a flock of sheep fed on a sort of rota which ensured there were always plenty ready for the table. 'Mutton hot and mutton cold, mutton young and mutton old, mutton tough and mutton tender' for all its lack of variety proved to Mrs Coopland more welcome than the usual and ubiquitous scrawny fowl.
29. Wood, *From Minnie*, 68.
30. ibid., 78, 53.

CHAPTER THREE: THE SPARK IGNITES

1. Taylor, *Chronicles*, 24.
2. MacMunn, *Mees Dolly*, 327–31.
3. Hibbert, *Great Mutiny*, 77, 78.
4. Taylor, op. cit., 24.
5. ibid., 23.
6. *Papers Relating to the Indian Mutiny* I.
7. See Moore, *At Meerut*, 828.
8. Hibbert, op. cit., 81.

9. Chick, *Annals*, 30–32.

10. Moore, op. cit., 828.

11. Steel, *On the Face*, 172.

12. Muter, *Recollections*, 17–18.

13. Tytler, *Englishwoman*, 113.

14. Muter, op. cit., 19.

15. Tytler, op. cit., 114.

16. Annie had come out eighteen months earlier to be her father's companion while her mother stayed at home to supervise the education of Annie's younger siblings.

17. *Illustrated London News*, 19 September 1857.

18. Chick, op. cit., 89.

19. *Illustrated London News*, 18 July 1857.

20. Chick, op. cit., 92.

21. ibid., 93.

22. ibid., 94–6.

23. Tytler, Through the . . . Mutiny, 73.

24. Haldane, *Story* [unpaginated].

25. Peile, letter in *The Times*, 25 September 1857.

26. ibid.

CHAPTER FOUR: ABLAZE

1. Kirk, Letter (ms.).

2. *FSUP* II, 161. The exact date of this proclamation is not known.

3. For an account (which is discredited by some) of the Jhansi massacre see Mrs Mutlow's testament in Chick's *Annals of the Indian Rebellion* (pp. 218–20). She was the Eurasian wife of a clerk in the British Political Officer Captain Skene's office, and seems to have escaped the rebels' notice when the other Christians being held prisoner (including her husband) were led out to be killed. She

spent the next few weeks hiding in a Hindu tomb, a garden, and on the city streets where she had to beg for food for herself and two young children. Captain Skene's khansamah also furnished an account of the massacre for Chick (p. 215).

4. Coopland, *Lady's Escape*, 79–80.
5. ibid., 84–5.
6. Muter, *Recollections*, 59–60.
7. *The Friend of India*, 24 September 1857.
8. Chick, *Annals*, 122–3.
9. Jackson, Reminiscences (ms.).
10. Chick, op. cit., 221 (see also Martin, *Indian Empire* II, 312).
11. ibid., 222–4.
12. Coopland, op. cit., 145.
13. Kirk, Letter (ms.).
14. Innes, Narrative (ms.).
15. Kaye, *History* II, 316.
16. Coopland, op. cit., 141–2.
17. Sharpley, Diaries (ms.).
18. ibid.
19. Vansittart, Diary (ms.).
20. Coopland, op. cit., 173–4, 184.
21. Bagley, Small Boy, 428–34.
22. Sharpley, op. cit.

CHAPTER VE: NEWS SPREADS

1. From Martin Tupper's poem 'Who Shall Comfort England?', found by the author in an unacknowledged newspaper cutting dated 31 August 1857.
2. Innes, Narrative (ms.).
3. ibid.
4. *The Times*, 8 November 1857.

5. Sligo, Reminiscences (ms.).
6. Captain Bailie, quoted in Hibbert, *Great Mutiny*, 131.
7. Young, *Delhi*, 184.
8. *The Times*, 7 August 1858.
9. Becher, *Reminiscences*, 131–6.
10. See note 4.
11. Fagan, Memoirs (ms.).
12. See Oriental and India Office Collections ms. 'Home Miscellane-ous' no. 75; also Rudrangshu Mukherjee's article in the journal *Past and Present* (August 1990), pp. 92–116.
13. Except, perhaps, for those women abducted from Cawnpore during the first massacre (see Chapter Six).
14. Kaye, *History* II, 119.
15. Hare, *Two Noble Lives*, 327.
16. *Illustrated London News*, 4 July 1857.
17. *The Times*, 25 August 1857.
18. Wallace-Dunlop, *Timely Retreat*, 251.
19. See note 1.
20. Kelly, *Delhi*, 28–9.
21. Bayly, *Raj*, 241.
22. *Punch*, 3 October 1857.
23. ibid., 12 September 1857.
24. ibid., 22 August 1857.
25. ibid.

CHAPTER SIX: THE CAWNPORE MASSACRES

1. Roberts, *Letters*, 28.
2. Larkins, Letter (ms.).
3. It was believed that the Nana was a Freemason, a member of the Lodge Harmony at Cawnpore, so he *must* have been a pukka Sahib.

4. Chalwin, Letters (ms.).
5. Parliamentary Papers (1857), 308–9.
6. Letter from a scrapbook of contemporary news cuttings in the author's collection.
7. ibid.
8. ibid.
9. Angelo, Diary (ms. and in *Notes and Queries*).
10. Hare, *Two Noble Lives*, 370.
11. The author and historian Andrew Ward suggests this woman may have been a Mrs Eckford. According to Cosens and Wallace (p. 22) 'Mrs Eckford set off . . . [from Fatehgarh on 23 May for Allahabad] by road, but was never heard of again. Her fate has never been discovered.'
12. *FSUP* IV, 508.
13. Bennett (née Horne), Ten Months, 1218–22.
14. ibid., 1223–4.
15. See note 6.
16. Thomson, *Cawnpore*, 107.
17. Trevelyan, *Cawnpore*, 85.
18. Kaye, *History* II, 354.
19. Emma is not recorded as having been present at the Bibigarh, nor having died in the entrenchment, and so the inference is that she was killed at the Satichowra Ghat.
20. There has been much discussion about the identity of this emissary from the Nana, who was seen stumbling towards the entrenchment with a baby at her breast. Some witnesses and historians are convinced it was Mrs Greenaway, a merchant's wife, imprisoned by the Nana in the Savada Koti with the Jacobis. But the evidence that it was her friend Mrs Jacobi seems more convincing. Amy certainly felt sure, as did another survivor of Cawnpore, W.J. Shepherd, and a member of the Jacobis' household, Moonshee Ralka Pershad.
21. Amy could not be sure of this: her parents and two-year-old

sister Mary certainly died at the Ghat, but what happened to the others we do not know.

22. Bennett, op. cit., 1225–32.
23. Thomson, op. cit., 168–9.
24. Colonel G.W. Williams was given the task in 1858, and produced 63 eyewitness accounts (given on oath) by Eurasians and natives.
25. Notably Mukherjee (see Chapter Five, note 13).
26. Russell, *Diary*, 281–2.
27. Kaye, op. cit., 269–70.
28. Williams, *Depositions*, no. 1 [in Forrest, *Selection*, vol. III].

CHAPTER SEVEN: THE CAWNPORE SURVIVORS

1. Hare, *Two Noble Lives*, 280.
2. Quoted from a scrapbook of contemporary news cuttings in the author's collection.
3. 'Nujoor Jewarree's Story', as above.
4. Hibbert, *Great Mutiny*, 209.
5. See note 2.
6. As above; the letter dated 28 October 1857.
7. Case, *Day by Day*, 315.
8. *Journal of the Society of Army Historical Research*, no. 143, September 1957.
9. See note 2; the letter dated 12 October 1857.
10. Hibbert, *Great Mutiny*, 213.
11. *Ayr Observer*, the letter dated 1 August 1857.
12. *Punch*, 12 September 1857.
13. Kaye, *History* II, 373.
14. For details of the Wheeler family tree I am indebted to P.J.O. Taylor whose *Companion to the Indian Mutiny* is in press as I write.
15. Williams, *Depositions*, no. 14 (in Forrest, *Selection*, III).

16. Chick, *Annals*, 184.
17. Printed at the Kaiserbagh, Lucknow, by the Vidya-Vinode Press, *c.* 1900.
18. Williams, op. cit., no. 1 (in Forrest, *Selection*, III).
19. R. MacCrea: see Yalland, *Traders*, 324.
20. ibid., 325.
21. Williams, op. cit., no. 4 (in Forrest, *Selection*, III).
22. ibid., nos. 6 and 7.
23. *Papers Relating to the Mutinies* III.
24. Chick, op. cit., 186–7.
25. ibid., 189.
26. ibid., 190.
27. Greenberger, *British Image*, 113.
28. See also Sutherland's ms. account.
29. National Archive of India, *Home Publication*, no. 1, 14 May 1858.
30. Bennett, Ten Months, 1232–3.
31. ibid., 1233–4.
32. ibid., 79–80.
33. ibid., 81.
34. ibid., 82–3.
35. In fact most historians seem to assume that the two narratives are by the same woman . . .
36. Horne, Narrative, ms., 83–5.
37. ibid., 86–7.
38. ibid., 88–9.

CHAPTER EIGHT: THE SIEGE OF LUCKNOW

1. Gubbins, *Mutinies*, 206.
2. Russell, *Diary*, 57–8.
3. Honoria Lawrence was Henry's cousin; they married in 1836 after having been deeply in love since their first meeting ten years

before, and enjoyed a partnership of equals unusual in their time and place. She was described as 'one in a thousand – highly gifted in mind, [and] of a most cheerful disposition', and she loved India and its people with a genuine and open-hearted passion.

4. Martin Gubbins being chief amongst them.

5. This was morally laudable but strategically foolish, providing the rebels with several vantage-points from which to attack the Residency during the siege.

6. Wells, Letters (ms.).

7. Henry Lawrence's granddaughter, Lady Stokes, visiting Lucknow in 1922 (see P. J. O. Taylor's book *A Feeling of Quiet Power*).

8. Mrs Germon's published diary consistently has 'Brien' for Bruere: perhaps her handwriting deceived the editor.

9. Germon, *Journal*, 26–9.

10. Gubbins, *Mutinies*, 204–5.

11. These poor doggies eventually went the way of all pets – save 'Bustle' Harris – when the order was given by Sir Henry that they be killed. Charlie had to drown them in the river. Bustle, however, was covertly given over to an officer for the duration of the siege, who promised to take full responsibility for the life and appetite of his charge; the dog, together with his master and mistress, survived.

12. Germon, op. cit., 29–30.

13. Kate was a silversmith's daughter from Bath, born in 1834.

14. Bartrum, *Reminiscences*, 13.

15. ibid., 22.

16. Germon, op. cit., 33–5.

17. Amongst them were Julia Inglis, Elizabeth Soppitt, and Emily Polehampton.

18. Germon, op. cit., 39–40.

19. This rendition of Sir Walter Scott's classic was followed by another, *Quentin Durward*; the bookcase from which they came was

probably placed like the rest against an outside wall of the building, to act as a shock absorber against enemy fire.

20. Germon, op. cit., 47–8, 53–5.

21. Lightning had struck twice in the same place for Sir Henry: the day before he was so badly wounded a shell had exploded (fairly harmlessly) in the very same room. When urged to move his quarters he refused, arguing that it could not happen again . . .

22. Germon, op. cit., 57–8.

23. Quoted by Kaye (*History* II, 604) from a private source.

24. Germon, op. cit., 58–9.

25. This is a little unfair: Mrs Boileau had had her share of troubles, having escaped from Secrora to Lucknow with her four children. Her account of the subsequent death of the youngest is heartbreaking (see Hibbert, *Great Mutiny*, 249–50).

26. Noted incredulously by Elizabeth Soppitt in Chick, *Annals*, 261. 'Certainly most of us had scanty wardrobes,' she says, 'but we managed to cover ourselves; she could be seen through.'

27. Case, *Day by Day*, 118.

28. Harris, *Diary*, 51.

29. Germon, op. cit., 82–3.

30. ibid., 94–5.

31. Bartrum, op. cit., 43.

32. *Jersey Times*, 10 December 1857.

CHAPTER NINE: MEANWHILE AND ELSEWHERE

1. Hare, *Two Noble Lives*, 256.

2. Martin, *Indian Empire*, II, 370.

3–6. Gilliland, Letters (ms.).

7. Durand, Papers (ms.) Bod. MS. Eng. hist. c.885, ff. 135r.–146v.

8. ibid.

9. This is how she signed herself in a letter to *The Times* on 26 September 1857.

10. Hare, op. cit., 303.

11. For information on Bonny Byrne see Cosens and Wallace, *Fatehgarh*, 11–14, and Taylor, *Star*, 123–42.

12. Probyn, Letters (ms.).

13. ibid.

14. Mill Memoir (ms.).

15. ibid.

16. Hare, op. cit., 249.

17. ibid., 234–5, 255–6.

18. Tytler, *Englishwoman*, 155.

19. Tytler, Through the . . . Mutiny, 156.

20. ibid., 158.

21. ibid., 120. There were those who strongly objected to Harriet's presence in camp, notwithstanding (or perhaps particularly because of) her condition (see Tytler, *Englishwoman*, 215).

22. A bell of arms was a small, thick-walled and circular edifice used for the storage of weapons and ammunition.

23. Tytler, Through the . . . Mutiny, 121, 135–6.

24. Tytler, *Englishwoman*, 149.

25. Tytler, Through the . . . Mutiny, 137.

26. ibid., 200.

27. ibid., 201.

CHAPTER TEN: THE RELIEF OF LUCKNOW

1. The words of a Highlander of the Relief Force to Mrs Boileau, whose first concern at seeing him was to ask whether Queen Victoria was still alive (Boileau Papers).

2. Bartrum, *Reminiscences*, 43–5.

3. ibid., 47–8.

4. Germon, *Journal*, 102–4.
5. Harris, *Diary*, 147.
6. Russell, *Diary*, 100–101.
7. Germon, op. cit., 111.
8. Inglis, *Siege*, 173–4.
9. Harris, op. cit., 144, 147.
10. Jackson, Reminiscences (ms.).
11. See p. 61.
12. Jackson, op. cit.
13–16. ibid.
17. Germon, op. cit., 120–1.
18. Christopher Hibbert (*Great Mutiny*, 349) quotes one amazed child at this point exclaiming to her mother, 'Oh, Mamma! There is a loaf of bread on the table. I am certain of it. I saw it with my own eyes.'
19. Bartrum, op. cit., 53–6.
20. ibid., 59.
21. ibid., 69–72.

CHAPTER ELEVEN: THE MEMSAHIBS DEPART

1. An Indian's advice to a friend of Ruth Coopland (Coopland, *Lady's Escape*, 248).
2. It still exists, lovingly preserved in the family's archive at the Oriental and India Office Collections.
3. Coopland, op. cit., 245.
4. ibid., 249.
5. See the letter 'from a Lady in Meerut' in *The Times*, 24 July 1857.
6. Coopland, op. cit., 276.
7. ibid., 284, 285.
8. Malleson, *History* I, 381.
9. *Papers Relating to the Indian Mutinies* III. See also Muir, *Records* II, 356.

10. Jackson, Reminiscences (ms.).
11. ibid.
12. Hare, *Two Noble Lives*, 370.
13. Figures quoted by Charlotte Canning (ibid., 236).
14. Transcribed in *Papers Relating to the Indian Mutinies* III.
15. Hare, op. cit., 340.
16. ibid., 345.
17. ibid., 350.
18. *Journal Kept During the Russian War . . .*, (London, 1855).
19. See Dampier, Diaries (ms.).
20. Tisdall, *Mrs Duberly*, 176.
21. See p. 100.
22. See Metcalfe, *Native Narratives*, 244.
23. *Freedom Struggle 1857*, 290.
24. Williams, Depositions, no. 28 (in Forrest, *Selection*, III).
25. See Chapter Four, note 3.
26. Lang, *Wanderings*, 93–4.
27. Witnesses quoted in Hibbert, *Great Mutiny*, 385, 383.
28. Hibbert, op. cit., 431.
29. See Taylor, *Star*, 223.
30. *FSUP* II, 260.
31. *FSUP* I, 465.

CHAPTER TWELVE: TOWARDS INDEPENDENCE

1. Count von Königsmark quoted in Diver, *Englishwoman*, 7.
2. Canning exasperated many families of the Mutiny's British victims by preferring a policy of justice rather than vengeance.
   'Your bloody, off-hand measures are not the cure for this sort of
   disease,' he insisted. 'Don't mistake violence for vigour.' (See
   Hibbert, *Great Mutiny*, 410.)
3. Coopland, *Lady's Escape*, 315.

4. Muter, *Recollections*, 244–6.

5. ibid., 257–8.

6. Bartrum, *Reminiscences*, 65.

7. Collier, *Sound*, 349.

8. See the Gilliland archive, Oriental and India Office Collections.

9. Becher, *Reminiscences*, 142.

10. Coopland, op. cit., 116–17.

11. Bamfield, *On the Strength*, 115.

12. A daughter of the Hirst family of Dehra Dun, and told to the author by her granddaughter, Mrs Joyce Menzies.

13. See p. 191 of the novel.

14. Tytler, *Englishwoman*, 181. Harriet died in Simla in 1907, aged 79. Her son, Stanley Delhi-Force, born in that ammunition cart in June, 1857, must have been one of the Mutiny's longest British survivors, dying in 1948 at 91.

15. See note 1.

16. MacMillan, *Women*, 225.

17. See Frank, *Lucie*, 192. Lady Lucie Duff Gordon, celebrated author of *Letters from Egypt* (1865), had played hostess (and champion) to Nana Sahib's envoy Azimullah Khan on his visit to Britain in 1854. A warm correspondence grew between them, and even after the Mutiny (in which Azimullah was perceived to be at the Nana's right hand) she remained loyal to the memory of a man she once greatly admired.

18. Annie Besant (1847–1933) was a British/Irish social and political reformer who emigrated to India to help champion the cause for independence. From 1917 to 1920 she was President of the Indian National Congress – until she decided she could not support Gandhi's policy of passive non-cooperation with the British. She was passionate on the Indian nationalists' behalf, and Dyer's action disgusted her.

Select Bibliography

SOURCE MATERIAL: MANUSCRIPTS

Locations:
Bod (Bodleian Library, Oxford)
BL (British Library, London)
CSAS (Centre of South-Asian Studies, Cambridge)
OIOL (Oriental and India Office Collections, London)
PC (Private Collection)
NAM (National Army Museum)

Angelo, Helena. Diary (PC).
Bartrum, Katherine. Diary and Letters (OIOC).
Boileau, Mrs George. Family Papers (CSAS).
Canning, Charlotte. Papers (BL and Leeds City Library).
Chalwin, Louisa. Letters (OIOC).
Corbyn, Caroline. Family Papers (PC).
Dampier, Charlotte. Diaries (PC).
Duberly, Fanny. Letters (BL).
Durand, Annie. Papers (Bod).
Ewart, Emma. Letters (OIOC).

Fagan, Sarah. Memoirs (PC).

Germon, Maria. Journal (OIOC).

Gilliland, Mary. Letters (OIOC).

Goldney, Mrs Philip. Narrative (OIOC).

Haines, Amy. Account (BL).

Horne (later Bennett), Amelia. Narrative (BL).

Innes, Lucy. Narrative (PC).

Jackson, Madeline. Reminiscences (OIOC).

Kirk, Ellen. Letter (OIOC).

Larkins, Emma. Letter (OIOC).

Lean, Maria. Letters (OIOC).

Lorne-Campbell, Mrs A. Letter (NAM).

Mill, Maria. Memoir (OIOC).

Monckton, Mrs. Family Papers (CSAS).

Nicholson, Esther. Reminiscences (PC and CSAS).

O'Donnel, Jane. Letter (NAM).

Peppé, Mrs William. Family Papers (CSAS).

Probyn, Charlotte. Letters (OIOC).

Sharpley, Edith. Diaries (PC).

Sligo, Marchioness of. Reminiscences (OIOC).

Sneyd, Elizabeth. Memoirs (OIOC, NAM).

Spry, Matilda. Letters (OIOC).

Strachey, Jane. Letters (OIOC).

Sutherland, Miss. Account (BL).

Thornhill, Mary. Papers (OIOC).

Timbrell, Agnes. Memoirs (OIOC).

Vansittart, Mary. Diary (OIOC).

Vibart, Mrs. Letters (OIOC).

Watts, Phoebe. Memoirs (PC).

Wells, Mrs W.W. Letters (CSAS).

Wood, Maria Lydia (Minnie). Journal (OIOC).

Young, Emma. Letters (PC).

SOURCE MATERIAL: PERIODICALS

(Not including letters published in contemporary newspapers: these are acknowledged in the relevant footnotes)

Angelo, Helena (ed. A. Harden). A Diary of the Indian Mutiny (*Notes and Queries, 1955*).

Anon. Through the Sepoy Mutiny (*Chamber's Journal*, 1931).

Bagley, F. R. A Small Boy in the Indian Mutiny (*Blackwood's Magazine*, 1930).

Bennett, Amelia (née Horne). Ten Months' Captivity . . . at Cawnpore (*Nineteenth Century*, 1913).

'Dolly, Mees'. An Untold Tragedy of '57 (*Cornhill Magazine*, 1927).

Moore, Kate. At Meerut During the Mutiny (*Nineteenth Century*, 1903).

Nicholson, Esther. An Irishwoman's Account of the Indian Mutiny (*Irish Sword*, 1934).

Tytler, Harriet. Through the Sepoy Mutiny (*Chamber's Journal*, 1931).

SOURCE MATERIAL: PRINTED BOOKS

Anon [Irwin, Mrs]. *Our Escape in June 1857* (Dundalk, 1862).

Bartrum, Katherine. *A Widow's Reminiscences of the Siege of Lucknow* (London, 1858).

Becher, Augusta. *Personal Reminiscences* (London, 1930).

Blake, Mrs. *Escape from Gwalior* (Private Circulation, n.d.).

Bost, Isabella. *Incidents in the Life of* . . . (Glasgow, 1913).

Brydon, Mrs William. *The Doctor's Lady*, ed. Geoffrey Moore (Bedford, n.d.).

Canning, Charlotte. *A Glimpse of the Burning Plain*, ed. Charles Allen (London, 1986). *See also* Hare, Augustus.

Case, Adelaide. *Day by Day at Lucknow* (London, 1858).

Coopland, Ruth. *A Lady's Escape from Gwalior* (London, 1859).

Duberly, Fanny. *Campaigning Experiences . . . during the Suppression of the Mutiny* (London, 1859).

Forbes, Mrs Hamilton. *Some Recollections of the Siege of Lucknow* (Axminster, 1905).

Germon, Maria. *Journal of the Siege of Lucknow*, ed. Michael Edwardes (London, 1958).

Greathed, Elisa F. See her own account in her edition of her husband's letters (London, 1858).

Haldane, Julia. *The Story of our Escape from Delhi* (Agra, 1888).

Hare, Augustus. *The Story of Two Noble Lives* [the Cannings] vol. 2 (London, 1893).

Harris, Mrs Georgina. *A Lady's Diary of the Siege of Lucknow* (London, 1858).

Huxham, Mrs G. *A Personal Narrative of the Siege of Lucknow* (London, n.d.).

Inglis, Hon. Julia. *Letters . . .* (London, 1858).

— *The Siege of Lucknow* (London, 1892).

Mawe, Mrs. See her narrative in G. B. Malleson's *The Mutiny of the Bengal Army* (London, 1857).

Metcalfe, Emily. *Memoirs* (London, 1895).

Muter, Mrs. *My Recollections of the Sepoy Revolt* (London, 1911).

Ouvry, Matilda. *A Lady's Diary* (Lymington, 1892).

Paget, Mrs Leopold. *Camp and Cantonment* (London, 1865).

Peile, Fanny. *The Delhi Massacre* (Calcutta, 1870).

Polehampton, Mrs Henry. See her letters and diary in the third edition of her husband's memoir, *Memoirs, Letters and Diary* (London, 1859).

Soppitt, Elizabeth. See her diary, attributed to 'An Officer's Wife', in the fifth edition of W. H. Fitchett's *Tale of the Great Mutiny* (London, 1912).

Spencer, Margaret. *Personal Reminiscences* (Clifton, 1905).

Tytler, Harriet. *An Englishwoman in India*, ed. Anthony Sattin (Oxford, 1986).

Wagentreiber, Fanny. *Reminiscences* (Lahore, 1911).

Wood, Minnie. *From Minnie With Love*, ed. Jane Vansittart (London, 1974).

BACKGROUND MATERIAL

Anon. *Englishwoman in India by a Lady Resident* (London, 1865).

Anon. [Maitland, Julia] *Letters from Madras, During the Years 1836–1839 by a Lady* (London, 1843).

Anon. [Mukerjee, Sambhu Chandra] *The Mutinies and the People or Statements of Native Fidelity . . . 1857–8 by a Hindu* (Calcutta, 1859).

Anon. [Wallace-Dunlop, Madeline and Rosalind] *The Timely Retreat; or, a Year in Bengal Before the Mutinies* by Two Sisters, 2 vols. (London, 1858).

Atkinson, G. F. *The Campaign in India, 1857–8* (London, 1859).

— *Curry and Rice* (London, 1859).

Bailey, S. *Women and the British Empire* (New York, 1984).

Ball, Charles. *The History of the Indian Mutiny*, 2 vols. (London, n.d.).

Ballhatchet, K. *Sex, Race and Class under the Raj* (London, 1980).

Bamfield, Veronica. *On the Strength: The Story of the British Army Wife* (London, 1974).

Barr, Pat. *The Memsahibs* (London, 1976).

Bayly, C. (ed.). *The Raj* (London, 1990).

Benson, A. C. (ed.). *The Letters of Queen Victoria*, vol. 3 (London, 1908).

Billington, Mary Frances. *Woman in India* (London, 1895).

Brown, Hilton (ed.). *The Sahibs* (London, 1948).

Chaudhuri, S. B. *Civil Rebellion in the Indian Mutinies* (Calcutta, 1957).

— *English Historical Writings . . . 1857–1859* (Calcutta, 1979).

Chick, N. A. *Annals of the Indian Rebellion*, ed. David Hutchinson (London, 1974).

Collier, Richard. *The Sound of Fury: An Account of the Indian Mutiny* (London, 1963).

Cosens, F.R. and Wallace, C.L. *Fatehgarh and the Mutiny* (Lucknow, 1933).

Cuthell, Edith. *My Garden in the City of Gardens* [Lucknow] (London, 1905).

Diver, Maud. *The Englishwoman in India* (London, 1909).

Durand, H.M. *The Life of Major-General Sir Henry Durand*, 2 vols. (London, 1883).

Eden, Emily. *Up the Country*, 2 vols. (London, 1866).

— *Letters from India*, ed. Eleanor Eden, 2 vols. (London, 1872).

Eden, Frances. *Tigers, Durbars and Kings: Fanny Eden's Indian Journals 1837–1838*, ed. Janet Dunbar (London, 1988).

Edwardes, Michael. *A Season in Hell: The Defence of the Lucknow Residency* (London, 1973).

— *Red Year: The Indian Rebellion of 1857* (London, 1973).

Edwards, William. *Personal Adventures during the Indian Rebellion* (London, 1858).

Falkland, Amelia. *Chow-Chow: Being Selections from a Journal kept in India . . .* 2 vols. (London, 1857).

Fane, Isabella. *Miss Fane in India*, ed. John Pemble (Gloucester, 1985).

Farrell, J.G. *The Siege of Krishnapur* (London, 1973).

Fay, Eliza. *Original Letters from India* (Calcutta, 1817).

Forbes-Mitchell, William. *Reminiscences of the Great Mutiny* (London, 1894).

Forrest, G.W. *History of the Indian Mutiny*, 3 vols. (Edinburgh, 1904–12).

— *Selection from the . . . State Papers*, 4 vols. (Calcutta, 1893–1912).

Frank, Katherine. *Lucie Duff Gordon* (London, 1994).

Freedom Struggle 1857: A Centenary Souvenir (Delhi, 1957).

Freedom Struggle in Uttar Pradesh [*FSUP*], 6 vols., ed. M.L. Bhargava, et al. (Lucknow, 1957–1961).

Further Papers Relative to the Mutinies in the East, 3 vols. (Calcutta, 1901).

Greenberger, A.J. *The British Image of India* (Oxford, 1969).

Griffiths, Percival. *The British in India* (London, 1946).

Gubbins, Martin. *An Account of the Mutinies in Oudh* (London, 1858).

Gupta, Pratul Chandra. *Nana Sahib and the Rising at Cawnpore* (Oxford, 1963).

Harris, John. *The Indian Mutiny* (London, 1973).

Hewitt, James (ed.). *Eye-Witnesses to the Indian Mutiny* (Reading, 1972).

Hibbert, Christopher. *The Great Mutiny: India 1857* (London, 1978).

Hilton, Edward H. *The Tourist's Guide to Lucknow*, 5th edn (Lucknow, 1905).

Holmes, T. Rice. *History of the Indian Mutiny*, 5th edn (London, 1898).

Hughes, Derrick. *The Mutiny Chaplains* (Salisbury, 1991).

Hyam, Ronald. *Empire and Sexuality* (Manchester, 1990).

India's Mutiny and England's Mourning (London, 1857).

Indian Domestic Economy (London, 1860).

Jones, Gavin. *My Escape from Fatehgarh* (Cawnpore, 1913).

Kaye, M.M. (ed.). *The Golden Calm: An English Lady's Life in Moghul Delhi* (Exeter, 1980).

Kaye, Sir John William. *History of the Sepoy War in India*, 3 vols. (London, 1864–7).

Kelly, Charles Arthur. *Delhi and Other Poems* (London, 1872).

Kerr, Barbara. *The Dispossessed* (London, 1974).

Kincaid, Dennis. *British Social Life in India, 1608–1937* (London, 1973).

Kindersley, Jemima. *Letters from . . . the East Indies* (London, 1777).

Ladendorf, J. M. *The Revolt in India* [Bibliography] (Zug, 1966).

Lang, John. *Wanderings in India* (London, 1859).

Leckey, Edward. *Fictions Connected with the Indian Outbreak of 1857 Exposed* (Bombay, 1859).

Lee, Joseph 'Dobbin'. *The Indian Mutiny* (Cawnpore, 1893).

Lewis, Ivor. *Sahibs, Nabobs and Boxwallahs: A Dictionary of the Words of Anglo-India* (Oxford, 1991).

Login, E. Dalhousie. *Lady Login's Recollections* (London, 1916).

Luard, Major C. E. *Contemporary Newspaper Accounts of Events during the Mutiny* (Allahabad, 1912).

M., D. *Scenes from the Late Indian Mutinies* (London, 1858).

Mackenzie, Mrs Colin. *Life in the Mission, the Camp, and the Zenana*, 3 vols. (London, 1853).

MacMillan, Margaret. *Women of the Raj* (London, 1988).

MacMunn, George. *Mees Dolly. An Untold Tragedy of '57* (London, Cornhill Magazine, 1927).

Maitland, Julia. *See* Anon.

Majumdar, R.K. *The Sepoy Mutiny* (Calcutta, 1957).

Malleson, Colonel G. B. *A History of the Indian Mutiny . . . Commencing from the close of the second volume of . . . Sir John Kaye's History* 2nd edn, 3 vols. (London, 1878–80).

Martin, R. Montgomery. *The Indian Empire*, vol. 2 (London, 1858–61).

Maude, Francis Cornwallis. *Memories of the Mutiny with which is incorporated the Personal Narrative of John Walter Sherer*, 2nd edn, 2 vols. (London, 1894).

Metcalfe, Charles Theophilus (trans.) *Two Native Narratives* (London, 1898).

Metcalfe, Thomas. *The Aftermath of Revolt 1857–1870* (Princetown, 1965).

Mills, Sara. *Discourses of Difference: An Analysis of Women's Travel Writing* (London, 1991).

Morris, James. *Heaven's Command: An Imperial Progress* (London, 1973).

Muir, Sir William. *Records of the Intelligence Department of the Government of the North-West Provinces of India . . . 1857*, ed. William Coldstream, 2 vols. (Edinburgh, 1902).

Mukerjee, S. C. *See* Anon.

Narrative of the Indian Revolt . . ., 6 vols. (London, 1858).

Papers Relating to the Indian Mutinies, 3 vols. (London, 1857–8).

Parks, Fanny. *Wanderings of a Pilgrim in Search of the Picturesque*, 2 vols. (London, 1850).

Pemble, John. *The Raj, The Indian Mutiny and the Kingdom of Oudh, 1801–1859* (Delhi, 1977).

Postans, Marianne. *The Moslem Noble: His Land and People* (London, 1857).

Rebellion 1857: A Symposium (Delhi, 1957).

Roberts, Emma. *Scenes and Characteristics of Hindostan, with Sketches of Anglo-Indian Society*, 3 vols. (London, 1835).

Roberts, Fred. *Letters Written during the Indian Mutiny* (London, 1924).

Robinson, Jane. *Unsuitable for Ladies: An Anthology of Women Travellers* (Oxford, 1994).

— *Wayward Women: A Guide to Women Travellers* (Oxford, 1990).

Russell, William Howard. *My Diary in India*, 1 vol. edn (London, 1957).

Sale, Lady. *A Journal of the Disasters in Afghanistan 1841–2* (London, 1843).

Scholberg, Henry. *The Indian Literature of the Great Rebellion* (New Delhi, 1993).

Sen, Surendra Nath. *Eighteen Fifty-Seven* (Delhi, 1958).

Seton, Rosemary. *The Indian 'Mutiny'* [Bibliography] (London, 1986).

Sharpe, Jenny. *Allegories of Empire: The Figure of Woman in the Colonial Text* (Minneapolis, 1993).

Sherer, J. W. *Daily Life during the Indian Mutiny* (London, 1898). *See also* Maude, F. C.

Smart, Jane. *Letter from a Lady at Madrass* (London, 1743).

Smith, Juliet. *Escape from Meerut* (London, 1971).

Sneade Brown, S. *Home Letters Written from India, 1828–41* (London, 1878).

Spear, Percival. *The Nabobs* (London, 1980).

Stanford, J. K. *Ladies in the Sun: Memsahibs in India 1790–1860* (London, 1962).

Steel, Flora Annie. *On the Face of the Waters* (London, 1896).

Surtees, Virginia. *Charlotte Canning* (London, 1972).

Tayler, Maria. *Women and War! A Reply to the questions How does War affect Women? and How can Women Prevent War?* (London, 1877).

Taylor, P. J. O. *A Companion to the 'Indian Mutiny' of 1857* (Delhi, 1996).

— *A Feeling of Quiet Power: The Siege of Lucknow 1857* (Delhi, 1994).

— *A Sahib Remembers* (Delhi, 1994).

— *A Star Shall Fall: India 1857* (Delhi, 1993).

— *Chronicles of the Mutiny* (Delhi, 1992).

Thomson, Captain Mowbray. *The Story of Cawnpore* (London, 1858).

Thompson, Edward. *The Other Side of the Medal* (London, 1925).

Thornhill, Mark. *Personal Adventures . . . during . . . the Indian Mutiny* (London, 1884).

Tisdall, E. E. P. *Mrs Duberly's Campaigns* (London, 1963).

Trevelyan, Sir George Otto. *Cawnpore* (London, 1865).

Trollope, Joanna. *Britannia's Daughters* (London, 1983).

Vansittart, Jane. *The Devil's Wind* (London, 1963).

Wallace-Dunlop, M. and R. *See* Anon.

Waterfield, A. J. *Children of the Mutiny* (London, 1935).

Wentworth, P. *The Devil's Wind* (London, 1912).

Wilkinson, Theon. *Two Monsoons: The Life and Death of Europeans in India* (London, 1976).

Williams, G.W. *Memorandum and Depositions on the Outbreak at Meerut* (Allahabad, 1858). *See also* Forrest, G.W.

Wylie, M. (ed.). *The English Captives in Oudh* (Calcutta, 1858).

Yalland, Zoë. *Boxwallahs: The British in Cawnpore 1857–1901* (Salisbury, 1994).

— *Traders and Nabobs: The British in Cawnpore 1765–1857* (Salisbury, 1987).

Young, Colonel Keith. *Delhi, 1857* (London, 1902).

Index